Communication for
Employees

ON THE MOVE

Communication for Employees

ON THE MOVE

RON BLICQ

Red River Community College
Winnipeg, Manitoba, Canada

Prentice-Hall, Inc., *Englewood Cliffs, New Jersey*

Library of Congress Cataloging in Publication Data

Blicq, R S   1925–
    On the move.

    Includes index.
    1. Communication in management. I. Title.
II. Title: Communication for employees.
HF5718.B53   658.4′5   74–32223
ISBN   0-13-634212-4

The names of people and organizations are imaginary
and no reference to real persons is implied or intended.

10   9   8   7   6

Prentice-Hall International, Inc., *London*
Prentice-Hall of Australia, Pty. Ltd., *Sydney*
Prentice-Hall of Canada, Ltd., *Toronto*
Prentice-Hall of India Private Limited, *New Delhi*
Prentice-Hall of Japan, Inc., *Tokyo*
Prentice-Hall of Southeast Asia (Pte.) Ltd., *Singapore*

Contents

Preface

Today's employees tend to move around. They are more ready to experiment than previous generations—to try doing different things until they find a job they like. They want a job that not only pays well but is personally satisfying.

But people on the move don't stop moving when they become permanently employed. Their movement just takes a different direction: upward within the company and, sometimes, outward into the world of small business ownership.

It's for these men and women I have written this book. People on the move continually break ties, meet new people, and make new friends, which means they have to communicate more and better than people who stand still.

R.S.B.

I

THIS BUSINESS CALLED "COMMUNICATION"

1

Communication:
What it Means
to You and Me

We spend much of our time communicating—with our families, friends, people we work with, employers, store clerks, long-distance telephone operators—the list is endless. In each exchange, ideas are presented and, we hope, understood. When you telephone for a replacement part for your automatic washer, or I complain to the service department that my Ecolift office copier is not working properly, or Chuck Harris writes for information on a new forklift truck, we each want the person at the other end to do what we expect of him. For this to happen we must explain precisely what we want. If we don't, you get the wrong part, I get the wrong service for my copier, and Chuck Harris never receives his information.

Of course, communication is a two-way street. If the person you are talking to is not reading or listening properly—if he is only half listening (while the other half watches the new secretary balancing coffee cups as she winds her way between the desks)—then your efforts to make sure he has the correct information may well be wasted. In this case getting the answer or result you want depends more on good luck than good management or good communication. All parties must be communicating efficiently for a proper job to be done.

When Greg Patterson brings Remick Airlines Flight 671 from Syracuse into Montrose Airport, his passengers complain about his rough landing. Greg is concerned too—not so much because the landing was rough but because he knows a fault exists in the landing gear.

In the flight office, he reports the problem to the ground main-tenance crew by making an entry in the aircraft log book. It might seem that all he has to write is: "Defective starboard landing gear." But Greg knows the crew chief needs more information than that. So he explains what the fault is like, any previous in-flight happenings that might have caused it, and possible effects it might have had on other parts of the aircraft. This is what he writes:

Severe wheel shimmy, starboard landing gear. Possibly caused by hard landing in crosswind at Utica, 0817, 16 May. Check effect of vibration on undercarriage structure.

If the problem is explained clearly, the maintenance crew will quickly identify what is wrong and repair the landing gear. Both Greg and the crew chief recognize that aircraft held on the ground cost money: the airline must keep its aircraft flying if it is to stay in business.

Even though you may think of yourself as only one of a firm's many employees, how well you communicate can affect how the firm prospers. A business peopled with good communicators is likely to be better run and make more money than a similar business staffed with poor com-municators. Good communication not only cuts costs but also reduces petty annoyances and frustrations. Indeed, being able to communicate well is important from the day you apply for a job right up until the day you retire.

Take a look at Andy and Bill—two machinists applying for the same job. First assume they have the same education, somewhat similar home backgrounds, and the same training, but that Andy is a much better communicator than Bill. On his application form he describes clearly what work he has done before, and then in the interview explains why he wants the job, how well his previous experience fits him for it, and why he believes he will make a good employee. Bill is not too sure what he should write about, and anyway he hates filling in forms, so he puts down just what the form asks for and no more. In the interview he shows up poorly because he answers questions with only "yes," "no," or a shrugged "I don't know." Because the interviewer learns a lot about Andy, he is much more likely to offer him the job.

The same can occur again and again in later life. Two crew chiefs, both the same age, of similar capability and training, and of the same seniority, have equal opportunity to fill a vacancy if both have the same communication abilities. But if one can explain a problem more clearly than the other, can write a better memorandum, and in general can talk more easily to the foreman and to others in the work group, he will almost undoubtedly be the one chosen for promotion.

Communication is such an integral part of our lives that we tend to take it for granted. It is not limited to writing and speaking, but includes illustrations (drawings, photographs, cartoons), actions, touch, gestures, and moving pictures. These mediums of communication are commonly used to inform, to explain, to instruct, and sometimes to ask questions.

But they are only half the communication process—the half in which we transmit information, much as a radio or television station transmits a program. A radio program goes nowhere—simply is not used—if there are no receivers within range of the station's transmitter. And even then the information conveyed by a radio receiver or displayed on a television screen is not used unless it is viewed by a human being who can understand and interpret it (see Fig. 1–1).

The person doing the "receiving" is always a listener, a viewer, or a reader. He is an essential component of any communication process, for without him there would be no reason for anyone to say anything out loud, draw pictures, or write words onto paper. Perhaps creative persons such as poets write purely for the joy of writing rhythmic words, and artists paint pictures of scenes or sights that have particularly moved them. But you and I are very unlikely to transmit any information without having good reason for doing so. Even these words are being written in the hope that some day they will be useful to a prospective receiver— which is you.

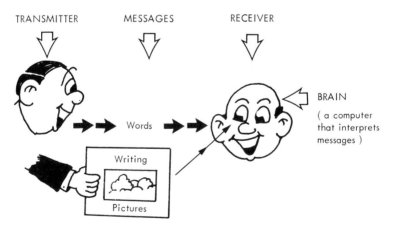

Fig. 1–1. The communication process.

2

Improving Communication as a "Receiver"

The "receiver" in the communication process takes in most information through his eyes and ears. (Smell and touch also are communication "senses," but they play a very minor role in business, the classroom, and normal day-to-day communication.) Receiving is automatic, and we seldom give it a second thought. We could hear right from infancy, and someone showed us how to read at an early age. How well we now read depends a lot on how well we were taught and how much reading we have done since then. But nobody ever really taught us how to listen, or bothered to explain that there is a difference between hearing and listening.

We hear sounds all the time, but we remember little of what we hear because we are not consciously listening. Only when there is an unusual sound, or one that is particularly loud, or a sound that we have been waiting for, do we consciously fine-tune our receivers. Then, instead of only hearing background noise that goes on all the time, we actively listen. You hear traffic, but you *listen* carefully to the sound of your own car's engine; you hear a jet pass overhead, but you *listen* if the noise falters or suddenly stops; you hear the radio in the next room, but you *listen* for an expected telephone call.

How often have you heard someone in a classroom ask a question that was clearly answered by the instructor some five minutes earlier? Where was the questioner when that topic was being discussed? He appeared to be hearing what was going on, but he obviously was not listening.

How well you listen may depend on the speaker. If he has a speaking voice that projects well, if he varies the pitch and the rhythm of his sentences, if he has a persuasive, interesting manner, if he is enthusiastic about his subject, and (most important of all) if he has organized his thoughts into a logical line of ideas, then you probably will find him easy to listen to and understand. Unfortunately, you will seldom encounter a speaker gifted in so many ways.

You will more likely be affected by the listening environment. Personal circumstances, such as the knowledge that a close member of your family is critically ill, or an argument that resulted in harsh words you now wish you could retract (but cannot, because you are sitting in a classroom far from a phone) can severely reduce your ability to concentrate. So can physical conditions: the room is too hot; you had a late night the night before; you are hungry; you have been sitting for much too long; or you need to go to the bathroom. Any one of these can cause the speaker's words to become the background noise to your private thoughts (see Fig. 1–2.)

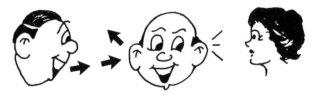

Fig. 1–2. Outside influences can cause you to detune your receiver.

LISTENING

There are three basic forms of listening, known as

Casual listening
Attentive listening
Critical listening

Casual listening is the kind of listening you do most of the time—when you do not intend to remember much you hear. You may listen just to pass the time, such as to the radio or to a general conversation in the lunchroom. You may hear the discussion of last night's game between the Chicago Black Hawks and the New York Rangers, but you do not listen very closely unless you are a hockey addict.

Attentive listening is the type of listening you do when you really want to learn something—when you want to remember exactly what is being said. When you listen attentively you get thoroughly "tuned in" to the person who is speaking, perhaps because he is a good speaker, but more usually because he is saying something that particularly interests you.

Critical listening is careful listening—thoughtful listening. In critical listening you continually assess, think about, and even analyze what is being said. You try to establish the value of the information, its usefulness, its accuracy, or even its credibility. You let your brain act like a sieve that permits useful pieces of information to filter into it but rejects facts you cannot (or do not want to) use.

Your interest in a subject will dictate the type of listening you do. You may start listening casually to a conversation, and then suddenly become attentive when the topic changes to a subject that directly affects you. Conversely, you may at first listen critically to a speaker who seems interesting and to have something important to say, but drift into casual listening as you discover he is only a political windbag.

During the morning coffee break Bev Skinner recounts how she fooled the tax collector when she filed her last return. Gavin Freeman listens *casually:* he is not really very interested in Bev's financial fiddling. He knows that Bev is an entertaining person to listen to; that she has a flair for telling stories and often has an attentive audience. But Gavin also knows that Bev exaggerates quite a bit, so he lets his listening be no more than casual.

When a friend describes a really good job opening at Adam Industries, Gavin listens *attentively.* He wants to hear exactly what the friend has to say about the job and where he should apply for it. He is likely to listen just as attentively when an instructor talks about taking part in employment interviews. He urgently needs to know what he should do, how he should act, and how he should reply to certain types of questions. His interest is high because the information directly affects him.

The same applies to apprentice electrician Rene Marchant, when the journeyman electrician he works with describes which terminals on the power control panel are "live." Rene needs to know what he can and cannot touch. Inattentiveness here could have fatal results.

Gavin Freeman listens *critically* when, as an employee, he attends a meeting at which the department manager explains organizational changes that are to take place. Some changes will affect Gavin, while others will not. This gives him something to think about: Will he have to adjust to a new foreman (although Gavin does not particularly like the present foreman, he recognizes that he is not a bad guy to work for)? Will the changes provide a better chance for him to become crew chief or will

other guys better qualified than he be brought in? And will this reor-
ganization mean higher pay? As each new item is mentioned Gavin
analyzes it to see how it applies to him, and perhaps makes a mental
note to ask questions later.

Sometimes we use all three forms of listening on the same occasion.
When Gavin Freeman goes to a union meeting, much of the business does
not affect him directly. He starts to listen attentively, but soon becomes
bored and only a casual listener. But when the talk turns to the wage
package the union will be demanding, he becomes an attentive listener:
like the rest of us, he is interested in what he will be paid. Then, just
before the meeting ends, the chairman introduces a topic that causes
Gavin to listen critically. This is a suggestion that the union support the
three-day work week. Gavin is immediately concerned he will lose some of
his wages, and he does a quick mental calculation to see how much. But
when the chairman goes on to explain that each day will be twelve hours
long, Gavin is immediately reassured that his take-home pay will be the
same. His thoughts then drift to some interesting implications: he would
have a four-day weekend (will he be welcome, hanging around the
house?); it may disrupt his car pool (will those who drive with him work
on different days than be does?); perhaps he could go back to school on
his days off (is this his chance to make up that high school physics course,
or possibly take a course in design drafting?).

Good listeners know how to listen because they identify early in
each situation what kind of listening is called for. They also know that
critical listening carries with it the danger that interest in the topic may
cause their thoughts to drift along private channels rather than concentrate on what is being said. When this happens, critical listening drops to
an even lower level than casual listening.

READING

How often have you been reading a textbook (even this one!) only
to find at the foot of a page that you have not "taken in" anything you
have just read? This is known as surface reading, which means that your
eyes scan the words, and your mind actually forms them, but your
thoughts continue on a private track, perhaps about a personal problem
or a more interesting topic.

As you read this—right now—it is possible you are only surface
reading. Perhaps you are also thinking about the little MG you looked at
last night and would like to buy, and your mind has already darted off to
consider how you could raise the cash to finance it.

You can correct this if, at the end of several paragraphs, you stop and ask yourself: What was that all about? If you are not sure, go back and look for topic sentences, which in technical books and instruction manuals are usually the first sentence of each major paragraph. Each should summarize what that particular paragraph is about (the remaining sentences explain more about the topic—see page 247). Go through them one by one, reading the whole paragraph if any topic sentence does not seem to make sense.

Try this technique right now by turning to the front of this chapter and reading only the first sentence of the first five paragraphs. They should tell you a "story," even if not in much detail. They are repeated here so that you can read them again quickly and see how there is a flow from one topic sentence to the next:

1. The "receiver" in the communication process takes in most information through his eyes and ears.
2. We hear sounds all the time, but we remember little of what we hear because we are not consciously listening.
3. How often have you heard someone in a classroom ask a question that was clearly answered by the instructor some five minutes earlier?
4. How well you listen may depend on the speaker.
5. You will more likely be affected by the listening environment.

NOTE TAKING

The average speaker delivers words much faster than you can possibly write (125 to 145 spoken words per minute, compared to 40 to 45 written words). If you want to record what he says, you will have to take notes only of the main points he makes. In the classroom, note taking is important because you hear a lot of things you will need to remember.

Taking Notes in Class

In the classroom you almost always take notes for only one person— yourself. So the words you write down should be information that will be useful for *you*. Listen carefully to identify each major topic the instructor introduces. Jot it down as a brief heading on the left-hand side of the page. Underneath it, jot down short headings that describe the major points he mentions. Leave a clear line between each and use abbreviations for long words (but make sure you will understand them later on). Try to keep these notes to the left-hand two-thirds of the page, if necessary drawing a vertical line down the page to prevent your pen from straying into the right-hand section. An example is shown in Fig. 1–3.

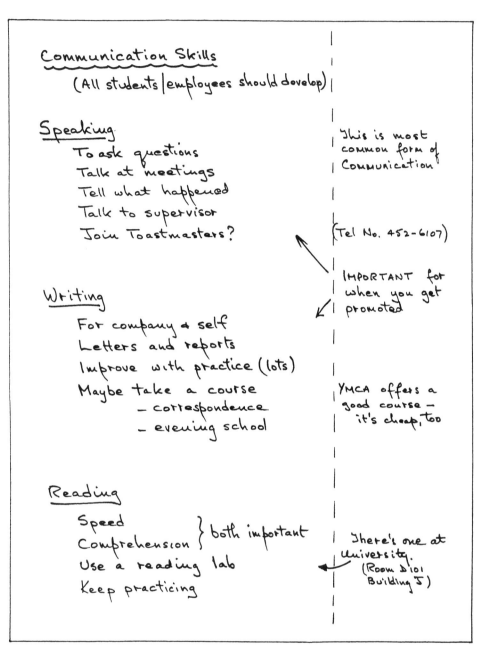

Fig. 1–3. Notes made during a talk (information in the right-hand column is written later).

When the instructor seems to have completed a topic, leave at least one inch before jotting down the next topic in case he goes back to the first one later on. This will permit you to nip quickly back to enter extra details. At the same time you will be automatically grouping information into topic areas.

As soon as possible after the instructor is finished, go back over your notes and expand them wherever you feel they are inadequate for studying. Use the right-hand side of the page to do this. If even then they seem to be a disorganized jumble, copy them into a permanent notebook so they will be readable in future.

Taking Notes in Industry

In industry you are likely to be taking notes for someone else. You may represent your department at a new equipment demonstration, or your fellow employees at a union meeting; you may attend a course; or you may visit a powerhouse, garbage disposal plant, or a printing press to study a new process. When you return you will be expected to tell your foreman or supervisor, and possibly a group of technicians, what you saw. You will have to answer their questions. And you may have to write a report. If you are to do an adequate job you will need to take notes. Here are some pointers:

1. Before going, find out exactly who you will have to pass information on to. Establish how much this person (or persons) knows about the topic, so you will not collect unnecessary information.
2. Also try to find out whether on your return you are going to have to explain orally what you saw, write a report about it, or do both.
3. Read recent literature about the subject, so that when the speaker starts you can quickly relate new ideas he presents to facts you already know. This gives you a confident starting point.

Because a speaker in industry may not arrange his information as carefully as an instructor in a classroom, you may have more difficulty in identifying each major topic he introduces. Watch for signs. A good speaker who has organized his material properly will offer a signal every time he comes to something new. He may pause and then start at a different speaking speed; he may use an introductory phrase such as: "The first step was to . . ." or "The second time we tried. . . ." He may have a visual aid such as a slide or flip chart on which he has already jotted down the main headings; or he may jot topics onto a board as he goes along.

Make your notes in the same way you would in a classroom, then write in extra details from memory as soon as the talk is over. If you have to write out a description or a report for your employer, do so while the notes and your memory of the talk are still fresh—preferably within 24 hours.

.   .   .

If you are really interested in listening to a particular "program," you must carefully tune your receiver. If you also want to take notes, you should first find out something about the program's subject so you will more easily recognize the key words and sentences when you see or hear them.

EXERCISES

Exercise 2.1

What kind of listening (casual, attentive, or critical) would yours be when each of the following topics is being discussed?

1. Last April's Academy Awards
2. The Indianapolis 500
3. Last night's news that for some people income tax is to be cut 10 percent
4. Baseball
5. Tips from one of last year's graduates on how to pass the examination in your toughest subject
6. Drag-strip racing
7. Football
8. The new Honda 350 motorcycle
9. The Winter Olympics
10. Trout fishing
11. A weekend job opening that pays $1.10 an hour more than your present job
12. Sky-diving

Exercise 2.2

Compare your answers in exercise 2.1 with those of other persons in the room; then answer these questions:

1. For most topics, has everyone else listed the same listening level as you? Why is this so?
2. Is there any one topic for which everyone has listed the same listening level?

3. On which topics are most persons in agreement? What does this indicate?

Exercise 2.3

Select one of your textbooks and find a passage containing at least five medium-length paragraphs (about 6 to 8 lines each).

1. Identify the topic sentence of each paragraph, number it, and write it down (see how this has been done on page 9).
2. Try to identify the "flow of information" through these sentences, then see if you can condense what they say into a single sentence (i.e., a Summary Statement).

Exercise 2.4

Without warning you beforehand, your instructor will show you a movie or TV talk, bring in a guest speaker, or read an article aloud to you. Take study notes on what you hear.

Exercise 2.5

Your instructor will tell you what subject is going to be discussed in a movie or TV talk, by a guest speaker, or by himself, and will warn you that you are to take study notes.

1. Before the subject is discussed, find some information about it.
2. During the "talk," take study notes as in exercise 2.4.
3. Compare the usefulness of the study notes taken in exercise 2.4 with those taken now. Why is one set better than the other?

3

Improving Communication as a "Transmitter"

In everyday life when we have something to say we usually just start. We say out loud what we think as quickly as the ideas come to mind. Or we scribble down a few words in a short letter to a friend without really stopping to make a plan. What we say often comes across smoothly and interestingly, partly because our character shows through. Unfortunately, this seldom happens in industry or business, where we need to speak and write much more carefully.

In the business world you will be expected to communicate in a businesslike way, and not to waste the listener's or reader's time by offering disorganized or unnecessary information. This simply means taking three preliminary steps before opening your mouth or setting pen to paper. They are:

1. Define the situation
2. Identify the receiver
3. Decide what you want to say

DEFINING THE SITUATION

Before attempting to speak or write, you should decide what kind of message you want to convey. Ask yourself whether you are trying to:

1. **Tell** somebody about something that has happened or is happening.
   Is your purpose to *inform?*
2. **Tell** somebody to do something, or how to go about doing it.
   Is your purpose to *instruct?*
3. **Suggest** to somebody how they should do something, or the best course to take.
   Is your purpose to *advise?*
4. **Remedy** something that has gone wrong or that has not been understood, or possibly change somebody's ill-advised thinking.
   Is your purpose to *correct?*
5. **Find out** something.
   Is your purpose to *question?*

If you are going to *inform* or *instruct,* you can be quite direct. This means saying right away what you have to say without adding any trimmings. The receiver wants facts and there is little point in giving him a lot of interesting but additional information.

If you are going to *advise* or *correct* (which includes reprimanding and complaining), you will need to explain more. That is, you will have to include more background information to make sure the receiver understands you and your reason for communicating. This is particularly true if you have to persuade or convince someone to agree with your line of thinking.

If you are going to *question,* you will have to make quite sure your question is perfectly clear, so the receiver will know exactly what is required of him. You may also have to insert some background information to help him understand the reason for your question.

Finally, you should ask yourself what results you expect from the receiver. When he has read or listened to what you have to say, should he be able to do something that he was not able to do before? Should he be able to carry out a new task? Or should he simply understand better why something has happened?

If you expect him to take some form of action or give you information, state *exactly* what you want him to do. Be specific—and avoid vague words. For example, you would give the receiver several opportunities to do the unexpected if you were to say: "I want you to contact Mr. Johnson shortly and let me know what his plans are." He may assume that by "contact" you mean telephone, when in fact you want him to go across the city and see Mr. Johnson. He may take "shortly" to mean this afternoon or tomorrow morning, when you really mean in half an hour. He may think that by "let me know" he is to write you a note, whereas you really intend him to telephone you. And he has to ask Mr. Johnson an impossibly vague question: "Mr. Johnson, what are your plans?"

A far better way to convey this message is to be specific: "I want you to go and see Mr. Johnson before 11 A.M., ask him what he plans to do this afternoon, and then telephone his answer to me by noon."

IDENTIFYING THE RECEIVER

Your interest in and knowledge of a subject may lead you to use terms that would be readily understood only by somebody of similar interest and background as yourself. Before you write or speak, you need to place yourself mentally in the receiver's shoes to find out how much you need explain and the kinds of words you can use.

Identifying a receiver does not mean knowing him as a specific person (unless you happen to know him personally). More often, it means establishing what type of person he is, what kind of position he holds, and how much he already knows about the topic.

If, for instance, you are an electronics technician describing a fault in a pocket calculator you have purchased, you should consider whether you will be addressing the sales manager or someone in the engineering department. In the first case you should try not to be too technical; in the second case you can afford to go into technical details. The same applies to a nurse describing a patient's symptoms: for the doctor she can use medical terms, but for the family of the patient she must use simpler words they can understand.

Many people fail to convey information clearly because they do not use this simple technique. It is particularly important before you write, because your receiver cannot always question what he reads.

MAKING A PLAN

No doubt in high school your teachers emphasized that you should never attempt to speak or write without first making a well-developed outline. They were right. But the methods they told you to use are probably unwieldy and too rigid for practical application in industry. The method suggested here and in the following chapters is simple to apply and will help you to be a better organized, more effective communicator.

Regardless of the purpose of your communication, or how long or short it will be, it can always be broken down into three basic blocks of information. These are shown in Fig. 1–4, and comprise:

1. **Main Message.** This says in very few words the information you most want to convey. Before it can be written you first need to know why

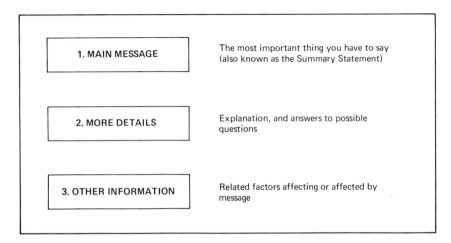

Fig. 1–4. Basic Information Blocks.

you are communicating the information and who it is for. In effect, it summarizes the whole message into a short *Summary Statement,* often only one or two sentences long. (For more suggestions on Summary Statements read "Placing the Message Up Front" in Chapter 15, page 239.)

2. **More Details.** This block amplifies and explains what has been said in the Main Message. It offers evidence to support what you are saying and answers questions the receiver would ask if given only the Main Message.

3. **Other Information.** This block can contain a variety of information connected with the Main Message, but not an essential part of it. It might suggest how or when something should be done, comment on costs of a project, or predict what will happen next.

These three blocks of information are basic units. Many others are illustrated in following chapters, each suitable for a different situation. Below are two communications on the same subject. In the first, the information is exactly as it was presented originally. In the second, the information has been rearranged into the three blocks shown in Fig. 1–4. Both communications are understandable, but the first takes longer to convey its message.

Original Communication:
Last summer I complained to Mr. Enright that there was a cooling problem in the office, and he had some changes made in the vents which helped a bit. Now it's winter and the operators are never satisfied, because they say it is too cold at floor level.

They are away on a course until next Friday. Could you

have the thermostat checked by then, and make any adjustments you need to raise the temperature? Don't try doing it on Monday, though, because the carpenters are putting in new windows that day.

Revised Communication:

Will you please check the thermostats in our office and make adjustments to raise the temperature.

Main Message

Some changes made in the vents last summer improved the cooling, but are now causing temperatures to be too low at floor level.

More Details

I would like this done before next Friday, but should warn you that Monday is not suitable because on that day the carpenters will be installing new windows.

Other Information

Apart from rearrangement of information, the revised communication is better because it sticks to essential information (it recognizes that to do his job the receiver does not need to know about Mr. Enright and the operators' complaints and movements). Deciding what information to include and what to leave out also is an important aspect of communication.

DECIDING WHAT YOU WANT TO SAY

Have you ever listened to somebody or read something and halfway through said to yourself: "What on earth is this person trying to tell me?" (Sometimes this can happen when you watch television or go to a movie; then the question becomes: "What am I supposed to be getting out of this?") In both cases the fault probably lies with the originator of the "message," who has probably failed to decide exactly what he is trying to say.

Before speaking or writing, try explaining in one sentence the main thing you want to tell the reader. Start with these six words:

I want to tell you that . . .

Now finish the sentence. This will force you to get right to the crux of the matter—to establish clearly what your main reason is for communicating information.

Here is an example:

I want to tell you that I won't be able to repair Sam Foot's refrigeration cooler by Saturday May 12 as promised.

Having said what has to be said, you can now ask yourself what the receiver of this bit of information might ask. The most likely questions would be:

> *Why can't you?*
> *What are you doing about it?*
> *When will you do it?*

If you then answer these questions, you will have a complete communication.

Here is another example:

> **I want to tell you that** Janice Scott has been transferred from the assembly line to the packing section, where she will not be affected by paint fumes.

Again try to think what questions the receiver of this information is likely to ask. Perhaps they are:

> *What were the circumstances that led up to this move?*
> *Why was it done?*
> *Who replaced Janice on the assembly line?*

The last question may not be necessary, because the message seems to concern Janice and what was done about her rather than the person who took her place. In a real-life situation you would have to decide whether or not this information is needed.

The words **I want to tell you that** force you to form the Summary Statement mentioned earlier. In practice, you would delete them from the Summary Statement before you say it or write it. But you will know they are there, silently helping you open with the Main Message. Can you identify which of these two persons started with a proper Summary Statement?

> *Dan:* Your order for 14 rolls of 22AWG wire was filled on May 27 and shipped by rail express the following day. We apologize for the delay.
>
> *Mike:* Referring to your telephone question of yesterday afternoon, we had difficulty in filling your order until May 27 and apologize for the delay. The 14 rolls of 22AWG wire were shipped the following day.

Only in front of Dan's opening statement can you comfortably insert the words **I want to tell you that.** Dan also starts with the information the receiver is most interested in: when the wire was shipped.

SAYING IT

Although it may not seem necessary to open with a Summary Statement when you are speaking to someone (because the listener can always ask questions if you do not explain things clearly), this is still a useful technique for speeding up communication. Not only will messages be conveyed more quickly, but you will also become known as an efficient communicator. See how differently Dan and Mike approach their supervisor to ask for time off:

Dan

Mr. Campbell! May I leave at noon on Thursday to attend the graduation ceremonies at Montrose University? My brother is graduating with his B.A., and since Dad died I'm the only one left to represent the family.

Mike

Oh, Mr. Campbell! May I see you for a minute? You remember when I joined the company last spring, you said I could go back to the Community College to get my diploma? [*Mr. Campbell nods*] Well the guys I took the course with phoned me last night to say the graduation will be this coming Friday. It's at 2 P.M. So can I leave at noon to go to it?

In the following chapters there are numerous examples of spoken communications that use information blocks to organize their messages, and open with Summary Statements that tell the listener right away what he most needs to know.

WRITING IT

The Summary Statement is particularly useful when writing to someone, because it helps you put the Main Message up front. But because information delivered so suddenly forces questions to the reader's mind, you must anticipate what these questions will be. This means you must look back at what you have written and try to view it as though you know little about the subject and are seeing the words for the first time.

Let's take a look at the events leading up to the Summary Statement announcing that repairs to Sam Foot's refrigeration cooler would not be completed by Saturday May 12:

When you promised Reg Campbell (your supervisor) to have the job done by May 12, you did so using a realistic estimate of the time that it would take. There was no way you could know that so many problems would arise—far more than you would expect from a routine repair job like this.

The project went well at first. You stripped the cooler down and found the breakdown was caused by a damaged valve in compressor unit number 2. You wrote a note to Reg Campbell ordering a replacement valve assembly complete with fittings, and he sent a telegram to the manufacturer so the item would be shipped quickly.

The next two days you were away from work with stomach flu. When you returned to work, you overhauled the cooler, expecting the valve assembly to come in at any moment. After a week it still had not arrived, so you asked Reg Campbell to send another telegram. "There is no point in doing that," he said. "The DEF Company was on strike all last week. They only returned to work yesterday morning. It will be another three days before the assembly comes in."

When it did arrive you had further problems. The connector on the new valve assembly would not lock with the connector on the existing pipe. You managed to force a join, but when you applied pressure it leaked badly. Then in trying to separate the connectors, you stripped the threads on the old one and grazed your knuckles badly on the new one. This meant you had to order two more identical connectors. Fortunately, a local supplier could get some and promised to bring them in by next Tuesday.

You reckon it will take you two days to fit the connectors onto the valve assembly and the existing pipe, then to reassemble and test the refrigeration cooler. This means you won't be finished until Thursday, May 17.

Your Summary Statement said:

I want to tell you that I won't be able to repair Sam Foot's refrigeration cooler by Saturday May 12 as promised.

Now let's try answering the three questions that would immediately jump to the reader's mind:

1. Why can't you?

> *Answer:*   There was a strike at DEF Company, which manufactures the refrigeration coolers. This prevented delivery of a replacement valve assembly until 10 May. The connector on the assembly did not fit the existing connector. I had to order replacement connectors.

2. *What are you doing about it?*

> *Answer:*   I have done all repair work. Installation of the connectors and testing of the cooler still have to be done. Delivery of the connectors has been promised for Tuesday May 15.

3. *When will you do it [complete the work]?*

> *Answer:*   It will take me two days to install the connectors and test the cooler.

If we put the Summary Statement and these three answers together, we now have this:

(I want to tell you that) I won't be able to repair Sam Foot's refrigeration cooler by Saturday May 12 as promised.

There was a strike at DEF Company, which manufactures the refrigeration coolers. This prevented delivery of a replacement valve assembly until 10 May. The connector on the assembly did not fit the existing connector. I had to order replacement connectors.

I have done all repair work. Installation of the connectors and testing of the refrigeration cooler still have to be done. Delivery of the connectors has been promised for Tuesday May 15.

It will take me two days to install the connectors and test the cooler.

This gives the full story, but it lacks continuity—which means reading smoothness. This is easy to remedy by inserting linking words, by deleting words and phrases that have been repeated in answering the questions, and by adding a closing statement that shows clearly when the job will be finished. Making these improvements is called "editing." How the same four paragraphs would look after editing is shown in Fig. 1–5. The final version, typed from the edited copy, is at Fig. 1–6 (page 24). The final version also follows the arrangement of information blocks suggested on pages 16 and 17. (see Fig. 1–4):

The *Main Message* is in paragraph 1
More Details appear in paragraphs 2 and 3
Other Information is in paragraph 4

• • •

If, before you speak or write, you know what you want to say, to whom you want to say it, and what he or she wants to know, you are likely to transmit useful information. If you also *plan* your message—

by dividing it into logical compartments—you will be even more likely to transmit clear, meaningful information that can be readily understood.

~~(I want to tell you that)~~ I won't be able to repair Sam Foot's refrigeration cooler by Saturday May 12 as promised.

A
~~There was a~~ strike at DEF Company, which manufactures the refrigeration coolers, ~~This~~ prevented delivery of ~~the~~ replace-
a
ment valve assembly until (10) May. Because the connector on the assembly did not fit the existing connector, I had to order replacement connectors.

except for
I have done all repair work, installation of the connectors and testing of the refrigeration cooler ~~still have to be done.~~ Delivery of the connectors has been promised for Tuesday (15) May.

ing
~~It will take me two days to~~ Install the connectors and testing will take two days. ~~the cooler.~~ The refrigeration cooler should be ready for Thursday May 17.

Fig. 1–5. Answers evolving from the summary statement, assembled, and edited.

EXERCISES

Exercise 3.1

In the following sentences, identify words that may not be properly understood:

1. Meet me in approximately two hours.
2. Place the desk near the south wall.
3. Calculate the price, then give me your answer as soon as possible.

I won't be able to repair Sam Foot's refrigeration cooler
by Saturday May 12 as promised.

A strike at DEF Company, which manufactures the refrigeration
coolers, prevented delivery of a replacement valve assembly
until May 10. Because the connector on the new assembly did
not fit the existing connector, I had to order replacement
connectors.

I have done all repair work, except for installation of the
connectors and testing of the refrigeration cooler. Delivery
of the connectors has been promised for Tuesday May 15.

Installing the connectors and testing will take two days.
The refrigeration cooler should be ready for Thursday May 17.

Fig. 1–6. Retyped version of edited copy in Fig. 1–5.

4. Make sure the doorway is high enough for an average man to enter without bumping his head.
5. The company president is expected soon. Be sure to clean up before he arrives.
6. The results show a fair percentage of failures.

Exercise 3.2

The paragraphs below contain information, but need Summary Statements (topic sentences).

1. I bought a minicalculator from Warren's Jewelers one month ago to-day. I have used it every day for four weeks without any problems, but this morning it started giving incorrect readings. Thinking the batteries were low, I replaced them, but it still displayed the same fault. I will have to return it to the manufacturer for warranty service.
2. At first, when the new contractor came in, everything was fine in the lunchroom. But gradually over the months service has become worse. I thought I was the only person to notice it, but now other employees are mentioning it. Some even go so far as to say it is intolerable. Maybe someone should tell the manager about it.

For each paragraph:
a. Write a Summary Statement (topic sentence).

b. Check that your sentence makes sense when you place the six words *I want to tell you that* in front of it.

Exercise 3.3

Use the information below to do this exercise:

1. The situation refers to Mr. Walters' order number 2728 dated May 20.
2. The materials he ordered were packed into eight cartons.
3. The cartons were shipped to him rail express on May 27.
4. The packing slip number for the shipment was M1401.
5. Mr. Walters lives in Orlando, Florida.
6. He telephoned me on June 3.
7. Mr. Walters informed me only five cartons had arrived by June 2.
8. I phoned the railway, and asked them to check on it.
9. The railway clerk said it was too soon; he was very rude about it.
10. The railway clerk phoned me June 5 to say he had news of the missing cartons.
11. Two cartons were found in the Carlton, Georgia railway station.
12. They were reshipped the same day (June 5).
13. I called the railway again today—they can't find the remaining package.
14. As of today, the railway is reporting the remaining package as missing.
15. This means that one of the eight cartons of materials we shipped to Mr. Walters on May 27 has been lost by or stolen from the railway.
16. Today I called our insurance agent.
17. Mr. Walters received two of the cartons today (June 8).
18. He is very unhappy—he needs the materials that were in the missing package.

   a. Assume you are informing your department manager what has happened. Identify which information is: Main Message
   More Details
   Other Information
   Unnecessary Information
   b. Arrange the existing sentences into a suitable order in three paragraphs: Main Message
   More Details
   Other Information
   c. By crossing out some words, changing others, and adding "linking" words, edit the paragraphs at (b) into three more readable paragraphs.

Exercise 3.4

Edit the following sentences into a more readable paragraph:

Before handing in your daily vouchers, check they are all filled out correctly. Not everyone is filling in all the lines on their vouchers. Every line must contain an entry. If you don't know the answer for a particular line, then enter "not known." Some entries need more information than there is space on the line. For these, write "see over" on the line. You can then write your entry on the back of the voucher. And one last thing: be sure to sign every voucher.

II

COMMUNICATING WITH
PROSPECTIVE EMPLOYERS

4

Finding Out Where the Jobs Are

Most of us look for a job rather haphazardly. Let's take the case of Gail and Dan Orlikow, who moved recently to another city when their father was transferred. Both wanted to find jobs. Gail is a 19-year-old clerk-typist who has one year's employment experience. Dan has just completed high school and wants summer employment before taking an electrical construction course at the local community college.

Gail used a standard approach, registering with the local employment agency and scanning the classified columns of the newspaper. But after four weeks she still had not received a job offer. Some positions she applied for had already been filled, or she was interviewed and then waited a long time before being told that the job had been filled by someone with more experience.

Dan tried a simpler technique: knocking on doors. That is, he systematically traveled down one of the major streets, stopping at any business he thought might offer him a job. The sixth firm he called on was Fred's Electric Service. To Dan's surprise, Fred invited him in, talked to him for ten minutes, then offered him a job as an electrician's helper.

Sometimes there is an element of luck in job hunting. What Dan could not know was that only the previous day an electrician's helper had quit to take a high-paying job in Alaska. Fred needed a replacement —and quickly. Normally he would have placed an advertisement in the classified columns of the newspaper, and then interviewed several applicants. But this would have taken time. By walking in at the right moment, Dan had presented him with a prospective employee who was easy to find and easy to hire. Because the impression he gave was of an inexperienced but personable young man, Fred hired him on the spot.

RESEARCHING JOB OPPORTUNITIES

For all the jobs that are advertised or listed with employment agencies, there are many more that are never advertised and are filled either by word of mouth (that is, by someone who knows about the job mentioning it to a friend) or by someone walking in at just the right moment. This "element of luck" is an important factor in finding a job, and one that comes into play when you go out and actively pursue job opportunities.

Gail's approach was good because she had a plan; but it was limited because it lacked imagination. It was too much like the plan used by other applicants. Dan's approach also was good in its own way; but it, too, was limited because it depended almost entirely on that element of luck. Both Gail and Dan could have improved their job hunting by researching where job opportunities might exist, and then pursuing them on a much broader front.

Where else could they have gone for information when they started to look for jobs? Gail used the two sources that occurred immediately to her: the classified advertisement columns, and employment agencies. But there are many other sources of information both she and her brother could have used. These are illustrated in Fig. 2–1.

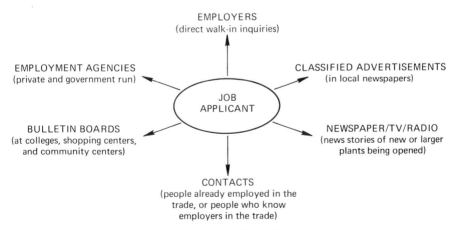

Fig. 2–1. Sources of job information.

APPROACHING EMPLOYEES

People already employed in the trade in which you want to find a job have a big advantage over you. As Fig. 2–2 shows, it's as though you are looking at them from outside—through a plate-glass window. As a new job applicant, you are part of the outer circle. Those already employed in the trade form the inner circle. Your aim should be to step through that plate-glass window; to make the grade from the outer circle to the inner circle.

This is what you are up against: to some extent, those in the inner circle know each other and are the first to hear when a job opportunity becomes available. Allen, at company A, is one of the first to know when a job opening occurs in his company. He has a friend, Bill, at company B, who is doing a lesser task but who probably could fill the position at company A. Allen may either inform his employer of Bill's suitability for the job, or go directly to Bill and tell him about the job being open. So Bill applies for it and is accepted. Then the job opening created by Bill's move is filled by Carl, from company C; and so on. While all this is going on, those on the outer circle seldom get to hear of all the jobs they might have filled. Eventually, of course, an opening does become available—usually one that no one on the inner circle wants. But of all the vacancies that occur, it is the only one filled by an unemployed person from the outer circle.

One way to make this step is to get to know people on the inner

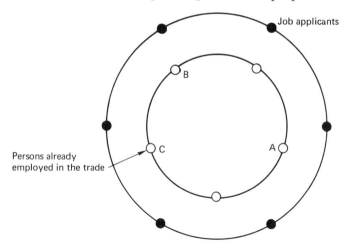

Fig. 2–2. Stepping from the unemployed outer circle to the employed inner circle is no easy task.

circle. If, for example, you graduated recently as an automotive mechanic, you might walk into a service station and chat with some of the mechanics. While doing so, ask if they know of jobs in either their own or other service stations, and who is likely to be hiring inside the trade. You will find them almost always helpful, and often keenly aware of the employment situation. Indeed, Allen, Bill, or Carl might well have called you about the job openings in their companies *if any one of them had known of you and your need for a job.*

APPROACHING EMPLOYERS

Although it may seem like a "long shot," the direct approach can pay dividends. A personal visit is probably better than a telephone call for two simple reasons: it is more difficult to explain oneself clearly over the telephone, and it is too easy for an employer to say "No" to someone he cannot see.

Dan used this approach as he walked down a major thoroughfare of his new city and stepped into the offices of probable employers. But he could have been more selective, and at the same time widened the range, if he had first sat down and made a list of employers likely to hire a person with his background.

Making such a list requires good imagination. You need to think far beyond the routine types of employers who hire applicants with your experience and training. (Note that this is *types* of employers, not employers' names; identifying possible employers by name comes later.) A student nurse would immediately list hospitals, clinics, doctors' offices, maternity homes, and mental institutions as likely places of employment; but she would not easily think of colleges, factories, and department stores, nearly all of which have their own medical facilities.

To make your own list, first take a sheet of lined paper and head it with the title Obvious Employers. On the upper part of the sheet write down the types of employers that immediately occur to you. For example, if you are a graduate of a food services course, or shortly will graduate, you would likely write:

Hotels and Motels
Restaurants
Bakeries
Caterers

At this point your ideas might suddenly dry up. This is when you need to bring the second part of the sheet into play, which you should title Not-so-obvious Employers. Now the ideas do not come easily, because thinking of other possible employers means stretching your imagination so that you consider all kinds of businesses and enterprises to identify whether in some remote way they might employ somebody like you. Sometimes it is worthwhile to bring in one or two friends and hold a "think-tank" session, during which you list even the most way-out suggestions. The idea, of course, is to get people to free their thinking machinery.

A person looking for work in the food services field probably would build up a list of not-so-obvious employers like those in Fig. 2–3. All these organizations have facilities for serving meals, and so employ persons experienced in food preparation. And this is by no means a complete list. Indeed, a list should never be considered complete: as the days go by you should continually add other types of employers as new ideas occur to you.

POSSIBLE EMPLOYERS

Public Institutions:

  Hospitals, colleges, jails

Residential Homes:

  For the elderly; for the underprivileged; for
  the retarded; for the blind

Airlines or companies preparing in-flight meals

Railways

Manufacturers of frozen dinners

Large organizations:

  Department stores, manufacturing companies,
  office complexes, government offices

Fig. 2–3. Not-so-obvious employers (food services).

A person with experience or training as an automotive mechanic, body shop worker, parts specialist, diesel mechanic, or spray painter would identify obvious employers as service stations, automobile dealer-ships, and automobile supply houses. But there would be a much wider range of not-so-obvious employers. Those for an automotive mechanic are listed in Fig. 2–4.

The next step is to convert your list of possible types of employers into a much longer list identifying the companies you will approach. For this information, turn to the Yellow Pages of your telephone directory, or refer to a city directory or business directory, both of which usually can be found in a public library. An automotive mechanic, for example, who is trying to find the names of furniture movers who have sizable vehicle fleets has only to turn to the heading MOVERS in the Yellow Pages of the telephone directory to find a substantial list.

For each type of employer listed on your sheet, now list the name, address, and telephone number of every company you are likely to visit. Also try to find the name of the person you want to speak to. Asking for a person by name not only personalizes your approach but also com-mands attention. If it is difficult to find, you may have to place a discreet telephone call to the company and ask the telephone operator for the name (and correct spelling) of the person who handles applications for employment.

PURSUING JOB OPPORTUNITIES

Job hunting can be a disheartening business. It is very easy to give up, or only make a token effort, if after a week or so all your attempts at finding a job seem to be fruitless. Yet this is the very moment when you should pursue your job hunting with increased effort. It can be dangerous to do it only when the spirit moves you (because the "spirit" tends to move you less, rather than more, when results are negative). Indeed, job hunt-ing should be done on a continuing basis, preferably with a plan that insures you do some every day.

The psychology of job hunting is comparatively recent. It came rapidly to the fore in the late 1960s, when numerous aerospace engineers were laid off, many of them middle-aged and having considerable ex-perience. Researchers found that some of these engineers made little or no attempt to find a new job. Or they filed two or three applications and then waited at home for the telephone to ring, much like a shy young girl waiting endlessly for a call from an imagined admirer. It proved very difficult to motivate these engineers to start from scratch; to convince them that employers would not come to them—that they must actively go out and sell themselves.

OBVIOUS EMPLOYERS

Local service stations
Automotive dealerships
Auto parts suppliers
Body shops
Auto rental outfits

NOT-SO-OBVIOUS EMPLOYERS

Government (federal, state, municipal) —
  Police and fire services
  Highway maintenance departments
  Parks and Recreation departments
  Office cars
Utilities —
  Electric power   Telephone
  Gas   Water
Furniture moving and storage outfits
Local delivery services
Long distance freight haulers
Transportation companies —
  Railways
  Airlines
  Motor coach lines
Retail department stores
Wholesalers
Chain stores (grocery and farm produce)

Fig. 2–4. A list of possible employers prepared by a job applicant with training in automotive mechanics.

Working with a Plan

It is best to work out a plan so your job hunting can be *seen* to be progressing. Although you may not seem to have any positive results, you will be able to see personal progress as you gradually cover territory.
You need to do two things:

1. Divide the day into two parts: one should be a regular time every day when you intend to stay at home to answer telephone calls; the other should be a longer time every day when you plan to call on prospective employers. The telephone time can also be used for making further plans for job hunting and for writing letters of application. It need not be long (no more than 2 hours), but it should be the same time every day so that you may inform prospective employers of it.
2. Identify on a map the location of offices you want to visit. Then take a certain section of the city, say several blocks of a major thoroughfare, and plan to call on all the possible employers along this stretch of pavement in one morning. The next day, take another part of the city and do the same thing. (You may liken this approach to a strategic military plan for systematically blanketing an area; in your case you would be mounting a campaign to find a good job.)

Taking the First Step

Even with a plan like this it is still possible to become depressed, to delay or even avoid going out at all, simply because making that initial contact by walking into a strange office is a lonely experience, and one that often results in a feeling of being unwanted. If you recognize this, and are aware that everybody you talk to in a strange office once went through what you are going through, it can help take the edge off the loneliness of your position. Remember, too, that all employers want to find good employees, and unless you make yourself known to an employer he may never know you exist. A door-to-door salesman would never sell his brushes, vacuum cleaners, or encyclopedias if he feared taking that active step which requires him to ring doorbells.

When calling on a company, ask the employee who confronts you (who probably will be a clerk or a typist) if you can speak to the person who handles job applications. At this point it helps to know this person's name, because instead of saying weakly: "May I please speak to the employment manager?" or "I'd like to speak to the person who looks after employment matters," you may say quite strongly: "May I speak to Mr. McGavin?" Your more positive approach will usually bring forth a positive response from the person facing you. You are then one step further inside the door.

EXERCISES

Exercise 4.1

Working alone, make a list of *types* (not names) of employers who might employ you in the particular trade for which you are being trained or have already completed a training course.

Exercise 4.2

Working in a group of four or five persons of the same or similar training as yourself, discuss possible *types* of employers. As a group, write out a list of *types* of employers who might employ you. Draw a horizontal line beneath the last entry.

Exercise 4.3

If several groups are making lists in Exercise 4.2, compare your group's list with those made by other groups. Add to the bottom of your group's list the names of additional types of employers thought of by other groups.

Exercise 4.4

Compare your personal list (Exercise 4.1) with the longer list you made in Exercise 4.2, and the even longer list you now have (Exercise 4.3). What observation about building up lists of possible types of employers can you make as a result of this comparison?

Exercise 4.5

From the list of types of employers built up in Exercises 4.1, 4.2, and 4.3, select the types you think could offer you the kind of work you would want to do. For each type, make a list of the names, addresses, and telephone numbers of employers you might ask for a job. (Use your local telephone directory or a trade directory to do this.)

Exercise 4.6

On a detailed map of your city, plot the location of each company listed in Exercise 4.5. IdentIfy groups of companies you could conveniently call on during a morning or an afternoon (i.e., during a three-hour period). How many companies would make a suitable-size group?

Exercise 4.7

If there are companies listed in Exercise 4.5 that you would telephone or write to rather than visit:
1. Explain why you would not visit them.
2. Indicate whether you would telephone or write to each of these companies.
3. Explain in each case why you have chosen to telephone rather than write, or vice versa.

5

Selling
Yourself
Well

There can be up to three stages in the hiring procedure, and you need to be successful at every stage if you are to be offered a job. If you fail to create a good impression at a particular stage your application simply progresses no further. You become one of the unsuccessful applicants.

CREATING A GOOD FIRST IMPRESSION

Appearance is an important factor in creating a good first impression. The way you shake hands, your tidiness and cleanliness, and your pleasantness, all contribute to the image that the interviewer will carry of you. It is not necessary that you dress in your best clothes—it's much better to dress comfortably but neatly in clothing that suits the type of work you want. A person looking for a job as a door-to-door encyclopedia salesman would obviously present himself to the encyclopedia company in a business suit; a girl applying for a job as a sales clerk in a store that sells clothing to the younger set should dress in clothing similar to the type being sold; and an auto body repair man would be suitably dressed if he appeared in presentable jeans and a sport shirt. The *condition* of the clothing you wear is particularly important, because its cleanliness and state of repair are signs of the quality of work you do. The same applies to personal cleanliness.

Making the Initial Contact Face to Face

When you first speak to persons who will answer "Yes" or "No" to your enquiry, tell them right away what they most need to hear from you. That is:

1. Say you are seeking employment;
2. Describe quickly what qualifications you have (those that suit the type of job they might have); and
3. Ask if there are any openings.

This initial statement should be brief but complete. For example:

> I'm looking for a job. I have had six months experience as a pot washer and general kitchen helper at the Memorial Home for the Elderly. Do you have any openings?

By concentrating everything in one short complete burst of information, you save time for the interviewer and offer a definite, forthright impression of yourself.

The interviewer, who in this case would most likely be the dietitian of an institution, can do one of four things:

1. She can say: "No. I'm sorry, we have no openings right now."

> If this happens, you should ask if she knows of other organizations that might be looking for help. It is unlikely that the dietitian does, but she probably knows the names of people in other organizations who hold positions similar to hers. These names can be very useful, and you should write them down before you leave. (Always try to carry away some useful information from every contact you make.) By following up these names you can learn of other names, one of which hopefully will lead to a successful interview and a job offer.

2. She can ask you to write your name, address, and phone number on a slip of paper.

> To an applicant this may seem promising, but is really little better than "No." The slip of paper can easily be lost, and anyway it almost immediately becomes only a name with no particular qualities about it to encourage the dietitian to call *you*, rather than another name on another slip of paper if an opening occurs. A better plan is to leave a Data Sheet containing information about you with the employer (this should be done regardless of the answer you receive), which she can turn to and read if she suddenly needs a new employee. There is more information about Data Sheets on pages 43 to 47.

3. She can ask you to fill in an application form.

This frequently happens in organizations that experience a fairly high turnover of help—which is very true of kitchen help. The dietitian would then hold your application as a person to interview if someone quits unexpectedly. She would be unlikely, however, to keep your application for much longer than three months.

4. She may interview you right away.

This could mean one of two things: either there is or shortly will be a job opening; or there is no job opening, but she is prescreening you to decide whether or not to keep your name on file should a vacancy occur.

Making the Initial Contact by Telephone

Not all initial contacts are made face to face. Sometimes it is more convenient to telephone (but "convenience" should be real, not a means for avoiding face-to-face contact).

If you choose to telephone, you should know that you are at a disadvantage compared to a person making a direct contact. Telephoning may save you from having to trudge from door to door, and the time and discomfort of sitting in an outer office waiting for someone to speak to you, but this convenience can be offset by hidden limitations. Some people do not project well over the telephone, even to creating an inaccurate image, while others have a hesitant telephone manner or sound unsure of themselves because they cannot see the person they are speaking to. Worst of all, a telephone applicant can be given the brushoff too easily.

Before telephoning, try to find out the name of the person who does the hiring and firing. (How? By calling up earlier and asking the switchboard operator.) Then when you confidently ask for him by name, your call will have a better chance of being put through.

For the uninitiated, getting past a switchboard operator or a secretary can be a formidable experience. If a secretary protects her boss from too many telephone calls, she may take it upon herself to screen you out. As a last resort, you can imply that you are either known to him or are returning a call by asking simply: "Is he in?" or "Is he back yet?" (The latter is a very natural question to ask, because it recognizes that a supervisor does come in and go out of his office fairly frequently. It is also subtle, because it seems to say that you are aware of his movements.)

When the employment manager answers the telephone, launch into the same burst of information that you would use for a face-to-face interview. The only difference is to identify yourself:

My name is Gail Orlikow and I am looking for work as a clerk-typist. I
have had one year's experience as a typist and part-time secretary at
Posner Furniture Wholesalers in Montrose, Ohio. Do you have any
openings?

Making the Initial Contact by Letter

In some circumstances you may have to write a letter of application. This happens when a company is in another city, if you are replying to a newspaper advertisement that asks for a written application,
or if you telephone the employment manager and he asks you to write
to him.

A letter of application is often the first step in the hiring procedure. If the employer likes what he sees, he probably will ask you to
complete an application form so he can judge you on the same basis as
other applicants. (He may also do this following an initial face-to-face
contact.) How carefully you prepare both your letter of application and
the application form tells an employer a lot about you. If either is untidy,
poorly arranged, or carelessly prepared, it may make him think you
will be an untidy, careless worker. If this happens, the door to step three
in the hiring procedure (the interview) remains shut.

A letter of application should have three parts:

1. **The initial contact** in which you state that you are applying for a job,
   and very briefly what your qualifications are to support your application.
2. **Some evidence** of your qualifications and past experience. Amplify what
   you said in the first paragraph by presenting facts about yourself, your
   training, and work that you have done. There must be no vague statements, for they leave too many questions in the reader's mind. For
   example:
   I have had plenty of experience in refrigeration work.
   How much is "plenty?" What kind of experience: installation? maintenance? repair? or only cleaning? And what kind of refrigeration
   work: small household refrigerators? large commercial units? or massive
   refrigeration systems?
   A better example of good evidence contains *facts* (who you worked for,
   how long you worked, and the kind of work you did):
   During my two years with Angle Services I carried out preventive
   maintenance and emergency repair of building refrigeration systems,
   primarily those in the Montrose and Kelvin Arenas, and in the
   Connaught Building.
   If you have a fair amount to write, you would do better to attach a
   Data Sheet containing details of your education and work experience
   rather than let your letter become too long.

3. **A closing statement** in which you indicate that you would like to come in for an interview and are available to do so.

Typical letters of application appear in Figs. 2–5 and 2–6. The comfortable, almost chatty style of the letter in Fig. 2–5, particularly in the first and last paragraphs, makes the reader feel that Gail would be a pleasant person to interview. And the evidence paragraph demonstrates her rather limited experience to good effect. The appearance of Gail's letter is important, too, because it testifies to her capability as a clerk-typist.

---

21 - 456 Guelph Avenue
Minneapolis, Minn.
55403

10 April 19__

Mr. Harvey Wilkin
Office Manager
Delta Distributors
201 Princess Street
Minneapolis, Minn.
55412

Dear Mr. Wilkin:

As a newcomer to Minneapolis, I am looking for work. Do you need someone with clerical/typing experience?

My previous employment has been as a clerk/typist with Posner Furniture Wholesalers in Montrose, Ohio, where for one year I did routine clerical and secretarial work, including typing, invoicing, filing, and record keeping. Prior to that I worked for two years as a part-time typist and file clerk for Rivercrest Realty, also of Montrose. My experience includes typing from a dictaphone, sending messages by Telex, and operating a 12-line switchboard. I have completed Grade XII (Ohio), Business option.

If there is a possibility of employment with Delta Distributors, may I come in for an interview? My telephone number is 457-6619, and I am at home every morning between 9 and 11 a.m.

Yours truly

Gail Orlikow

Gail Orlikow

Fig. 2–5. A general letter of application for employment.

Ken Goulding's letter (Fig. 2–6) also would get a good response because he sounds believable.

Preparing a Data Sheet

There are two uses for a Data Sheet: to attach to a letter of application, and to hand to a prospective employer that you visit. The same form can be used for both occasions. It should be typed neatly so that the reader gains the impression of a well-organized, presentable applicant before he reads a word about you.

A Data Sheet contains information that will help an employer assess the kind of person you are. Although details of your work experience and education are important, he will also be interested in your interests and hobbies. From these he can gain an insight into you as a complete person rather than just a narrow view of you as an employee having had certain work experience.

Data Sheets should be similar to the example in Fig. 2–7, and generally contain the following parts (see page 47):

1. Personal Information

The minimum information here should be your age, address, telephone number, and marital status. Additional items you might like to include would be personal statistics (height, weight, etc.) and Social Security number.

2. Education

It is usually sufficient to show the highest school level you achieved, the name and location of the school you then attended, and the year. Details of primary education may be included, but are not necessary.

For courses taken and diplomas received since graduating from high school, you should list the title of the course, where and when it was taken, and the type of diplomas you received (e.g., diploma, certificate, etc).

3. Work Experience

Because this is the information an employer most wants to read, you should tell him what kind of work you have done as well as where you were employed. Here are some suggestions:

273 Argyle Street
Reece, Minn. 55747

May 11, 19___

Mr. Andy McGuire
Wilding's Motors Inc
20 Craven Road
Weekaskasing Falls, Wis. 53144

Dear Mr. McGuire:

I am applying for the position of Automotive Mechanic in your Weekaskasing Falls service station, which was advertised in the May 8 Reece Enquirer.

Currently, I am attending a 10-month Automotive Mechanic's course at Reece Community College, and will graduate on June 28. My progress has been good, with marks mostly in the "B" range (Mr. D. Craven, one of my instructors, can provide a reference for me).

As I grew up on my father's farm near Eau Claire, Wis., I gained considerable mechanical experience operating and doing maintenance on all the farm machinery. I worked for my father for two years before taking the automotive course, and for the past eight months have been a part-time welder in Mr. B. Mugrin's machine shop at 121 Ferrymoor Road, Reece, Minn.

I would like to live and work in Weekaskasing Falls, and look forward to an interview with you when you are in Minneapolis. To contact me, please leave a message at (218) 775-1160.

Yours sincerely
Ken Goulding
KEN G. GOULDING

Fig. 2–6(a) Letter of application replying to an advertisement.

The letter on the opposite page is in reply to this advertisement in the Reece, Minn., Enquirer:

WILDING'S MOTORS INC.

invites applications from

AUTOMOTIVE MECHANICS, BODY SHOP PERSONNEL,

AND PARTS COUNTERMEN

to fill positions that will be created in a

new facility to be opened in

WEEKASKASING FALLS, WISCONSIN

Applicants should have at least some related experience in the automotive field. Good starting wages plus fringe benefits and relocation expenses. Interviews will be held in Minneapolis. Apply in writing to:

Andy McGuire, Wilding's Motors Inc., 20 Craven Road, Weekaskasing Falls, Wis. 53144

Note how Ken Goulding introduces that he has welding experience. He could have said:

I also have experience as a welder.

or

I have also done some welding.

Instead, he mentions where he works, for how long he has done this work, and the name of the person he works for. Details such as these, providing they are not overdone, turn an unknown applicant into a believable person that Andy McGuire would want to talk to.

A person with more work experience than this may prefer to write a shorter letter and attach a Data Sheet (also known as a Resumé or Biography) like that in Fig. 2–7. When a Data Sheet is used, the "evidence" paragraph of the letter simply summarizes the most important points in the Data Sheet.

Fig. 2–6(b) Comments on letter of application on opposite page.

a. Arrange periods of employment in reverse order (start with present or most recent job and work backwards to your first job).
b. Cover the whole period from the time you started work (don't leave any blanks for the employer to wonder about).
c. For each job you have had, give:

   The name and location of the company (underline the company name);
   The length of time you were employed (give start and finish dates);
   The name of your job position (e.g.; packer, lab assistant, instrument man);
   The kind of work you did.

   When describing work, give enough information so the reader can see what your *responsibilities* were. For example, Frank Wittering's entry for Franklin Fisheries ("June 1974 to date" in Fig. 2–7) would have been much less descriptive if it had only said:

   Worked on refrigeration and deep freeze plant

   By using the verb *servicing*, Frank demonstrates much more clearly the kind of work he was doing.

4. Interests

Enter here your interests or activities outside work or school. An employer will be particularly interested to read that you have been a member of the YMCA, YMHA, YWCA, Scouts, or other community organizations, and especially so if you have been active in the organization (group secretary, for instance) rather than just a member.

5. References

When entering the names of persons who have agreed to act as references for you, include their position or a comment to show employers who they are and why they will give a realistic reference. Simply to give a person's name and address seems to imply that the person is only a friend (and so may not give an unbiased opinion).

Filling in an Application Form

Because we are all familiar with our own backgrounds and experience, and because everyone is tired of having to fill in forms, there is a tendency to take short cuts when filling in an application form for an employer. Yet there is a great danger that an application form filled in hurriedly or carelessly may tell the wrong story about you as a potential employee. If, for example, there is a space on the form that asks

DATA SHEET

FRANK G. WITTERING

Personal Information:

Age: 23

Address: 411 Chamblay Avenue, Gamble, Minn; Tel. 489-6027

Marital Status: Married, no children

Education:

High School Graduation, Walker Collegiate, Ohio, 1971
Certificate in Refrigeration & Air Conditioning, Montrose, Ohio,
    Community College, June 1974

Work Experience:

June 1974 to date	Franklin Fisheries, Gamble, Minn. Maintenance technician servicing refrigeration and deep freeze plant.
Sept 1973 to June 1974	Taking Refrigeration course at Montrose Community College.
May 1972 to Aug 1973	International Nickel Company, Thompson, Canada. Underground worker in mine, assisting in excavating ore deposits.
June 1968 to May 1972	Palliser Printers, Walker, Ohio. Printer's helper, doing binding, cutting and stitching in bindery, and some small offset press work and hand typesetting for newspaper. Part time for three years (while at high school); full time for one year.

Interests:

Mostly modifying stock cars and sometimes driving them. Member of 4H
Club from 1967 to 1970; president of Walker, Ohio, Club for one year.

References:

Mr. G. Wilimovsky Plant Superintendent Bluebell Frozen Goods Reece, Minn., 55747 (previously Chief Plant Engineer at Franklin Fisheries)	Mrs. Janice Verigny Owner Palliser Printers Walker, Ohio 43374

Fig. 2–7. A typical Data Sheet (also known as a Biography or Resumé).

for your present biweekly wage, don't enter an hourly rate just because it happens to be the rate you know. The impression the employment manager will gain is that either you resist or are not good at following instructions (whereas it may simply be that you didn't trust yourself to multiply your hourly rate of $3.42 × 37½ hours per week × 2 weeks).

For the same reason, try to answer every question rather than leave any blank spaces. If you don't know the answer to a question, write "not known"; or if it simply does not apply to you, write "does not apply," "not applicable," or its abbreviation "N/A."

Many job applicants feel that it is unnecessary to put much into the "Hobbies and Interests" section of an application form. This section is there to help the employer see if you are a well-rounded person with a reasonable range of interests. It also provides him with a topic to talk about during the initial moments of an interview. You can help him and yourself by writing down interests (such as community activities), sports, and hobbies that you can talk about knowledgeably.

PREPARING FOR AN INTERVIEW

The final stage in the job selection process is the employment interview. In the full process this is the third stage, and the only one during which you present yourself personally before a prospective employer. In the preceding stages he has gained only a "paper" impression of you based on your letter of application, Data Sheet, or job application form; now he wants to see how you measure up. He has probably narrowed down the list of applicants to those who have demonstrated on paper that they are fully qualified for the job, or have impressed him because they have other interesting qualities. He will now see them in the flesh, and will base his decision on whom to select partly on what he has already read, but primarily on what he sees. This, then, is your main chance to do a good selling job.

Preparation is of vital importance for a successful job interview because it influences how well you present yourself. Preparation involves learning something about the company that has a job opening, preparing to answer difficult questions, and knowing what questions you want to ask.

Learn Something About the Company

During an interview, opportunities may suddenly occur for you to comment on or ask questions about the company. You should have some idea of its size, plants in other cities, and principal products. It is also useful to know something about its history, and items that have recently been in the news.

Some interviewers test an applicant's knowledge of the company by asking seemingly innocent questions. For example, when an applicant for a job as a lineman's helper was asked what other type of work he thought he could do, he replied that he would like to work on the company's production line. But he had not researched the company and so did not know it only installed and maintained electric power lines. Indeed, he really was not quite sure what a lineman's helper does! He had simply noticed in the advertisement that the pay was good and had jumped in quickly to be one of the first applicants.

How can you find information about a company? One source is the local business directory; another, the trade and commerce department of the municipal government; a third, the information desk of the local library. The amount of research you do will depend upon the company's size: obviously, little research is needed for a two- or three-man company, other than perhaps to discover what its principal product is and who owns the company.

Prepare for Difficult Questions

"Difficult" questions are those that ask about your motives and test whether you have really thought about the job you are applying for. For example, it is common for an interviewer to ask why an applicant wants to work for that particular company. If the applicant takes too long to answer, the interviewer may think he has not thought about it enough to be seriously interested in the job. Similarly, if you are already employed but are looking for another job, a prospective employer is likely to ask why you want to leave your present job. If you are unprepared, you may hesitate or offer an inadequate answer; to the interviewer you may seem to be hiding something.

The third most likely question is:

What wage are you looking for?

or:

If we offer you a job, how much do you think we should pay you?

Many applicants hesitate to answer this question. They fear that if their figure is too high they may eliminate themselves as applicants; or, conversely, if it is too low the employer will take advantage of them and offer less than he planned to pay. Neither should be true. Most companies have a specific starting wage for each job, which is what they will offer an inexperienced applicant. An experienced applicant can, of course, expect a higher starting wage.

Why, then, does an employer ask this question? He is probably testing you to see if you evaluate yourself properly, and whether you have prepared adequately for the interview. To answer his question, you should decide beforehand what pay you would like in light of the going rate for the kind of work you will be doing (the labor board and persons employed in similar positions are useful sources for this information). For an unskilled job, the going rate may be the minimum wage established by the government, or, if a union represents the employees, a rate established by agreement between the union and the company. If it calls for some experience, it probably will be higher. So don't be alarmed if during an interview you discover you have estimated the wage incorrectly. If your figure is too high, the employer will suggest a starting wage and ask if it will be acceptable. The same should happen if you quote a wage that is lower than he normally pays.

You should also consider fringe benefits. These can be small things, like the amount of paid holiday you will have each year, whether the employer pays all or part of your health insurance premiums, whether there is a group insurance plan, whether there is a company pension plan and, perhaps most important, whether there are prospects for you to move up within the firm. All should be considered as additions to the basic wage, which means you need to look at the question of pay as a total package rather than simply take-home pay.

Know What Questions to Ask

Toward the end of an interview you will probably be asked if you have any questions. This is the moment when your mind goes completely blank as you frantically try to remember what you planned to say. Before the interview, you should have jotted a few brief, easy-to-read questions onto a slip of paper or card, and placed it in your pocket or handbag. Some people think this should not be done because it looks like a crib sheet. I cannot agree. To the interviewer, it is simply another sign that you are prepared for the interview.

TAKING PART IN THE INTERVIEW

So much for preparation. Now for the interview itself. You will want to impress the interviewer that you are the right person for the job, but nervousness can make you appear unnaturally quiet, hesitant, or awkward. Your voice seems squeaky, you sweat, you don't know what to do with your hands, and you seem to say all the wrong things. Much of this is normal, and can be partly overcome by knowing that your outward appearance is good and that inside conditions are under control. Here are a few pointers.

Dress Comfortably

Wear clothes that suit the job you are applying for. But be sure they are neat and clean. Someone answering an advertisement for a short-order cook should not arrive in greasy coveralls (from working on his car) and expect to get the job; neither should a high school student seeking employment as a nurse's aide wear Bermuda shorts and a halter top (although this might be suitable attire if she was applying for a job as an outdoor swimming pool assistant).

Appear Confident

Create the impression of a confident person, even though you may be feeling anything but sure of yourself. Walk firmly into the room, shake hands definitely, look directly at the interviewer, and settle well back in the chair when you are asked to sit, so that you are not poised uncomfortably on the edge. Then look your interviewer expectantly in the eye, inviting him to ask the first question.

Control Your Voice

Speak up. Too many applicants seem afraid to speak above a whisper, which makes the interviewer lean uncomfortably forward to hear them. Others rush their words out, as if in a hurry to get the interview over. You should speak clearly and distinctly at a moderate pace, pausing when necessary to think out exactly what you want to say.

Answer Questions Properly

Because some applicants are very nervous they tend to answer questions too briefly, saying only "Yes," "No," "Oh, fine," "Uh-huh," and so on. This prevents an interviewer from learning much. In the short time he has with you, an interviewer wants to find out something about you: he wants to know what you think and hear your opinions. It is up to you to help him.

A skillful interviewer will pave the way by asking questions that cannot be answered "Yes" or "No." (Such questions often start with words like "How" and "Why.") If you are faced by a less skillful interviewer, you would be wise to answer questions that call for only simple answers with additional information that he probably wants but has not asked for. For example, a machinist asked if he has experience working on a turret lathe would probably say: "Yes," or "Yes, I have." But to this he should add additional information, such as: "Yes. I used a turret lathe for 14 months at —— company, making ——s and ——s."

If you do not know the answer to a question, don't bluff; instead, say directly that you do not know. An honest admission that you don't know is much better than a hastily made-up answer that may seem like a "snow job."

THE INTERVIEW'S PARTS

An interview normally breaks into three parts:

1. A short opening, during which the interviewer does a reasonable amount of the talking.
2. A long middle, during which you as the applicant are expected to do most of the talking.
3. A short closing part, during which you and the interviewer exchange final questions and answers.

In the first part the interviewer may try to discuss your personal life, your background, your interests, or your hobbies. He will choose one of these topics because you should be able to talk more easily about them than your work and the job you are applying for. His plan will be to relax you as much as he can during the initial two or three minutes.

In the middle part of the interview he will want you to talk far more than he talks. He will expect you to discuss or talk sufficiently about each topic for him to gain a good impression of work you have done (he will be particularly interested in the responsibilities of each job and your ability to work without supervision), the type of person you are, and how you got along with your previous employers and the people you worked with.

In the closing stage the interviewer normally summarizes the main points about the job and offers information on topics not covered earlier. (This frequently covers routine items such as hours of work, fringe benefits, and length of probationary period.) He will also ask if you have any questions. This is a signal for you to check the little question card you made earlier. It also alerts you to the fact that the interview is nearly over.

Before you leave, the interviewer should inform you how soon he will let you know if you have the job. (You should always assume that there are several applicants for a job, and that a final decision will not be reached until after the last one has been interviewed.) If he forgets to do this, you should ask.

An interviewer will seldom give any indication of your suitability during the interview. His policy should be to let each applicant feel he is being given full consideration and has an equal opportunity to be given the job. Sometimes an interviewer may realize that a particular applicant simply is not suitable for the job he has in mind, and may quietly play down the applicant's chances without coming right out and saying so. His purpose will be to prevent such an applicant from walking away from an interview in a "glow," feeling that he has a good chance for getting the job when it is unlikely that he will be selected.

An applicant should make it clear by his manner that he is sincerely interested in finding work, and in learning more about the job and the company that will employ him. But if during the interview he realizes it is not the kind of job he wants, and decides that he would in no way take the job even if it is offered to him, he should tell the interviewer that he wants to withdraw his application. This helps both the interviewer and those who do want the job, because it shortens the list of applicants. (When an interviewer is told by an applicant that he is not interested in the job, the interviewer normally asks why—in case he has created a false impression about the job and the company. Indeed, he may even try to persuade the applicant to reconsider.)

WAITING FOR A CALL

After a seemingly successful interview, an applicant may lull himself into thinking he has the job "all tied up." So with a false sense of security he sits at home waiting for the employer to call him. Eventually it comes as a shock to receive a courtesy letter saying that the job has been filled by someone else. It also becomes much more difficult to start all over again and actively pursue other jobs.

The remedy is obvious, but not easy to apply. It involves continually searching, making initial contacts, filling in application forms, and attending interviews. To do this successfully means working with a plan, like the one described on page 35. Remember: it is extremely short-sighted to chase only one job at a time.

EXERCISES

Exercise 5.1

Select a small company, then write out a good opening statement you would say to the boss or one of his managers:

1. When you meet him face to face.
2. When he answers the telephone.

Exercise 5.2

Draw up a Data Sheet or Biography describing yourself (see pages 43 to 47). Decide whether you have enough work or other experience to warrant attaching the Data Sheet to a letter of application. If so, attach it to the letters requested in Exercises 5.4 and 5.5.

Exercise 5.3

Select a company you would like to work for, then research and list information about the company that would be helpful when writing to it and talking about job prospects during an interview.

Exercise 5.4

Write an unsolicited letter of application to the company in Exercise 5.3.

Exercise 5.5

From the classified advertisements in your newspaper, select a job you would like to apply for (alternatively, select one of the advertisements on the opposite page), then:

1. Write an opening statement for a telephone enquiry.
2. Write an opening statement for a face-to-face enquiry.
3. Write a letter of application. (If you are replying to a newspaper advertisement, clip it out and attach it to your letter.)

Exercise 5.6

Assume you are called in for an interview by the company you applied to in Exercise 5.4 or 5.5.

1. Draw up a list of questions you would want to ask during the interview.
2. Select the three most important questions, and list them in downward order of importance.

HELP WANTED

DISTRIBUTION OPERATIONS CLERK

National Paint Co. has an immediate opening within its distribution function leading to varied challenging positions. We require a neat, conscientious aggressive person capable of responsibility and a genuine desire for advancement. Starting salary open to qualifications. Apply with full particulars to Box 607

LARGE IMPORT AUTOMOTIVE GARAGE REQUIRES MECHANICS OR MECHANICALLY INCLINED PERSONNEL TO WORK ON IMPORT AND DOMESTICS.
P. O. BOX 2051, DORVAL STATION

AUTO BODY REPAIR PERSON WITH HAND TOOLS. FULL TIME EMPLOYMENT. NO FLAT RATE. GOOD WORKING CONDITIONS. APPLY BOX 536

REQUIRED IMMEDIATELY

Responsible individual who is interested in performing finishing and packaging operations in the collecting department of a printing plant operation.
Apply Box 638

SECRETARY with accounting knowledge for 1 girl CONSTRUCTION OFFICE. NATIONAL COMPANY. Good salary and benefits. State background and experience to Box 545.

GENERAL LABORER FOR DIVERsified sprinkler irrigated farm. Permanent employment, training on the job provided. House and utilities supplied for married couple in Southern Alberta. Good future for right person. Write Box 524

JR. ACCOUNTING CLERK

Require a junior accounting clerk age 19-22, to handle under supervision accounts payable, costing and coding of invoices and to assist in collections. Prerequisites are min. 1 yrs. office exp. in accounting work OR successful completion of a basic accounting course. Drivers licence also required. Apply in your own handwriting giving resume of personal & job history and salary expected to Box 546.

REGISTER FOR FLEXIBLE EMPLOYMENT IN THE FOLLOWING AREAS:
Indust. engineering
Electr. Drafting
Mech. drafting
Accounting
Couriers
Sales
etc.

Please reply to Box 626

DISTRIBUTOR FOR A NATIONAL Food Co. reqs. imm. a young reliable person to assist in warehouse and deliveries within the city limits. Exc. working cond. Good starting salary with a good chance for advancement. Apply Box 643

WE HAVE 3 POSITIONS OPEN FOR, 1 qualified sign painter with ability to do layout work. 1 person with a real desire to learn sign painting. 1 person to learn the paper posting trade, in our outdoor advertising posting service. Good working cond. & benefits. Apply Box 10.

WATCH MAKER

Exp. watch maker req., good opportunities in expanding business. Apply, Box 632.

DRIVERS NEEDED FOR 1, 2, OR 3 EVENINGS PER WEEK FOR LIGHT DELIVERIES

Hours 6-9 p.m.
Must have a good driving record.

Apply to Box 649

COMPETENT BOOKKEEPER-TYPIST for permanent part-time employment in well located downtown office. Competitive wages. applications strictly confidential. Box 526.

RECEPTIONIST

Typing and an outgoing personality required. Reply to Box 573

DRIVER FOR FLOWER SHOP. MUST know city. Box 402

SERVICE STATION PERSONNEL wanted. Some mechanical knowledge preferred. Days & evgs. Age 20 & up. Please write to Box 721

EXPERIENCED DENTAL TECHnician wanted. Good opportunity. Top wages and benefits. Apply P.O. Box 550.

LICENCED PRACTICAL NURSES REquired for day & evening shifts. Reply stating experience, marital status etc. to Box 552

DELIVERY PERSON, MALE OR FEmale for automotive supply firm. Chance for advancement. Write Box 653.

NCR 171 ACCT. MACHINE OP., accts. receivable & office procedures. Reply to Box 612

REQUIRED IMMED - 2 QUALIFIED service technicians with automatic transmission exp. Reply in writing to Box 637

JUNIOR ACCOUNTANT
LARGE PRECAST CONCRETE MANUFACTURER

Offers a cost accounting, position in its West Kildonan office. Good starting salary and company benefit plans. Some experience and own transportation necessary. Apply in confidence stating qualifications and experience to Box 617

Experienced parts truck driver required immediately. Grade XI Education preferred. Must be reliable, bondable, ambitious and have clear driving record. Write to Box 604.

PERSON NEEDED FOR GENERAL office duties - answering phone, typing, filing & knowledge of bookkeeping Reply to box 579

Florist shop requires reliable energetic person for full-time employment. 40-hr. wk. including Saturdays. Experience preferred. Reply stating qualifications to Box 625

REQUIRE PERSON WITH GRADE XI education and mechanical ability for specialized trade. Will train applicant. Starting rate to $500. per month if qualified. Apply Box 622

DRIVER SALES PERSON TO SELL auto supplies to service stations, etc. Must be bondable. Write to Box 650.

PERSONS 19-25 WANTED TO TRAIN on heavy duty cutting machines. Full time only. Apply Box 609.

ORDER DESK CLERK

For auto glass department. Must have knowledge of cars and trucks, and a clear driver's licence Box 603

WANTED DRIVER FOR FAST FOOD service with own car.
Write to Box 507

III

COMMUNICATING
AS AN EMPLOYEE

6

Communicating with Other Employees

When you jump from the outer circle to the inner circle (see page 30), you shed your role of unemployed application and suddenly become an employee. At first you communicate only with employees who work with or near you, and occasionally with your immediate supervisor. But as the days pass you meet more and more employees at every level, and have dealings with them on business, personal, and social matters.

YOUR FIRST DAYS ON THE JOB

For those initial days or weeks on a new job, you should look around, watch others, and listen. Look around to find out where things are—the lunchroom, washrooms, water fountain, library, coffee machines —and where your supervisor can be found. At the same time watch others to see what they do: what time they stop for coffee, lunch, and end of day; where they go to get spare parts; the routes that those who live near you take to get to work. Getting to know things like these will make you feel comfortable in your new surroundings, and quickly add to your sense of "belonging."

Listen to what your supervisor and other employees have to say. You may choose to listen *casually, attentively,* or *critically* to those you work with. Try to identify who gets an attentive ear from other employees, and to whom they listen only casually. Then when you want to ask a question (like: "Who do I see to borrow company tools overnight?"), you will know who to turn to.

But listen *attentively* to your supervisor, who at first will patiently explain procedures and methods, but will expect you to know them after only a few days. And never be afraid to ask questions. A supervisor would much prefer you to ask, even though the answer may seem painfully obvious, than to make a costly error.

Three days after starting at Waddington's Wholesale Grocers, Kathy Winowski was asked by her boss to run off (meaning print) 20 copies of an important order, and to do it right away. She knew the company had its own printing machine (she had read about it in the company newspaper), but she did not know where it was. So she asked Gary Davidson, the chief clerk, who directed her to the print room in the basement. The printer told her he could do the job but that she would have to wait because he already had a rush job on the press. So Kathy waited, and waited, and waited—until the printer had finished printing 8,000 copies of a form.

Meanwhile, her boss was fuming impatiently upstairs, having expected her back in ten minutes. He thought she was using the small office copier in the legal department down the hall, and now he didn't know where she had disappeared (most likely taking a very long coffee break, he thought). If Kathy had asked him, rather than someone else, where the machine was, then he would have directed her to the right place. Or if she had thought to ask the printer how long his rush job would take, she probably would have gone back to her boss and told him of the delay.

This need to anticipate what is wanted—to think ahead and ask questions whenever you are in doubt—is an important aspect of in-company communication.

TAKING PART IN COMPANY SOCIAL ACTIVITIES

Most companies hold social activities, depending on the number of employees and their sociableness, and on management's encouragement. Although no one will expect you to attend every activity that your company plans, it is a good thing to take in at least some of them.

Surprisingly, you may find that the guy in the machine shop who yelled at you for moving his toolbox is a top-notch golfer who gladly shows you how to correct your stance, and then invites you to go around the course with him next Saturday. Or that the crusty old man you've noticed in the paint shop becomes a boisterous cook behind a barbecue. And the acid-tongued cashier who quarreled with you in the cafeteria last week beams at you at the Christmas dance. Suddenly, people you have seen only in their work environment are different: they haven't changed, but in shedding their protective workaday roles they seem to have become more "human."

The opposite also is true: you have become a different person in their eyes. To the machinist, the spray painter, and the cashier, you are no longer just the "new employee" but someone who enjoys relaxation just as much as they do.

The chemistry that makes all this happen is, quite simply, communication. Social affairs provide an opportunity for people to meet and talk to each other in a way that they generally cannot do in the more restrictive atmosphere at work. Such communication is not always spoken: it can be a nod of approval, a grin, a raised glass, or a hand on one's sleeve. But the effect is far-reaching, because when you meet again as employees the following day or next week you have something in common: a shared experience.

Management is well aware that social activities promote good working relationships. Employees get to know each other better, and have the chance to talk to their supervisors on subjects of common interest. (These should never include "work" topics; they may be mentioned in passing, but a social event should not become an extension of the office.) All-company social affairs also give managers a chance to circulate among the employees, and to talk more comfortably with them than they can possibly do in the day-to-day business atmosphere.

JOINING AN EMPLOYEES' COMMITTEE

Company parties, golf tournaments, and bowling leagues don't just happen: they need willing persons to run them. In larger companies, social committees are elected into office by all the employees. In smaller companies social activities occur more casually, with someone just suggesting that everyone go bowling or to the beach for a picnic, and others volunteering to take part in various ways.

The longer you are an employee of a particular company, the more likely you are to be asked to help out at a forthcoming affair, and later even to serve on the social committee. You may feel you are too new, or don't know enough employees, or are too inexperienced to do a good job. But you would be wise to accept.

What are the advantages?

* There is no better way to meet people and to get known yourself.
* Your enjoyment of the event is greater.

* You get invaluable experience in planning and organizing an activity and taking part in meetings.
* You get noticed as a "doer" rather than a "watcher" (a plus in your favor when the company later looks for someone to promote from the shop floor).
* You get a chance to exercise your communication abilities.

The social committee may not be the only organization that needs you. There may be a sickness and retirement gift fund that requires helpers to collect a small amount on paydays from everybody who belongs to it. Or there may be a saving and lending organization, known as a credit union, whose purpose is to offer moderate-interest savings accounts for employees with money to spare, and low-interest loans for those needing extra cash. Employees are elected to an executive committee, which then appoints a supervisory committee, credit committee, and delinquent loan committee, all staffed voluntarily. Although nobody from company management may serve on these committees (to prevent any suspicion of company involvement) the credit union may employ an independent manager, who in turn may have paid assistants.

Serving as a committee member of a company credit union offers excellent experience in business management. Its operations are very similar to those of any properly run business, in that it has to keep records of how its affairs are run and of every decision made by its committees. Each committee appoints a chairman to run its meetings (they are run slightly more formally than, say, those of the social committee), and a secretary to write the committee's decisions into meeting "minutes," which become a permanent record for inspection by the credit union management committee and independent auditors.

Employees holding positions as committee chairmen and secretaries need to be good communicators. Most learn their roles when, as committee members, they watch the previous chairman and secretary in action. It is more useful, however, to have some knowledge of what to do before you serve on any of these committees. Here are some suggestions.

How to Be a Committee Member

When you are first elected or appointed to a committee, it is usually as a committee member. This gives you the chance to see how things are done, for in time you may be chosen to be secretary, or possibly chairman, and will need to know the procedure for holding meetings.

Committee members discuss each point introduced by the chairman or the person he calls on to make a proposal, and decide whether they are for or against whatever is being suggested. Their role is to *listen critically,* to ask questions where necessary, and to contribute to the discussion *when they have something useful to say.*

If, for example, the suggestion being discussed is a proposal to increase the credit union manager's salary by $30 a month, you might want to ask what his salary is now, or when he last received a pay increase. Or, if you know the salary being paid to the manager of another credit union and the other members do not, you would want to speak up and tell them what you know.

As a committee member you may be asked to get some information for the next meeting. If you have a lot of facts and figures to present, print them neatly onto a large card for display or have them typed onto a sheet of paper and make enough copies to give one to each member. This is much better than reciting figures that no one will be able to remember. Your display card or handout in this case might look like Fig. 3–1.

When your turn comes to report your findings to the meeting, you can either hold up your card or hand out your sheets. But you should not let everyone draw their own conclusions. Rather, you should explain briefly what the comparison of salaries means:

> I've averaged the salaries of five other credit union managers, plus ours, and found that our manager earns about $90 a month less than average. But he has some 600 fewer members' accounts to look after.

SALARY COMPARISON – CREDIT UNION MANAGERS		
CREDIT UNION	No. OF MEMBERS	SALARY
POMONA	320	$ 875
NEEDLE TRADES	960	1050
CROSSTOWN	2340	1240
VALLEY FIELD	1650	1095
WINCHESTER	700	1020
OUR MANAGER	470	950
AVERAGE	1073	$1038

Fig. 3–1. Display card or handout sheet for use at a meeting.

You can say this either just before you hand out the sheets, or after the committee has had a few moments to study them.

Then, when the discussion is over, the chairman will ask all the committee members to say whether or not they think the manager should be paid more. He will quote a definite figure, which he will have obtained by listening to what is said during the discussion. If, for example, the discussion indicated that most members felt $30 a month to be a reasonable increase, in a very informal committee the chairman might simply ask:

Well, what do you think: shall we give Bill another thirty bucks?

If most of the members say "Yes," then the suggestion is approved.

In a more formally run committee, proposals or suggestions are called "motions." Each motion has to be proposed by a committee member and seconded by another one, whose names are recorded in the minutes of the meeting. If you are the person who first suggested that the manager's pay be increased, you may be asked by the chairman to make a formal proposal, in which case you simply say:

I propose that Bill Stark's salary be increased by $30 a month.

If another person agrees with you, he indicates this by saying:

I second that.

The chairman then asks the committee to vote on your motion, saying something like this:

Proposed by Andy Sandal [you], seconded by Don Trail, that the credit union manager's salary be increased by $30; that is, from $950 to $980 a month.

He then asks how many approve the proposal, saying:

Who is in favor?

He repeats the question to find out how many are against the proposal:

How many against?

If the majority approve (members indicate their approval or disapproval by raising a hand when asked if they are in favor of or against the motion), the chairman says:

Motion carried.

If the majority vote is against the proposal, he says:

Motion defeated.

How to be Committee Chairman

As chairman of a committee your role should be to run the committee's meetings, but not control them. Many newly elected chairmen tend to forget this. They remember that as a committee member they took an active part in discussing each proposal, not noticing that the previous chairman (if he was doing his job properly) allowed the discussions to run their course, interrupting only if members strayed from the topic or became engaged in a heated argument.

The chairman has three main things to do:

1. **He must prepare a list of topics** (commonly known as the agenda—see Fig. 3–2) to be discussed at the meeting. The first item is usually approval of the previous meeting's minutes. Then comes a list of items to discuss. Finally, there is a single entry: "Other business," which gives committee members the chance to introduce new items not on the agenda.

2. **He must run the meeting,** which means introducing each topic in turn (usually in the order listed on the agenda), inviting the members to discuss it, sensing when there has been sufficient discussion, and, if a motion has been proposed, asking the members to vote on it. He starts by calling the meeting to order and asking the secretary to read aloud the minutes of the previous meeting. When this has been done he asks the committee to approve the minutes as being correct (in a formal meeting he asks someone to propose, and someone else to second, that the minutes be approved), and then goes on to the next item. He introduces each item like this:

   The next item is a proposal from Andy Sandal that the credit union manager's salary be increased.

   He should then ask the person making the proposal (Andy, in this case) to give more information or explain why he has made it. At the end of the discussion he should repeat the proposal, ask for someone else to second it, and call for a vote as described on page 63.

   If several changes to a proposal are suggested during the discussion, the chairman must make it quite clear what the agreed change is and who suggested it before calling for a seconder and asking the members to vote:

   The motion proposed by Andy Sandal, as amended by Carol Rayner,

MONTROSE MANUFACTURERS CREDIT UNION

Notice of Executive Committee Meeting
February 12, 19__, 4.30 p.m.

AGENDA

1.   Approval of Minutes, January 15 meeting.

2.   Proposed amalgamation with Pomona C.U.

3.   Manager's salary.

4.   Other business

R.G. Burns, Chairman

Fig. 3–2. Agenda for a committee meeting

is for the credit union manager's salary to be increased by $30 a
month effective March 1st, and a further $10 a month effective
September 1st.

3. **He must sense when there has been sufficient discussion,** then call for a
vote to be taken.

You will find that the most difficult part of your job as chairman
will be to communicate the impression that you are running the meeting
without suppressing comments from any of the committee members. You
may also have to quieten an overly talkative member and encourage a quiet
person to take part.

How to be Committee Secretary

The secretary is not only a secretary but also a committee member like everyone else. He (or she) can take part in the discussion and vote, but must not become so involved as to forget to take notes.

If you are appointed secretary, your chief worry will probably be how to take down correctly everything that is said. The answer is quite simply that you don't have to. The most important things to record are:

1. The wording of each item or proposal, and the name of the person who introduced it.
2. Any changes that are made to the original proposal and the names of persons suggesting the changes.
3. The names of persons proposing and recording motions, and whether each motion is carried or defeated.
4. Any important factors mentioned that are likely to be followed up, and the names of persons who will be taking action.

Don't try to write the minutes in proper sentences while the meeting is going on. Make short notes, using the person's initials and the letters "P," "A," or "S" to indicate who proposed, amended, or seconded a motion, and the letters "C" or "D" to show whether the motion was carried or defeated. The only words you must record accurately are the exact words of the motion (if necessary you can ask the chairman to repeat them, to be sure you have them right).

Then, when the meeting is over, you should write the minutes out fully from your notes, checking any doubtful points with the chairman. It is wise to do this immediately after the meeting, while the words are still fresh in your mind. Minutes of a meeting are shown in Fig. 3–3.

BELONGING TO THE UNION

Much has been said and written about unions. Some people believe in them very strongly; others feel they restrict a person's individuality. You may be required to belong to a trade union in order to be an employee in certain companies. In others, you may be required to pay "dues," which are membership fees, but you do not have to belong to the union or take part in union activities if you prefer not to.

In some companies there is only one union, which normally is part of a much larger union. Your company's union would be called a "local" and have a number (for example, Local 230 of the UAW–United Auto Workers Union). Even then, the union does not represent everyone in the company: office staff, supervisors, managers, and professional staff

MONTROSE MANUFACTURERS CREDIT UNION

Minutes of

Executive Committee Meeting, February 12, 19__

In attendance: Reg Burns - Chairman
                   Rose Bayliss - Secretary
                   Don Trail
                   Carol Rayner
                   Andy Sandal
                   Paul Chevrier
                   Dave Kane
Absent: Carl Rutledge

1. The chairman opened the meeting at 4.35 p.m.

2. Minutes of the January 15 meeting were read by R. Bayliss.
    P. Chevrier questioned whether a proposed interest-free loan of
    $2000 to D. Bronsky was necessary in light of his recent sweep-
    stake win. The chairman replied that D. Bronsky had already been
    approached and had agreed to refund the full sum before the end
    of the month.

3. Proposed by D. Kane, seconded by A. Sandal, that the minutes be
    approved as read. Carried.

4. The chairman announced he had been approached by the executive of
    Pomona C.U. with a proposal that the two rather small credit unions
    should amalgamate. After lengthy discussion, a subcommittee of
    P. Chevrier, C. Rutledge and C. Rayner was formed to consider
    amalgamation and report its findings at the March meeting.

5. A. Sandal reported his comparison of credit union managers' sala-
    ries [see chart, attached]. Proposed by A. Sandal, amended by
    C. Rayner, seconded by D. Trail, that the C.U. manager's salary be
    increased by $30.00 a month from March 1, 19__, and a further
    $10.00 a month from September 1, 19__. Carried.

6. There being no other business, the chairman closed the meeting at
    5.15 p.m.

Rose Bayliss

R. Bayliss [Ms.] - Secretary

Fig. 3–3. Minutes of a meeting.

such as engineers traditionally have not belonged to unions. In recent years, however, such groups have been indicating that they, too, want to form or belong to a union.

In companies that employ persons with numerous different skills (such as electricians, plumbers, steamfitters, and machinists) the employees may belong to one of several unions, depending on their trade. The "local" of each of these unions operates from a central, independent office, and has its members working in several companies.

How to Communicate with the Union

Your line of communication with the union is usually through a shop steward, who represents all the union members in the area where you and he work. In union terms, this area is commonly referred to as a "shop." There may be several shop stewards in your company, each elected to office by the union members of the shop where he works. You are likely to meet your shop steward first when he signs you up as a new employee, and hence a new union member. Later you will see him at union meetings, where he may sit at the front table as part of the union executive.

At these union meetings you can express your opinion, propose and second motions, and vote when called on to do so. When the shop steward's term of office ends you can propose the name of the same person or that of someone else to be the next shop steward, or somebody may even propose your name for the position. Other positions on the executive of the union "local" are also open to you, and the likelihood of your being elected to them increases as your time with the company lengthens and you get known by more and more employees who are union members.

Day-to-day communication with your shop steward will be routine except when you have a work problem that cannot be resolved through normal dealings with your supervisor. If you have such a complaint (that is, if you feel that either your supervisor or the company is treating you unfairly), you can take it directly to your shop steward. He will ask you to explain the problem to him and, if he thinks your complaint is valid, he will write it onto a special form which he will present to the company.

The exact procedure for doing this is written into the "contract" between the company and the union. Every employee is given a copy of the contract. It describes all the agreements made between the company and the union, and the steps that must be taken to resolve any differences that occur. Such differences handled this way are referred to as "grievances."

Your problem is then discussed between the union and the company, and the company replies in writing to indicate whether or not it agrees your grievance is valid.

How the Union Can Communicate for You

The union has machinery to carry your case through successively higher negotiation levels—right up to formal arbitration—if it feels strongly that your grievance is legitimate and the company does not agree. A typical grievance might evolve from the situation described below.

Fred Winters is a paint sprayer in a cabinet factory. He feels that a recent change in the design of the spray booth has been causing too high a concentration of paint fumes, and this in turn has been giving him headaches. He has mentioned it several times to his supervisor, who is sympathetic but does nothing about it. Then one day the supervisor asks Fred to work overtime.

"Sorry," Fred replies. "But eight hours of these fumes is all I can take."

"Can't help that," the supervisor answers. "The Philmore job's got to be done today."

Fred grumbles some more about it, but finally agrees to stay on.

"But I won't be in tomorrow," he warns, "if I've got another of those headaches."

"Don't look for any sympathy from me," the supervisor snaps back. "You've just got a bad attitude."

The following day Fred has both a severe headache and stomach cramps, so he phones in sick. He is absent only one day, and his supervisor looks at him suspiciously when he books in again. Then on payday Fred discovers the supervisor has docked him one day's pay. (He has a right to do so, because there is a rule in the contract with the union that says an employee has to be sick for two days to gain sick leave. In practice, however, the rule is seldom applied.)

At coffee break, Fred complains bitterly to Danny in the next booth about the treatment he is getting.

"But I'll get my own back," he adds, "Next week I'll just be off sick for two days. See what he can do about that!"

"I'd rather have the money," Danny comments. "Anyway, he'll know what you're doing. Then he can say he's right about you having a bad attitude. I heard what he said to you the other day—maybe you've got a grievance. Why don't you talk to the shop steward about it?"

Danny is right. It's much better to get a problem out into the open than to let it smolder beneath the surface.

The important thing is to know *who* to go to when you have a personal problem or a complaint. Employers are generally aware that their employees must have some way to communicate with the company, and will provide an avenue for them to do so. They are also aware that employees must feel that the person they go to will not only take the time to listen but also will *understand* why the problem is important to that particular employee. In Fred's case communication was easy because he was in a union. In a company where there is no union, there may be a special committee (with representatives on it from both management and employees) to deal with grievances. Or, if there are no proper arrangements, the door to the personnel manager's office should always be open.

Although he is a member of management, the personnel manager (who may also be called the industrial relations manager) has an unusual role in that he may be approached by any employee, and will represent him in dealings with the company if there is no union to speak for him. Personnel managers often have special talents that enable them to get along well with all kinds of people.

And what happened when Fred went to the shop steward? The union felt that Fred had a good case and filed a grievance. Fortunately, Fred's supervisor was realistic about it and realized he had been hasty, so he went to Fred and they talked about things generally, and the spray booth in particular. The outcome was that Fred got back his one day's lost pay, and some further changes were made in the spray booth to improve air movement.

The outcome might have been different if Fred's supervisor had taken a firm line, which could have happened if he had been the kind of person who feels that to apologize is to "lose face." The company probably would have had to support the supervisor because he had acted within the terms of the contract. The union probably would have carried the grievance further. Eventually, the problem would have been resolved —probably in Fred's favor—when someone thought to test air movement in the spray booth. But in the meantime communication would have become practically nonexistent between Fred and his supervisor and restrained and suspicious between the union and the company. Normal face-to-face communication that can so easily iron out small differences would have been exchanged for formal interchanges that lower morale and reduce a pleasant work atmosphere to a stilted "business arrangement."

THE COMPANY'S VIEW

Most companies want to develop each employee to his or her full potential. In time this may mean that you will be moved to different jobs within the company to broaden your experience, given increased responsibility as your experience develops and your abilities become evident, and perhaps eventually promoted to a junior supervisory position. Gradually, the company learns much about you as an employee and a worker; but it also wants to see how you get on with people around you.

Employers are particularly interested in your activities in situations that parallel those you are likely to experience when you shoulder greater responsibility. A person who takes part in promoting and organizing social activities is already demonstrating administrative abilities. If he also serves on committees, he is already learning what is expected of him when, as a supervisor, he attends department meetings. And if he serves in an executive position on a committee, he is already assuming leadership responsibilities.

From your point of view, then, there are two advantages to establishing good communication with other employees:

1. You gain experience that will be extremely useful in your personal self-development.
2. You get noticed by your employer as a potentially promotable prospect.

But—and this is a very big BUT—your reasons for taking part in employee-oriented activities must be genuine. Doing so purely to get yourself noticed and then promoted will defeat your objective, because your attempts at establishing good interpersonal relationships will be hollow. They will soon be recognized for their true worth by your fellow employees, and probably by management as well.

EXERCISES

NOTE: When an exercise calls for you to give a spoken answer, your instructor will tell you who is playing the role of "receiver."

Exercise 6.1

Can you act on these instructions? If not, what questions would you ask before doing so?

1. "Meet Mr. Miller and his party at the airport, and drive them back to the office." (You know nothing about Mr. Miller and his party.)
2. "Please tell the people in your area that I want to speak to everyone as soon as you have had lunch."

3. "Send copies of this invoice to the Accounts Department."
4. "Order a replacement valve direct from the manufacturer in West Germany." (Assume you know the manufacturer's name and address.)
5. "If you find signs of serious damage, report it."
6. "Get me a firm price for half a dozen steel filing cabinets."

Exercise 6.2

You are the employee who did not receive the promotion described in exercise 7.8 (page 94). You are also a member of the union. Because the personnel manager does not give you a satisfactory answer (he mumbles something about Bill Mace's previous experience being taken into account), go to your shop steward and ask him to put in a grievance for you.

Exercise 6.3

Because your employer has recently lost a large manufacturing order, you are one of 20 employees who have been told they will be laid off in two weeks. At lunch you sit with Bill Vanderhorst, who joined the company one week after you. To your surprise, you find that Bill has not been laid off.

Go to the employment manager and complain you are being given unfair treatment. Use the following information:

1. You joined the company exactly one year ago.
2. You've never had any written reprimands, but you are "pretty sure" Bill has (he often arrives late for work).
3. Bill is known to be "well in" with his supervisor, Cam Watkins.
4. You are not particularly friendly with your supervisor, Will Danzig, but neither is there any difficulty between you.
5. Will Danzig is known to be particularly fair in his dealings with employees.

NOTE: If you prefer, you may assume you are a union member, in which case you will complain to your shop steward rather than the employment manager.

Exercise 6.4

At lunch hour, many of the employees in the plant where you work eat their sandwiches in Kingsbury Park, one block south of the building. Today you are sitting with a group of guys from the machine shop and some of the girls from the production line. It's warm, and someone humorously suggests going for a swim at Moray Beach. The idea grows that a swim and barbecue should be held right after work one evening next week. At first it is suggested as a joint venture limited to employees in the machine shop and on the production line. But a later suggestion includes everyone in the plant. The plan is to promote it as a company social function, so that the Employees' Club will support it financially.

As everyone packs up and strolls back to the plant, you (as a member of the social committee) are asked to suggest the idea to Sam Warrick, who is chairman of the Employees' Club.

1. Suggest this social function to Sam.
2. Write a memo to Sam, which he can use as a proposal at tomorrow's meeting of the Employees' Club.
3. At the meeting, explain the suggestion in greater detail to the other committee members.

Exercise 6.5

You are a member of the social committee at your company. At a previous meeting you volunteered to survey the 70 employees to find out what kind of summer social activity most favor. The results of your survey are: family picnic—16; evening riverboat cruise—23; swimming party—3; dance—16; no opinion—8; horseback riding—4. Most people surveyed also said they would like to have two social affairs during the summer.

At this week's meeting you have to tell the committee what you have found out.

1. Prepare a chart or handout to use at the meeting.
2. Tell the committee the results of your study.

Exercise 6.6

Assume you are one of the employees of a small but very democratic company. It is 1 p.m. when you go into the little lunchroom. You are there because yesterday Vic Davis (the company owner) sent everyone a memo that said:

I want to meet the staff at 1 p.m. tomorrow to discuss plans to try out a compressed work week.

You notice that three other people are present: Dan Kane, Mel Wilson, and Jane Tempor. A minute later Bev Dearden and Carl Rostowski come in, followed almost immediately by Vic Davis and Rick Brown, the accountant. Vic is chairman and he asks you to take the minutes of the meeting. The conversation goes like this:

Vic: Who's missing?
Dan: Winston Carstairs. He's gone to a union meeting.
Vic: Oh. Now—before we get down to the main topic, I understand congratulations are in order.

Everyone looks up expectantly.

Vic: (*continuing*) Two of our members tell me they've decided to form a "company" of their own. (*slight pause*) Bev and Carl are to be married in the fall.

There is a general hubbub while everyone jumps up and congratulates the newly engaged couple. When things have quieted down, Vic continues:

Vic: Now for the main reason for this meeting. I'd like to know if you want to try the shorter work week. To put the record straight right from the start, I'm not trying to force it on anybody. The eight of you can decide for yourselves what you want to do.

Dan: Do we have to decide right now?

Vic: No. Today's meeting is mainly to introduce the idea; to let you start thinking about it.

Rick: How soon do we have to decide?

Vic: Well, I'd like to know by the end of the month.

Jane: I'm not quite sure how the compressed work week works. I mean, do you put in shorter hours?

Vic: No, no! The number of hours you put in each week remains exactly the same. In a compressed work week you come in maybe for only four days, but for ten hours a day.

Rick: Or only three days, for twelve hours a day.

Vic: In which case you would put in a fourth day every third week—to average out at forty hours a week.

Dan: (*humorously*) Or maybe only two days a week . . .

Carl: For twenty hours a day . . .

Dan: And five-day weekends. Oh, man!

There is general laughter at this point.

Jane: What I don't understand is—do you come in early or late?

Vic: That's for you to decide.

Jane: You mean we can start at 6.00 a.m. and quit at 4.00?

Dan: 6.00 a.m.! Nobody is going to get me up at that unearthly hour!

Jane: Or 10.00 a.m. and quit at 8.00?

Dan: That's better!

Vic: When you start and finish is up to you, really. And which day you choose to take off . . .

Dan: Monday!

Jane: Friday!

Dan: Can't stand Monday mornings!

Jane: So I can get my apartment cleaned up before the weekend.

Bev: (*quietly*) Wouldn't it be better to stick with what we've got now? At least everyone knows where they stand.

Mel: My brother's working a four-day week over at Ace Industries.

Jane: How does he like it?

Mel: (*shrugs*) Don't know, really. I never asked him.

You:	How long has he been on it?
Mel:	Oh, quite a while. Six months, I guess.
Jane:	Could you find out, Mel?
Mel:	Sure.
Vic:	See if you can also find out how other people at Ace Industries like it. We'd be interested in the overall reaction to the compressed work week, as well as your brother's.
Mel:	OK. How soon do you want to know?
Vic:	In a week. I was planning to meet with all of you again at the same time next week. When you have had time to think about it.
Dan:	I think the whole idea is for the birds! I suggest we quit wasting time—stick with what we've got.

Vic looks questioningly around the table (he's taking a vote):

Rick:	No. Let's go ahead.
Jane:	I'd like to think it over.
Mel:	I'm interested.
Bev:	I'll wait to see what Mel's brother says.
Carl:	I agree.
You:	It's worth looking into.
Vic:	I guess we go ahead, then. (*to you*) Put that into the minutes will you?
Carl:	You know—there's one aspect we've not mentioned: flextime.
You:	Did you say "flextime?"
Carl:	That's right. It was in the news a while back. Some government offices are trying it.
Jane:	I've never heard of it.
Carl:	I don't know much, either. I heard it on the radio.
Rick:	I think I can explain. "Flextime" is short for "flexible time." All it means is that everyone comes in and leaves when they want.
Vic:	Yes. But there's also a "core" period when everyone has to be in. Like 10.00 a.m. to 3.00 p.m.
Rick:	Each person decides what time they want to come in—on a day-to-day basis.
Jane:	You mean, today I can come in at 6 a.m. and tomorrow at 10 a.m.?
Rick:	If you like. You just put in eight hours from the time you come in. It's your choice.
Dan:	But you must be in between 10 and 3?
Rick:	Or some time like that—depends on what "core" time Mr. Davis chooses.
Bev:	Wouldn't that make even more of a mess? For carpools, I mean.
Carl:	Maybe not so bad as fixed times. At least everyone can choose when they come in.
Jane:	It won't affect you, Bev. Not if you're going to be married.
Carl:	We'll have our own car pool—come in together.
Jane:	Oh, I didn't mean that. (*pause*) What I meant was: will Bev still be working?

Bev: (*annoyed*) I wasn't exactly planning to sit at home all day . . .

Jane: Sorry, Bev! I was thinking of a company rule. (*She turns to Vic*) Mr. Davis—isn't there a rule that says two people from the same family can't be employed by the company?

Vic: Well, yes . . .

Bev: Oh! I didn't know that!

Carl: But I thought it only applied to someone who's already employed bringing in a relative as a new employee.

Vic: That's true. If you're already employed, I won't hire your wife; or brother, sister, father, mother, son, or daughter. I haven't run into a situation before where two employees marry.

Jane: Better start looking for a new job, Carl!

Carl: Me?

Dan: I agree! If I had to choose between Carl and Bev, I'd go for the scenery every time.

Vic: I think I can say right now—the rule doesn't apply to Bev and Carl. (*He turns to Rick*). Will you go over to the government administration office and talk to Dixon Best? See how they are handling "flextime" and let us know at the next meeting.

Rick: OK.

Vic: (*to everyone*) Anything else?

Dan: I'd like to know if you can "bank" hours: work eleven hours one day and maybe five the next.

Rick: I'll look into that, too.

Carl: I know with "flextime" you can't miss a day. You still work a five-day week.

Vic looks around to see if there are any further questions.

Vic: OK. We'll meet again a week from today. Same time.

As everyone leaves, Vic turns to you.

Vic: When you write up the minutes, make sure Winston gets a copy.

The exercise: Write the minutes of the meeting.

7

Communicating
with Your Employer

The days have gone when a company simply hired hands to do its work but cared little about them, their opinions, and their personal lives. Today, management wants to know what its employees think about their work, and what they say to each other about the company and its policies. It wants them to realize that they are important, that the company cannot function properly without them, and that the company is interested in each person as an individual.

Modern employers are well aware that a poor work environment is bad for productivity. Discontented employees create problems, and problems increase business costs. So management tries to create a line of communication between itself and its employees. It sends out newsletters and posts announcements on bulletin boards to keep them up to date on company plans.

But in return it needs to hear from its employees. It wants to hear their complaints, ideas, and suggestions; it wants to know if they like the company's new scheme for employee insurance, or plans for a Christmas party, or suggested changes in pension benefits. Unfortunately, this upward line of communication often is not well used, partly because management may not be listening carefully enough, but mostly because employees either do not know how or are afraid to communicate with management.

In practice, you as an employee will communicate with your employer for four reasons—when you want to:

Ask a question
Offer a suggestion
Make a request
Pass along information

In all these cases, the person you will normally go to is your immediate supervisor. And in nearly all cases your communication with him will be spoken. Only if you offer a suggestion or make a request that he has to take to someone else for an answer, or inform him of something that needs to be remembered (such as details of an accident), are you likely to write to him.

ASKING A QUESTION

Karen McCawley has an urgent order to pack and ship some wallpaper to a hardware store in a neighboring city. But the order does not say how the package should be sent, and she wonders whether it should go by bus, by rail, or perhaps even by air. So when the supply manager happens to pass her table (Karen does not know he is hurrying to a meeting, and that he is already late), she stops him. This is the conversation that ensues:

Karen	*Supply Manager*
Oh, Mr. Samuels!	
	Yes, Karen? (*he pauses, but wants to move on*)
I've got a shipment here for Westrock Hardware . . .	
	Oh?
In Montrose . . .	
	Oh, yes . . .
How do you think I should send it?	
	(*impatiently*) Doesn't it say on the order?
No—it doesn't say anything.	
	Let me have a look. (*he impatiently flicks the order sheet around to see it better*) Oh! This is an *Urgent* order.
Yeah! It says *Urgent* right on it.	
	Then how much does it weigh?
Oh, I don't know. I haven't weighed it yet.	

*(sighs, smothering his exaspera-
tion)* Well, if it's 10 pounds or
over send it express—either rail
or bus, whichever is the faster. If
it's under 10 pounds, send it by
air.

Just a minute—I'll write that
down . . . *(pause while she
writes, repeating what he has
just said)* Thanks, Mr. Samuels.

OK, Karen. *(and he hurries off)*

The whole exchange has lasted 73 seconds—57 seconds longer than
necessary. If Karen had prepared herself to ask the question, Mr. Samuels
would have spent much less time on a very trivial matter, and she would
not be wondering why he seemed so irritable.

Being prepared means:

1. Knowing what you want to ask.
2. Being ready to supply information you may in turn be asked.

In Karen's case, she should have known the weight of the parcel and
made it clear to Mr. Samuels that she was talking about an "urgent"
order. Let's take it again from the top:

Karen	*Supply Manager*
Oh, Mr. Samuels!	
	Yes, Karen?
How do I ship this order to Montrose? It's marked *Urgent,* but there are no shipping instructions.	
	How much does it weigh?
Thirteen pounds.	
	By rail express or bus—whichever is faster.
Oh. Thank you.	
	OK, Karen.

Total time: 16 seconds. Even if Mr. Samuels had also explained that 10
pounds was the dividing line between air and surface transportation, it
would have taken only 12 extra seconds.

When you need to ask a question, try to think of it as three short
blocks of information arranged in the order shown in Fig. 3–4. If the

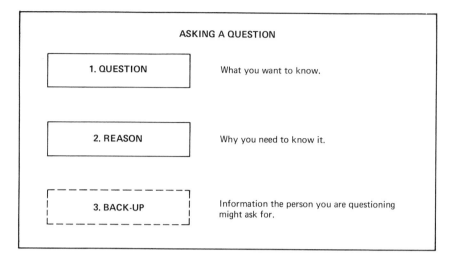

Fig. 3–4. Information blocks for asking a question.

question is short, the first two blocks can be asked together (as Karen was able to do in the second example above):

How do I ship this order to Montrose?   1. QUESTION

It's marked URGENT, but there are no   2. REASON
shipping instructions.

The third block (Back-Up) is held in readiness in case the person being questioned asks for more information. In Karen's case, this comprised the weight of the package (which Mr. Samuels needed) and the name of the hardware store and the order number (which he did not ask for). You should always have back-up information ready before you ask a question, to save time in case you are asked for it.

Although most questions are asked out loud, occasionally you may need to write a question down. This sometimes happens to Mark Lavallee, who seldom sees Bob Reevor, the other maintenance technician in a small but busy telephone assembly plant. Mark works the evening shift, Bob the day shift.

Throughout the summer the air conditioning equipment has run around the clock. But as fall approaches the evenings grow cooler, and by 9 P.M. Mark has learned to switch off the air conditioner before the girls on the assembly line start complaining that the plant is too cold. Now he wonders whether he should switch it on again before he shuts the plant at midnight. His question to Bob, which he pins to the maintenance room notice board, is this:

Bob—

Do you still want me to leave the air
conditioner running all night?

1. QUESTION

I usually switch it off about 9 P.M., or
as soon as the temperature drops below 72°F.

2. REASON

—Mark

In a written question, the Back-Up block has to be omitted (because the reader cannot immediately ask a question) or the information must be built into the REASON block.

MAKING A SUGGESTION

Most suggestions made by employees are for reasons affecting their work, although occasionally they may be for the promotion of social activities. Mark Lavallee, for example, has noticed that every time he is called over to repair or replace a telephone test set, an assembler has to stop work and wait for him. If Mark is already working somewhere else in the plant, then the "downtime" (the length of time that work stops) becomes excessive. He reckons that a planned withdrawal of test sets—so that they can be inspected and serviced before they fail—would probably cut out most of this downtime.

So at coffee break one evening Mark described the problem, then introduced his idea to Dale Meacham, the shift supervisor. Dale listened carefully, then fired some questions back at Mark: How often would you have to replace the sets? Wouldn't that interfere with the assembly operation? Would you need any extra sets as spares? How many?

By now Mark had begun to wonder whether it was such a good idea after all. But Dale sensed this, and explained to him that a suggestion is only an idea until it has been thoroughly thought out.

"You need to second-guess what you'll be asked," he added. "Then you can be ready with the answers. Otherwise the person you're talking to may think it's not such a good idea after all."

Dale went on to describe how a suggestion needs to be planned as three blocks of information, plus a reserve, and drew the sketch in Fig. 3–5. He added that sometimes it is possible to combine blocks 2 and 3, particularly if the suggestion is simple and its explanation is short.

So Mark went away and did some calculations. First he wanted to know how often he'd have to service the test sets so he could be reasonably sure they would not break down between servicings. And then he had to calculate whether there were enough spare test sets to do this.

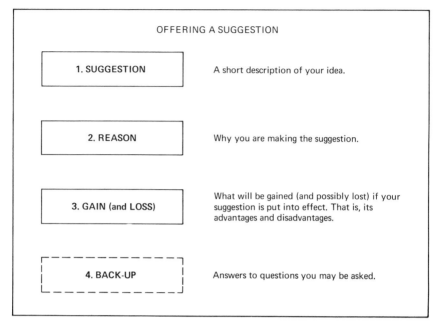

OFFERING A SUGGESTION

| 1. SUGGESTION | A short description of your idea. |

| 2. REASON | Why you are making the suggestion. |

| 3. GAIN (and LOSS) | What will be gained (and possibly lost) if your suggestion is put into effect. That is, its advantages and disadvantages. |

| 4. BACK-UP | Answers to questions you may be asked. |

Fig. 3–5. Information blocks for offering a suggestion.

Finally, he wanted to find out if there really would be a saving in time—for himself as well as the assemblers. When he had all these facts at his fingertips (and arranged in the proper order), he hunted his supervisor down again. This time he came straight to the point:

Dale! I think that if we could service the telephone test sets regularly—rather than wait for them to fail—we could cut out a lot of downtime on the line.

> 1. SUGGESTION

I've noticed that every time one of the test sets fails, work stops at that station until I can get over to fix it. If I'm busy, it may be 45 minutes before I'm there.

> 2. REASON

I reckon I could get there before most of the breakdowns occur, if at each station I was to take out the old set and put in a newly serviced one every 17 days. I'd need to do six stations a week—that's one most nights, sometimes two. The only problem is, to keep the changes going in rotation I'd need two more test sets than we have now.

> 3. GAIN and LOSS

Dale had some questions to ask, but this time Mark was ready with his answers:

Dale: That sounds good, Mark, but when do you propose
to change the sets? Wouldn't that stop the line too?

Mark: No, I've already thought of that. I could do the
changeover when the line stops for lunch. It
doesn't matter when I take my break.
What about the extra two test sets—how much is
that going to cost?

Mark: A little over $500. They list at $265 each.

Dale: (*thoughtfully*) So for an investment of $530 we
could virtually eliminate downtime due to test set
outage. Hmmmmm—sounds interesting!

> | 4. BACK-UP |

When a suggestion is relatively easy to put into effect, the employee's
supervisor can usually decide if he wants to try it out. But with Mark
Lavallee's suggestion it was not that simple: some money had to be spent
first, and to get approval to spend that money Dale had to go to his
department manager or someone even higher up in the company. And he
could not do it just by asking; he had to request it in writing.

As the employee who made the original suggestion, it can easily
happen that your part in "thinking up" an idea may become lost. But if
your supervisor asks you to write him a memorandum (commonly called
a "memo") describing your suggestion, your name still remains in the
picture and you get the credit for the idea.

Writing a memo may at first seem to be much more difficult than
just telling your supervisor about your suggestion. But this need not be
so. You can still use the same information blocks to shape your suggestion
into the memorandum, which is exactly what Mark Lavallee did. When he
had finished writing his suggestion, and had had it typed, it looked like
this:

From: Mark Lavallee   *Date:* 19 February 19___

To: Dale Meacham   *Subject:* Planned Servicing of
        (Evening Shift Supervisor)   Telephone Test Sets

I suggest that we replace each telephone test set on the
assembly line every 17 days, rather than wait for test sets to
fail before replacing them.

> | 1. SUGGESTION |

This would reduce much of the downtime that now occurs
when a test set fails (downtime varies from 25 to 50 minutes
per breakdown, and on average one test set breaks down
every night). I could do the changeovers at mid-evening
break, when the line is shut down for 45 minutes.

> | 2. & 3. REASON and GAIN |

If the test sets are replaced and serviced in rotation, we

would need to buy two additional sets to be sure that
sufficient freshly serviced ones are always available. The
cost would be $265 each, or $530 total.

```
┌──────────────────┐
│    3. LOSS       │
└──────────────────┘
```

Mark Lavallee

Some of the information previously in block 3 has now been combined with block 2, and the answers Mark had ready as back-up information (block 4) have become part of the memo. This is essential in any situation where the reader cannot easily question the writer.

Before sending this memorandum to his department manager, Dale Meacham would probably check Mark's calculations and add a comment of his own—most likely a recommendation that the change in methods take place. If Mark is to receive recognition for having devised the idea, it is better to have him write the memorandum, and for Dale to add a comment to it, than for Dale to write it. If Dale did the writing it would probably look as though he originated the idea, even though he may mention that it is Mark's suggestion.

MAKING A REQUEST

Employees make requests mostly for personal reasons. They want time off to attend a meeting, go to a funeral, or take a driving test; they want to take an evening course, and hope the company will pay all or part of the cost; they want to transfer to another job in the department; or they simply want an increase in pay. Because a request often asks for a favor, you may find it difficult to state your request immediately. Information blocks like those in Fig. 3–6 can help you come straight to the point.

The most important information block is No. 1—Request. There is a great tendency to lead gently up to it (to prepare the listener to accept it) rather than to come straight to the point. Compare these two approaches, one made by Steve Cahill to John Craven, the day shift supervisor; and the other by Karen McCawley to Sid Samuels, the supply manager:

An Indirect Approach	*A Direct Approach*
STEVE: Mr. Craven! Could I speak to you for a moment? I've been in your department for three years now—ever since I	KAREN: Mr. Samuels! Could I have the day off next Friday? My sister is getting married in the evening, and I'd like to have

joined the company. I kind of like it here—the guys are a great bunch to work with. But, you know how it is—sometimes you hanker after a change. You've got to be thinking what you're going to do next. So, when I heard that Bob Reevor is leaving and Mark Lavallee is taking his place on the day shift, I got to thinking maybe I could handle Mark's old job. I took the same kind of course that he did at technical school. That is, of course, if you haven't got someone else already lined up for it. I mean—do you think I should apply for it?

the day clear to help her get ready.

Steve's rather disorganized approach is, perhaps, a little exaggerated. But it does illustrate how in trying to lead gently up to his request Steve has almost lost the point he is trying to make. Even worse, his long and

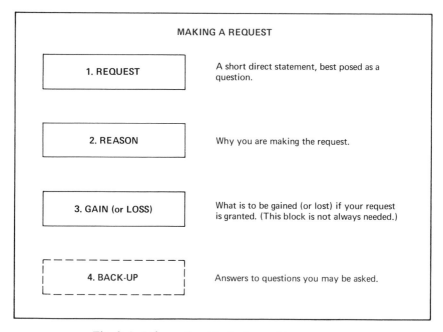

Fig. 3–6. Information blocks for making a request.

roundabout approach might cause a busy listener like John Craven to drift off frequency *so that he does not hear the request* when it finally reaches him. Here is how Steve should have worded his request to make it more direct:

A Direct Approach

| 1. REQUEST | STEVE: Mr. Craven! Could I speak to you for a moment? I'd like to apply for Mark Lavallee's job on the night shift. |

| 2. REASON | I've done most jobs on the line, and feel it's time I tried something different. Mark and I took the same course at technical school, so I'm sure I could handle his job all right. |

John Craven would then talk to Steve about the job and probably ask him a few questions to see if he really could handle it, such as:

CRAVEN: Do you know exactly what Mark's job involves?

| 4. BACK-UP | STEVE: I've a pretty good idea: I've talked to Bob Reevor about it—he does the same work as Mark, but on the day shift. I know how to replace and service the test sets, and I did routine maintenance for three weeks on the night shift when Mark was on vacation last year. Mr. Meacham could tell you how I made out. |

Only in very small firms are transfers arranged following a spoken request like this. Most likely, Steve would be asked to fill in a company "Request for Transfer" form, or to apply for the position in writing. Such an application would be written as a short memorandum, like this:

From: Steve Cahill   *Date:*   4 April 19___
To: Mr. J. Craven   *Subject:*   Request for Transfer

I am applying for transfer to the position of maintenance technician on the evening shift from 15 April.

Steve Cahill

In this instance Steve has to write only the information for block 1: the Request, because the company knows him and his suitability as an employee. He can, if he wishes, add a few words of evidence (but he must be careful not to overdo it):

I am familiar with the work, having acted as standby for Mark Lavallee for three weeks last August.

A more complete request using all four information blocks is that written by Ernie Dagg, who wants a week off (if possible with pay) to attend a leadership course sponsored by the Boy Scouts. He knows he is asking for quite a lot, but he has two major factors in his favor:

1. Most employers recognize that a company has social obligations to the community in which it is located.
2. Persons who are active in community activities usually become very responsible employees with lots of promotion potential.

How Ernie wrote his request, making block 4 (Back-Up) part of it instead of holding it in reserve as he would have done if he had been speaking, is illustrated below.

From: E. Dagg   *Date:* 24 September 19___
To: Mr. G. Samuels   *Subject:* Request for Leave

May I have one week's leave to attend a leadership course sponsored by the Boy Scouts of America? The course is being held in Atlanta, Georgia from 28 October to 1 November (see attached description).

1. REQUEST

As Leader of 212th Boy Scout Troup in Malvern, I have been selected by the Central Region to be their representative on this year's course. When I have completed it, I will be eligible to hold a position on the regional committee.

2. REASON

3. GAIN

I would be away over the month-end period, so someone would have to do the monthly stock count and complete the record cards for me. Steve Cahill has done part of it before, and I could show him all of it before I go.

and LOSS

All my expenses during the course will be paid by the Boy Scout organization. But I would appreciate it if the company could keep me on at least part pay for the week I would be away.

4. BACK-UP

E. Dagg

Will the company approve Ernie's request? And will it keep him on the payroll? The answer to both questions might well be "Yes." The clue is in the Gain section of Ernie's second paragraph: The company stands to gain from Ernie taking leadership training like this, because it will also prepare him to step into a supervisory position in the company.

GIVING INFORMATION

An employee passes information along to his supervisor when he needs to tell the company about something that is happening or has happened. For example, when clerk-typist Jeannie Lord realizes at 2.15 P.M. that she will not be able to finish both of two rush jobs due to go out with that afternoon's mail, she goes to the chief records clerk (who is her supervisor) to inform him about it. She says:

Information Blocks

Pete! There's no way I can get all my work done by 4.15 today.

1. SUMMARY

I started right away on your order for Vancourt Electronics, but had to stop to do a rush job for Ms. Swarz, which I haven't finished yet. It's also my turn to be relief switchboard operator—in fact, I'm going on the switchboard right now.

2. & 3. SITUATION and EVENT

When I get back, I'll have time only to finish Ms. Swarz's job, unless you can persuade her that yours should be done first.

4. RESULT

Jeannie has used the information blocks in Fig. 3–7 to tell her story. They start with a Summary Statement that tells the listener right away what he most needs to know (this is the Main Message described in Chapter 3—see page 16). The three following blocks then describe the circumstances, occurrence, and effect in greater detail. Jeannie has combined blocks 2 and 3 (Situation and Event) because their content is closely interwoven.

In Patrick Dugan's case, an unusual occurrence at his workbench has caused him to telephone his supervisor (Ron Ludwig) to inform him what has happened:

Hello—Ron? There's been a small accident here which has pretty well stopped my work for the rest of the day.

1. SUMMARY

The electrician was around just now replacing fluorescent lamps.

2. SITUATION

He dropped one across my bench. It shattered and dropped bits of glass into the vat.

3. EVENT

I've had to throw out the liquid, which means I'll have to start the tests all over again. There's no time to heat up a new vat by the end of the shift, so I can't finish today's batch.

4. RESULT

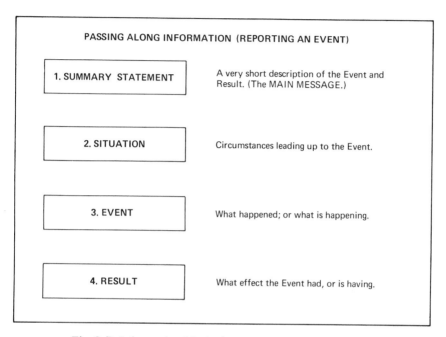

PASSING ALONG INFORMATION (REPORTING AN EVENT)

1. SUMMARY STATEMENT	A very short description of the Event and Result. (The MAIN MESSAGE.)
2. SITUATION	Circumstances leading up to the Event.
3. EVENT	What happened; or what is happening.
4. RESULT	What effect the Event had, or is having.

Fig. 3–7. Information blocks for passing along information.

A verbal report is sufficient for a minor incident such as this. It gives Ron Ludwig the information he needs to decide whether he will tell Patrick just to clean up the mess and continue the job tomorrow, or ask him to work overtime tonight so he cán finish the batch.

If the flying glass had injured an employee or damaged equipment, Ron would have asked Patrick to write a brief account of what happened. To do this, Patrick would have used the same information blocks he used for his spoken report (Fig. 3–7). And, although he could simply have taken a plain sheet of paper and headed it with a title (such as "Details of Accident in Room 301"), he would more likely have prepared his short report as a memorandum, as illustrated in Fig. 3–8.

Passing along information about an event or occurrence is simply reporting what has happened. In the written form, it is the first of several kinds of reports you may eventually write as a supervisor.

But reports are written not only by supervisors. They may be, and often are, written by employees on the job—particularly those carrying out

THE RONING GROUP

From: ___Pat Dugan_____   Date: _____27 November 19_____

To: ___Ron Ludwig_____   Subject: __Damage to Vancourt Calibrator__

                                                    Model RA-12

A small accident that damaged my Vancourt Calibrator stopped
work on Batch No. 81 at 3.10 p.m.   ①

The incident occurred while an electrician was replacing
fluorescent lamps in the overhead fixtures.   ②

A lamp slipped from his hands, striking the calibrator and
breaking the glass of its meter dial. Glass from the shattered   ③
lamp and meter dropped into the vat.

This means that today's batch will have to be re-run, and
tomorrow's batch cannot be started until the meter shop has   ④
repaired the calibrator.

                              Pat

Fig. 3–8. A memorandum to inform a supervisor of an incident and its effects.

assignments on their own. For that reason parts of Chapter 11 ("Communicating About Your Work") also apply to you, and should be read
with this chapter. They are:

Reporting an Event (page 145)
Reporting a Field Assignment (page 147)
Reporting Progress (page 149)
Reporting an Inspection (page 151)

EXERCISES

NOTE: 1. *When an exercise calls for you to give a spoken answer, your*
          instructor will tell you who is playing the role of "receiver."
       2. *Additional situations an employee might face are presented*

in the exercises for Chapters 10 and 11. References to these exercises follow Exercise 7.14 (page 99).

Asking Questions

Exercise 7.1

When you started working on the first of the month you were told you would be earning $3.40 per hour. You calculate this as $136 a week, or $272 on the 15th of the month, which will be your first payday. Allowing for deductions, which you generously estimate at about $40, you expect your first check to be close to $232.

But when it comes, it is for only $114.48. The slip attached to it says:

Gross pay:	$136.00
Deductions (tax, insurance, pension)	$ 21.52
Net pay:	$114.48

Your supervisor comes by at the moment, so you ask him why it is so low. He suggests you see the accountant in the front office.
What do you say to the accountant?

Exercise 7.2

When you were hired by Mr. Richards, the employment manager, in September, one of the fringe benefits he told you about was that employees have three weeks vacation from their very first year. Now it is the following spring, and employees are talking about their vacation plans. You say you are going to use your three weeks to go to Fairbanks, Alaska.

"Think again!" says Hank Commit. "You won't get three weeks! When did you start?"

You tell him it was September 1.

He shakes his head knowingly: "About eight days—that's all you'll get. They count your time only to the first of April."

Disappointed, you look for your supervisor to find out just how long a vacation you will have this coming summer.

What do you say to him?

Exercise 7.3

You are a driver for Ace Industries, and it is your job to drive the company's mail to Postal Station C at 3.00 p.m. every day. This duty is sandwiched between other important jobs, and you have just enough time to make the delivery, which takes you 25 minutes (round trip).

To allow everyone to have a full week off between Christmas and New Year, Ace Industries is closing down from December 24 to January 1. To make up the lost days, it has been agreed between the union and the company that employees will work three Saturdays in November.

On the morning of the first Saturday, you discover that the postal station is closed all day. By making enquiries you also realize that

1. The only postal station open is the office on Main Street, and it is open only from 10.00 a.m. to 2.00 p.m.
2. It takes 20 minutes each way to drive to this postal station.
3. Mail collection in the plant is scheduled for 2.30 p.m. every day.
4. Routine mail is no problem: you can deposit it in a corner mailbox.
5. Special delivery and registered mail constitute your problem, because they must be taken to a postal station. (There is a fair amount of special mail like this every day.)

Ask your supervisor what you are to do.

Offering Suggestions

Exercise 7.4

You work for a company that rents office machinery and small industrial equipment to businesses in the city. Your job is partly to deliver and pick up equipment, and partly to do maintenance on it.

Requests for equipment often come in late in the afternoon, for delivery first thing the next morning (companies like to start their rental period from 8.00 a.m.). Each morning you take the bus to work, then pick up the company delivery truck and often retrace your route toward your home as you make deliveries.

Suggest to the company owner that you be allowed to take the truck home at night, with the next morning's deliveries in it, then start delivering on the way in to work.

Exercise 7.5

The company you work for has a small printing department which prints most of the forms used by the company. Some of these forms are odd sizes, and you notice that they are printed on larger sheets which are trimmed to size. The offcuts are thrown out (you see them in the garbage cans). You would like to fish them out of the garbage and take them home, but cannot because there is a security check on materials carried out of the company.

1. Ask your supervisor for permission to be given all offcuts in future so you can take them to your sister, who wants to use them in the nursery school where she is taking a training course; or

2. Suggest to your supervisor that the offcuts be saved and glued together into odd-shaped but still useful scratch pads.

Making Requests

Exercise 7.6

When you graduate from your local community college, you do not receive your certificate because you failed one subject (English). You are told, however, that you can write a supplemental examination on a date yet to be announced.

In the meantime, you are hired by Kelvin Industries. During the pre-employment interview you discuss the deficient subject with Mr. Dawlish, the personnel manager. He says the company expects you to clear this deficiency, and that he is hiring you on the understanding that you will have your certificate within three months.

Yesterday you received a letter from the Department of Education announcing that your supplemental examination is scheduled for 9.00 a.m. next Tuesday in Room D-101 of the community college.

Ask your supervisor for the morning off:

1. Verbally.
2. In writing (as a memorandum).

Exercise 7.7

In your spare time you are a model railroad hobbyist, and you belong to a club that builds and operates an extensive HO rail layout in a glass-enclosed area of a shopping mall. The club is redesigning much of the layout, and is building a complex locomotive turntable that needs precision machinery. Because the company where you work has some expensive machine tools that you can operate, the club president asks if you can do the job at your place of work during a couple of evenings or over the weekend.

You think you probably could, but know you would have to have company approval. You would also have to obtain approval for the two railroad hobbyists who designed the turntable to come in with you. There are sketches of the turntable, but no machine drawings, so they would have to give you instructions while you are doing the job. This means you have to ask for permission to: (1) come in at night or on weekends to do a private job: (2) bring two persons in with you who are not employees; and (3) use company equipment.

1. Ask your foreman for approval.

Your foreman, Kurt Jenks, thinks it will be all right for you to come in and use the equipment, but he's not sure about the other people. Because only the production manager can give final approval, he suggests you write a note explaining what you want to do, which he will take to the manager.

2. Write a memorandum to Kurt Jenks, requesting his approval.

Exercise 7.8

You have been employed in the Production Department of Ray-On Industries for four years, and on several occasions have been complimented by the foreman on the quality of your work. Other employees have come and gone, until now you are the senior employee at Assembly Station D.

Last Monday, the crew chief at your station was told he is being promoted to foreman and will be transferred to another department. You believe you have good reason to expect that you will be made crew chief in his place.

1. Go to your foreman and ask for the position.

This morning when you came to work you were shattered to discover that Bill Mace had been made crew chief. What really burns you up is that he's been in the department only seven months, and a company employee for only a year and a half. Mary Collins, one of the assemblers, says she thinks she knows the reason. "He's the chief accountant's nephew. That's why!" she says.

2. Go to your foreman and ask why you did not get the job.

He is embarrassed and does not give you a proper answer. You question him some more, until he suggests you see the personnel manager.

3. Tell the personnel manager about it and ask why you were passed over.

Exercise 7.9

The company where you work is located in a large building in an older part of the city that is almost entirely occupied by small manufacturers, wholesalers, and business offices. During the day the streets are filled with traffic and the sidewalks with pedestrians. But at night the area is empty, silent, and poorly lit.

Recently there has been a lot of overtime, with the Production Department operating until 9.00 p.m. several times a week. This means the employees have to leave in the dark through a heavily shadowed lane (the building's night door opens onto the lane). They also have to bring a snack with them because the company has never installed eating facilities. There is a privately run cafeteria on the main floor of the building, but it and other cafes that dot the area all close before 6.00 p.m.

You are particularly concerned about all this overtime, because next week you are starting an evening course at the community college which will tie you up from 7 to 9:30 p.m. on Tuesdays and Thursdays.

At the 6.30 p.m. break, employees often complain to each other about the bad lighting in the lane, the need for cabs to drive women employees to the bus stop on Main Street, and the lack of sandwich and coffee machines in the company's rest room. From time to time someone asks a supervisor or the personnel manager if something can be done, but they are always told it depends on how long the overtime schedule goes on.

This evening, it is generally decided to needle management the following day so the company will finally realize there is a problem. Employees will go to their respective supervisors or managers, and to the personnel manager, with various questions or requests. The group wants you to ask questions drawn from this list:

1. Ask your supervisor if evening work is going to continue for long.
2. Suggest to your supervisor that the company install coffee and sandwich machines.
3. Ask the personnel manager if he can arrange for police to patrol the lane between 8.45 p.m. and 9.15 p.m. on overtime nights.
4. Ask your supervisor to order cabs to drive women employees to the bus stop.
5. Request that the company pay for the cabs (ask the personnel manager for this, assuming that your supervisor orders cabs for you).
6. Request that your supervisor arrange for better lighting in the lane.
7. For yourself, request your supervisor not to put you on overtime on Tuesdays and Thursdays.

Conveying Information

Exercise 7.10

You are employed as a pump attendant at Parkway Service Station, and this week you are working the midnight to 8 a.m. shift. The owner of the Station is Carl Runcorn, and he normally comes in just before you leave.

An early customer this morning asks you to fill his car with gas, check the oil, and replace a burned-out oil pressure warning lamp behind the dash. You don't know which is the correct size lamp (you can't find the chart for his automobile), so you take the display carton containing some 150 bulbs into the car with you.

Some time after the customer has left, you realize you have left the carton on the floor of his car (on the passenger's side). You remember he used a credit card, and so you check through the credit slips until you come across two on which there is a charge for a lamp bulb. Unfortunately, you can't tell which was for that particular customer. You jot down the following information from the slips:

Walston Oil Company Credit Slip No.	218847	218816
Name of card holder:	Will J. Shayko	Paul Klieg
Card Number:	2 718 406 227	2 501 711 308
Car License No:	(not entered)	BJ 2815

1. Explain this to Carl Runcorn when he comes in.
2. Assume Runcorn is coming in late today (too late for you to wait for him). Write him a memorandum explaining what has happened.

Exercise 7.11

You are driving home from a field assignment and it is late afternoon (you are driving your own car, for which the company pays you 12 cents a mile). In Morgantown you notice that your right front wheel has developed a squeak.

You stop at Morgantown Auto Repair, 276 Westbury St. (lessee owner: James K. Connor) to have it checked. His technician replaces both bearings. The Work Order (WO) number is 27611. The cost is $22.65, which you pay in cash.

You drive another 120 miles, then stop for the night.

Next morning, you drive 200 miles until just west of Brandon, when the car begins pulling violently to the right. You stop and check the wheel: it is quite hot. Obviously, you can drive no farther, so you ask a passing driver to telephone a service station in Brandon.

A tow truck takes your car into Brandon Autos, 54-8th Avenue, where inspection shows excessive clearance between the bearings and the drum of the right front wheel. The drum has been dragging on the brake shoes. The repair man says: "Whoever did this didn't seat the bearings properly. They probably torqued tight, but worked loose on the road." You pay $34.50 for the repairs, plus a towing charge of $13. The WO number is 4132.

Because of the two repair jobs, you arrive in your home city one day later than expected. Today, you are back to work and filling in your expense account. You want to claim the cost of one of the repair jobs (you feel if your regular service station had done the job, the second repair job would not have been necessary).

1. Go to your supervisor and explain to him why you were late returning, and that you want to claim some of the repair work.
2. Your supervisor asks you to give him a written request claiming the cost of the repair work (and towing charge) in Brandon. Write this memorandum to him. (Assume that you attach copies of both work orders to it.)

Exercise 7.12

Until recently, your office owned a rather old office copier that was cheap to operate but very slow and did not make good copies. You knew your supervisor wanted the company to rent a better copier, but he was never able to convince the manager that it was necessary (the manager's view has always been that a better machine would encourage employees to do a lot of private copying at company expense).

Three months ago the old copier caused a holdup on an important job. Your supervisor used this incident to persuade the manager to rent a Mobex copier. The manager reluctantly agreed, but he warned your supervisor, who in turn warned all the employees, that if copying costs increased too much with the new machine it would go back. As a safeguard, your supervisor placed a book beside the machine, in which he instructed users to write the number of copies they made each time, and the "copy counter" meter reading when they finished.

This morning when you arrive at work, Marlene comes running up to you. "Come down to the copier," she says, "Quick!"

Around the machine, scattered all over the floor, are hundreds of copies of a manufacturing order; an order you were copying the night before, just before you left. You had put it on the machine and dialed AUTOMATIC because you needed twenty copies. But it had made only seven copies when there was a power cut which lasted until after everyone had gone home.

You realize now that you forgot to switch the machine off. "It must have started up again when the power came on," you say to Marlene, "and kept on going until it ran out of paper."

"But it didn't stop," she says. "It was still clicking over when I came in just now, even without paper."

You look at the reading on the copy counter, and compare it with the last reading in the book. "Oh, no!" you gasp. "It's counted over 5,000 copies during the night."

"You know how much that will cost?" asks Marlene. "At 8 cents a copy —about $400!"

You pile up all the copies of the manufacturing order, and count out the twenty you needed. Then you look for your supervisor.

1. Tell him what has happened.
2. At his request, write him a memorandum explaining the occurrence, which he can later take to the manager.

Exercise 7.13

You are a driver for Delta Delivery Service, and your job is to deliver customers' goods to destinations around the city.

This morning you make a delivery to the shopping center at Poplar Park, then travel north on Walnut Street to Craven Avenue. The time is 10 a.m., so you decide to grab a quick coffee at the Mini-Inn at Craven and Walnut. Craven Avenue is packed with cars so you leave the van in the parking lot behind the Mini-Inn.

Ten minutes later you come out to find your van has gone. At this moment you realize that you left your keys in it. (It is normal practice to leave the keys in the truck overnight in Delta's parking compound; without thinking, you have followed this practice.)

You phone the dispatcher at Delta. His name is Vic Orrison, and he is also your boss.

1. Explain to Vic what has happened.

Vic arranges another van to pick you up. He also reports the theft to the police. At 2.15 p.m. the police phone in to report they have found your van, complete with keys, on the Twilite Drive-In Theater property, 15 miles south of the city.

You are driven out to fetch it. You find it is undamaged. A Chevy bumper you had to deliver is still in the truck, but a tachometer and odometer you were to deliver to the Walston Oil station at Acacia Road and Riverton Street are missing.

The van is a Chevy Custom 10, license number T4210. Its mileage is 23206.

2. Write a short report describing this happening for Vic.

Exercise 7.14

You are a mechanic at Wilding's Motors. The time is 8 a.m. Cars for the day's work are being driven from the reception area to each mechanic's respective work stall.

A 1972 Buick Wildcat is driven up to the second floor by a car jockey and put into your stall (number 39). You are instructed to remove the air cleaner and detach the gas line from the carburetor. You now have to pick up some spare parts you will need for the car, so you close the hood to the first notch and walk downstairs to the Parts Department.

While you are away, a car jockey is told to move the Buick from your stall and place it in stall 36, three stalls down the row. Neither he nor the dispatcher know of the work you have done. The car jockey moves the car, unknowingly spraying gas all over the hot manifold. He gets out of the car and walks away.

You meet him as you return and, just after you pass him, the engine explodes and catches fire (the heat has ignited the gasoline vapor with explosive force). Mechanics rush in with fire extinguishers. All windows on the floor have been blown out. The fire department arrives and the police investigate.

1. Your boss (his name is Rod Stuart) rushes up and asks you what happened. Tell him.

2. More bosses arrive, with more questions. Rod intervenes: "Go into my office," he says to you, "and write down exactly what happened." Do so. (Prepare it as a memorandum from you to Rod.)

NOTE: *You should assume you would not yet be aware of some of the actions in the sequence of events described above.*

*   *   *

Additional Exercises

Some of the exercises at the ends of chapters 10 and 11 could also apply to employees who are not yet supervisors. They are:

Type of Exercise	Ex. No.	Page
Making a Request	10.3	140
Reporting a Field Assignment	11.3	162
	11.4	162
Reporting Progress	11.5	165
Reporting an Inspection	11.7	166
	11.8	167

8

Communicating with Customers

The amount of contact you have with your employer's customers depends on the type of job you have. For certain jobs, you are right in the front line and deal directly with customers. For example, employees continually meet customers if they

* Service major appliances and equipment at a customer's office or residence; i.e., washing machines, dryers, stoves, refrigerators, air conditioners, and furnaces.
* Repair, renovate, or clean buildings and permanent fixtures in them (such as windows and carpets).
* Sell over a counter, either in a parts distributorship or a retail store.
* Deliver materials, parts, and supplies.
* Take telephone orders.

Prominent in this category are employees who provide personal services such as nursing, hairdressing, barbering, and dental hygiene. For these people there is continuous, direct contact with customers, who sometimes are called "patients."

In other jobs you may deal with customers only part of the time. This occurs mainly when the customer comes to your employer to have work done. You may be "in the back" doing the work, while someone else takes the work in and returns it to him. You meet the customer only if you have to explain what is wrong with his equipment, what work needs to be done to it, or what work you have already done. And just occasionally you may stand in for the person who normally deals with customers.

Employees having only occasional customer contact are those who overhaul or repair trucks, automobiles, small appliances (toasters, irons), bicycles, shoes, clocks, watches, and so on.

The amount of customer contact employees in various occupations are likely to experience is shown in Fig. 3–9. These are only general examples, for much will depend on the type of work your employer does. An electrician employed by a major appliance repair company would probably have a lot of customer contact time, whereas an electrician employed by a manufacturer to install and maintain electrical equipment on a production line would probably never meet customers. It is in service industries much more than production industries that employees are most likely to come face to face with customers.

When you are in the front line, the impression a customer has of you may become the impression he gains of the company you represent. If you are pleasant but businesslike, the customer will subconsciously think of the company as a pleasant, businesslike company to deal with. Similarly, if your appearance is neat and tidy, he will imagine a clean, well-organized company (of particular importance in the food industries). But if you are sloppily dressed, disorganized, or have a rude or abrupt manner, the customer will tend to imagine a haphazard, poorly run business. This, more than anything else, may cause him to turn to a competitor.

Employees in the front line are also the first persons to bear the burden of pressure when there are too many customers. If you are already busy with one customer and other customers are waiting for your attention:

1. Try not to become flustered, or appear to hurry your existing customer.
2. Try to keep a mental picture of the order in which customers come in. This may prevent a "pushy" customer from cutting off less assertive ones who arrived earlier.
3. If you are alone, ask your present customer to excuse you for a minute while you find someone else to help.
4. Don't be afraid to turn to everyone and say *loudly and cheerfully:*
   > I'm sorry you're having to wait so long.
   > *and:*
   > I'll be with you as quickly as I can.
   > *or:*
   > Excuse me for a minute while I find someone else to help you.
   > *and, when you return:*
   > Somebody will be with you in a minute.

LIKELY AMOUNT OF CUSTOMER CONTACT
(Not including persons involved in direct selling)

Many Contacts

Barber	Photographer
Beautician	Plumber
Carpet and tile installer	Radiologist
Dental hygienist	Receptionist
Electrician	Refrigeration technician
Hairdresser	Reporter
Librarian	Service station attendant
Meatcutter (butcher)	Switchboard operator
Nurse	TV Serviceman
Painter, decorator	Waitress

Occasional Contacts

Advertising and graphic artist	Electronics technician
Air conditioning technician	Instrument technician
Automotive mechanic	Radio operator
Carpenter	Stenographer
Clerk-typist	Surveyor
Diesel mechanic	Upholsterer
Draftsman	Watch repairman (horologist)

Few or No Contacts

Accountant	Machinist
Aircraft mechanic	Sewing machine operator
Autobody repairman	Sheet metal worker
Baker	Spray painter
Bricklayer (mason)	Stationary engineer
Cook	Steelworker
Heavy equipment operator	Welder

Fig. 3–9. Probable extent of customer contact for various occupations.

Your intent should be to prevent customers from feeling you are being discourteous by simply ignoring them. Make them feel you are aware they are there and are doing your best to help them.

Telephone callers should always be given courteous treatment, because their impression of you and the firm you work for will depend entirely on what they hear. They cannot see you working under pressure; neither can they know that the jangle of the ringing telephone may have been one irritant too many in the middle of a hectic afternoon.

No matter how rattled you may be, you should never indicate your annoyance by being abrupt. A telephone caller will sense it immediately from the tone of your voice and the words you use. Instead, politely say you are occupied at the moment, and that you will call back in, say, 20 minutes. But you must say this before the caller has a chance to explain in too much detail why he or she is telephoning, otherwise it will sound as though you are trying to avoid providing the service being asked for.

If you are very busy and simply cannot handle another call, try it like this:

YOU: Western Supply. Wanda Brandt speaking.
CALLER: Can you give me some information and prices on power tools for tree pruning?
YOU: I certainly can, but I'll have to call you back in a few minutes. Could you give me your name and telephone number, please?

Always request the caller's number rather than ask for the caller to phone again later. This not only shows interest on your part but also ensures that your company does not lose contact with a possible customer. A customer asked to phone again later may never do so, having telephoned a competitor in the meantime. The important thing to remember, of course, is that you *do* call back, and reasonably soon.

Here is another example:

YOU: Welland and Welland. Ron Brown speaking.
CALLER: This is Mrs. James, 2728 Rembrandt Road.
YOU: Yes, Mrs. James.   (1)
CALLER: You know, there's something wrong with that carpet you installed for me last week . . .   (2)
YOU: There is, Mrs. James? Let me get your file out, will you? Then I'll call you back. OK?

If you can, try to say you will call back when you first respond— at (1). But sometimes, as in this case, the caller does not pause long enough for you to do more than simply acknowledge who is calling. Then you will have to listen for a suitable point in the caller's remarks. In the above example, this was when Mrs. James paused momentarily at (2).

CALMING THE DISSATISFIED CUSTOMER

Unfortunately, not all customers are pleasant or easy to deal with. Indeed, some can be extremely difficult—even rude—and this can place you in a very difficult position. No matter how awkward or rude a customer chooses to be, you must never be rude in return. Your role is to apologize if you have really done something wrong, or express your regret if the customer thinks you have committed an error (even though you haven't). You can do it like this:

> I'm sorry, Mr. James; I supplied you with the wrong size bolts. I'll exchange them right away.
>
> or
>
> I'm sorry you feel like that, Mr. Hearst. But the strike at the Lakehead has completely cut off our supplies. There's no way I can get you a replacement.

If a customer is particularly difficult, or is provoking you to the point of losing control, suggest that he talk to your supervisor. (Bring the supervisor to the customer if the problem occurs where you work, or ask the customer to telephone your supervisor if you are at the customer's place.) But do this before it is too late—*before* you become so angry that you say things you later regret.

Remember that a customer who gets mad may be just "letting off steam." Perhaps things have been going wrong for him all day, and the error you make proves to be the proverbial "last straw."

You can help him and yourself by listening attentively to show that you really want to set things straight. He will calm down much more quickly if he sees you are genuinely concerned that things have gone wrong than if you seem to be only casually interested in him and his problems.

Many customer problems can be avoided if clear communication exists between employee and customer. As an employee, you need to be told exactly what is to be done for a customer. In turn, he needs to know how much you are going to do and what it is going to cost. All this must be established before any work is done.

FINDING OUT WHAT THE CUSTOMER WANTS

Before starting on a job, ask the customer or your supervisor to explain what you are to do, and whether there is a limit to the amount of time you are to spend on the job. The latter can be important if, for example, you are servicing a customer's equipment that is old or needs extensive repair. If the cost of repair work turns out to be more than the equipment is worth, the customer will rightly be annoyed if you have built up a hefty labor bill before checking whether or not there is a limit. (The customer's annoyance will be matched by that of your boss when he discovers that you have put in a lot of work which, if he is to maintain the customer's goodwill, he probably cannot bill to the customer.)

When Bill Walkin was sent in to paint John Gilmore's apartment, John told him which color was to go in each room, then went away on a short business trip. In two days Bill ran out of every color of paint, and telephoned his boss to send more. The boss grumbled to Bill that he was putting the paint on too thick, but sent over seven gallons anyway.

The reason became clear on the following day, when John Gilmore returned with several rolls of wallpaper under his arm. He explained that only three walls should have been painted in each room, because wallpaper was to be hung on the fourth wall. (Only then did Bill remember John saying something about all east walls being "accent" walls.)

The moral is clear: always make sure you understand exactly what you are to do. Ask your supervisor first, because he has the customer's original instructions and your company will bill according to them. If the customer tells you to do things differently, or to do extra work, check with your supervisor to see if it is all right to do so.

MAKING SURE THE CUSTOMER KNOWS THE FACTS

When a customer places a service call, his main interest is to get his equipment or machinery operating again as quickly as possible. If he is in a hurry, you may have him breathing down your neck, which can be very unsettling. So you hurry, and put in a lot of new parts, and when you leave him he is very happy.

But not for long. Two days later your employer sends him a bill for the work you did, and he is appalled at the high cost. In the urgency of the moment you forgot to warn him just how much it was going to cost. This means your company now has a dissatisfied customer.

No matter how urgently a customer wants a job done, when you have taken things apart and found out what is wrong, stop for a moment and tell him

1. What the problem is.
2. What needs to be done to overcome it.

3. How much it is going to cost (you may have to get this information from your supervisor).

He may not like the bad news, but at least you are giving him the opportunity to choose whether you are to go ahead or stop work. Then, when the bill comes in, it will not cause a shock that may affect the customer's opinion of you and your company.

More information on how to communicate with customers appears in Chapter 12 (starting on page 170). This is the point at which, if you have a problem to resolve or a difficult customer to cope with, your supervisor can take over. Nevertheless, the ideas it offers should be read by all employees, because one day every one of us may face a problem or be in a situation in which we cannot turn to someone else for help.

EXERCISES

NOTE: Your instructor will tell you who is playing the role of "receiver" for each of these exercises.

Exercise 8.1

You are alone in the office when the telephone rings. The caller doesn't announce who he is, but simply demands to speak to Mr. Atkins, the manager. You explain that he is not in and ask if you can be of assistance.

"No. I've had enough trouble with your outfit," the caller replies. "Put me straight through to your manager."

You explain that Mr. Atkins really is not in, and won't be back until 2 p.m. "If you would care to leave your name and telephone number," you add, "I'll have him call you as soon as he comes in."

"Now, don't give me that," he snaps back. "Just let me talk to him. Right away."

1. What do you say now?
2. What do you tell Mr. Atkins if the caller does not leave his name, and he:
   a. Simply hangs up?
   b. Says: "Don't you worry, I'll make sure Mr. Atkins hears about the runaround you've given me!"?

Exercise 8.2

You are talking to Mrs. Wilshire, who is a new customer, when Harry Renshaw charges in. A big, blustering man, he is full of his own importance and constantly demanding immediate attention. He is also one of your company's best customers.

He strides over to where you and Mrs. Wilshire are talking and, without even waiting for a pause in the conversation, says:

"Run upstairs and find me three sacks of No. 12—there are none on the floor. Put them straight into my station wagon: I've backed it up to the door. And charge them to my account."

1. He obviously expects you to act immediately. What do you say to him?
2. He does not wait for you to reply, and is already on his way out the door. Do you call him back? If so, what do you say to him?
3. What do you say to Mrs. Wilshire:
   a. If Harry Renshaw is standing there?
   b. If he leaves immediately?

Exercise 8.3

When Harry Renshaw (of the previous exercise) comes in early in the morning to order a Vancourt 212 Soil Sifter, you tell him there is a two-month delivery delay. He says he cannot wait that long and demands that you sell him the display model. You check with your supervisor, who says OK, and you tell Mr. Renshaw it will be delivered tomorrow.

It is now 5 p.m. and you have a problem: the display model has disappeared. The company owner has since sold it to a friend.

Visit Mr. Renshaw and tell him what has happened.

Exercise 8.4

When Mr. Downs comes in the door carrying the separator you sent him yesterday, you sense right away that he is displeased.

"This is the third separator you've sent me, and it's still not the right one," he barks at you. "I want a model 280C. Can't you fill a simple order like that?"

This is the sequence of events leading to Mr. Downs' confrontation with you:

1. The first separator you sent was a 283 instead of a 280C.
2. The second separator was a 280C, but was damaged.
3. You remembered calling the warehouse yesterday, and saying to Harry over the intercom: "He wants a 280C—got that? Check that it's not broken, and make sure all the parts are there." Now Mr. Downs is returning another model 283—not the 280C he wanted.

At this moment you suddenly realize that the similarity in sound of "280C" and "283" has caused Harry to send out the wrong model.

1. What do you say to Mr. Downs?
2. Assume Mr. Downs lives some distance out of town and has shipped the separator back to you. Write him a letter of apology and explanation.

Exercise 8.5

It was raining this morning when you delivered the outboard motor your company had repaired for Mr. Terry. Mrs. Terry asks you to take it to the backyard and fit it onto her husband's boat. She does not go with you.

The boat and a new car are sitting side by side in the garage. It's a squeeze to carry the outboard motor between them, but you manage it without touching either.

It is now mid-afternoon and Mrs. Terry confronts you in the store. She accuses you of damaging her husband's new car: there is a long, deep scratch along the front door and fender. You tell her you were very careful and did not touch the car, but she insists that the mark was not there yesterday, and drags you outside to examine it. She demands that either you or your company pay to have the car repaired. (It is your opinion that she has damaged the car—possibly backing out of the garage—and is using you as a scapegoat.)

Reply to Mrs. Terry's increasingly shrill demands that you "do something about it."

IV

COMMUNICATING WHEN YOU BECOME SUPERVISOR

9

Communicating
with Employees

The first step up into even a very junior supervisory position has
far-reaching effects on relationships. All of a sudden you are accepted
by the company as the new infant on the management team: you are a bit
wet behind the ears, but given time you'll grow. In time you will learn
how to communicate with management and other supervisors, just as a
child in its early months has to learn how to communicate with its
parents and brothers and sisters.

But as a newly appointed junior supervisor you may find it difficult
to adapt to the change in relationship between yourself and those who
until yesterday were your co-workers. This doesn't happen overnight: it
evolves slowly, as you gradually become familiar with your new role and
realize that your loyalties are now split. Whereas before you were "one
of the guys," you are now separated from them by an invisible barrier.
You may still work closely with them, but your loyalty to the company
now has to take first place over your loyalty to the employees.

In this atmosphere it is not surprising that a new supervisor often
feels isolated. His position is lonely because it effectively separates him
from his buddies but doesn't make him feel close to the other members of
the management team. His role is particularly important, however, because he bridges the gap between management and the labor force. When
management hands down instructions, it is the supervisor's task to hand
them on and explain them to employees. And when the workmen have a
beef, it is the supervisor's job to be in close enough contact with them to
hear of the problem and to draw it to management's attention.

A new supervisor may be chosen to become foreman both because he

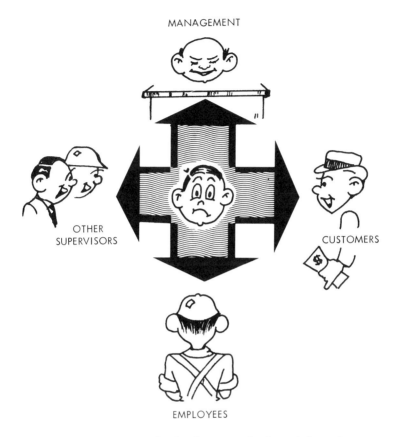

MANAGEMENT

OTHER
SUPERVISORS

CUSTOMERS

EMPLOYEES

Fig. 4–1. Communication is a supervisor's stock in trade.

is good at his work and because he seems to have the qualities that make a good leader. But the tool that will prove most useful to him is the ability to communicate with all kinds of people. As Fig. 4–1 illustrates, he will need to communicate downward (to the employees), upward (to senior management), and sideways (to other supervisors and to the company's customers). Because very few foremen, shift bosses, and crew chiefs are given training in how to communicate *before* they are promoted, this section is provided to prepare you for that difficult communications role when your turn comes to climb up the first rung of the promotion ladder.

WHEN YOU SHOULD LISTEN

Employees need to feel that there is someone in the company they can talk to. They may want to complain about somebody, ask for something, make a suggestion, or simply "bend your ear" for a moment. Busy though you may be, as a supervisor you must always be ready to listen to them.

When you listen to an employee he wants to feel you are interested in what he has to say, and that you do not begrudge the time you are giving him. However, being interested does not mean becoming so involved that you no longer appear to be a detached, unbiased observer; or, if an employee comes to you with a complaint, that you cannot prevent yourself from taking sides—either for or against him.

For example, when Janice complains to Anne (her supervisor) that all the "dirty" jobs end up on her desk while Maria gets the easy ones, Anne suspects there is some truth in her complaint. She realizes that Maria, who usually arrives at work a few minutes earlier than Janice, may be sorting out the best jobs for herself. But Anne does not attempt to say so, or even suggest to Janice that she is on her side. She listens carefully, displays interest and concern, and tells Janice she will look into it.

Listening to the Hesitant Employee

Sometimes it is difficult for a supervisor to tell whether a person who comes in and talks for no apparent reason is simply trying to kill time or really has a difficult problem to talk about. Not everyone is aware that they should open a conversation with the Main Message (see Chapters 3 and 7), which means you may have to listen for a while to see if there is a reason behind the employee's visit. If you obviously attempt to hasten the conversation, you will probably make it more difficult for an employee with a real problem to get around to it.

Take Len Burn, for example. His wife has to go into the hospital for a week, and she's worried about how he is going to manage alone with their three small children. A neighbor has offered to look after the kids from 10 A.M. every day, but the Burns cannot find anyone to come in earlier than that. The only way he can manage is to start work at 10:30 for a week. But he also knows that this is the company's busy period, which makes it doubly hard for him to ask Don Connaught for the time. Then when Len tries to talk to Don about his problem, he starts out on the wrong foot:

Len	*Don*
Guess you're pretty busy . . .	
	You said it!
Always like this, this time of year.	
	Uh-huh.

The only year I can remember
it being worse was '72.

You've been here longer than I
have.

Yeah! Twelve years, next September.

Longer than most.

Uh-huh.

Here there is a slight pause: Don is waiting to see what is on Len's
mind. He has worked with Len long enough to know that he usually
makes better conversation than this. (Note how Don's replies carefully
echo what Len is saying—they quietly encourage him to continue. Don
knows better than to pass opinions or say anything that may make it
seem that *he* is steering the conversation.) Don's gentle comments are a
form of listening.

Len	*Don*
It—er—it being so busy—that's what makes it so difficult for me to ask . . .	
	Ask what, Len? (*gently, encouraging Len to go on*) (1)
I need some time off—only two hours a day—for a week—when my wife goes into hospital . . .	
	(*encouragingly*) Into hospital? (2)
So I can look after the kids until the baby-sitter comes in. I'd be in by ten-thirty every day. And it would be only for a week.	
	(*thoughtfully*) I see . . .
I know it's a bad time . . .	
	How soon would this be, Len? (3)
In about two weeks—as soon as there's a bed in the hospital.	
	You've got quite a problem! Let me look into it, will you, Len? Come and see me again before you leave tonight. OK? (4)

Although Don has not said much in this conversation, he has really
been communicating all the time. At the points marked (1) and (2) his
echo-type comments are really saying "Go on, I'm listening." At point (2)
he might easily have been tempted to ask "When?" but he has wisely

waited until (3), when Len has finished explaining. Then, in his few brief comments at point (4), he is really saying three things:

1. "I understand, Len. You have my sympathy."
2. "I can't give you an answer right away, but I'll do something about it." (*Don may already have made up his mind to say "Yes," but he cannot even hint at it until he has approval from his department manager—just in case there is some reason why Len's request and Don's recommendation have to be turned down.*)
3. "I'll not send you home tonight still wondering what's going to happen." (*This means he's going to act immediately, and plans to give Len an answer at 4.30 P.M.*)

In these examples it appears easy to be a listener. But the opposite is true. It is difficult not to say something, or to grunt no more than a non-committal "Uh-huh" when the person speaking to you is struggling to find the right words. But to say something at the wrong moment may turn his conversation off course—so that it becomes your conversation rather than his—at which point you have stopped being a listener.

Listening to the Angry Employee

An angry employee who comes to you with a complaint may let his anger mask the real problem. Something has happened to cause his anger, and you need to find out what it is. But his anger may create an offensive, chip-on-the-shoulder attitude, cause him to use abusive language, or prevent him from clearly explaining his complaint. And, if his anger is directed at you or the company, you may find it difficult not to be provoked into responding with equal anger.

No matter how provocative an employee may be, you must not let yourself be drawn into an argument with him. Your role is to listen attentively, and to show interest in and concern for his problem. Let him "blast off" until he runs out of steam. Then, when he has calmed down enough to speak more clearly, ask him to repeat his complaint so you can get the details straight. Make sure he understands that you want facts, and let him see that you are jotting down notes.

As he retells his story, ask questions to find out exactly what has happened (bearing in mind that he is speaking only from his own point of view). Note details such as the names of people involved, who else saw what was going on, the time and place of each occurrence, and so on. But throughout, maintain your impartiality by neither commenting nor passing an opinion.

When the employee has finished, tell him you want to be sure you
have the facts straight. Then repeat the complaint to him, like this:

> I gather, Hank, that your problem started last Monday, when you couldn't
> find your time card. Right?

(Hank nods his head)

> It wasn't there in the evening, either, but it was there on Tuesday morn-
> ing. You told the time clerk on Tuesday that it wasn't there the day be-
> fore, and he said he'd sign you in. OK?

(Hank again nods his head)

> Then this morning you found you've been docked a day's pay. You saw
> the accountant and he said it was because you missed a day: Monday, to
> be exact.

> You went to see the time clerk this morning, but now he says you never
> talked to him on Tuesday. In fact, he said you are a liar and you weren't
> in at all on Monday.

At this point Hank interrupts to ask that the word "liar" be changed.
He explains that the time clerk didn't exactly say that—not in so many
words—but Hank felt it was pretty clear that he meant it.

By repeating the facts back to the employee you give him an opportunity to correct something he may have said in the heat of the
moment which he later would recognize as not entirely accurate.

When the employee feels that your description of his complaint is
correct, you can tell him you will look into the problem and talk to him
again (and here you should set a definite time to see him). The employee
may still be smoldering inside when he leaves you, but he will at least
know that you have given him a fair, unbiased hearing and that you are
doing something about his complaint. For more information about
complaints and how they are handled in a union shop, see "Belonging to
the Union" in chapter 6 (page 67).

WHEN YOU NEED TO EXPLAIN

When a new employee joins your group, you will need to tell him
about the equipment he is to use and how you like things done. You will
also make similar explanations to existing employees when new equip-

ment is brought in or changes occur in procedures. These explanations fall into two categories: those describing hardware (from nuts and bolts to machinery) and those describing methods (from mail handling to X-ray testing of metals).

Listeners expect descriptions and explanations to be easy to understand (for if they are confusing, listeners quickly "switch off their receivers" and then make mistakes or ask a lot of unnecessary questions). This means that you, as the person doing the explaining, need first to think about what you want to say and then to arrange the information in a logical order that will help listeners understand even complex explanations.

Describing Equipment or Machinery

Regardless of whether a piece of equipment is simple or complex, its description should cover three main points: Purpose, Construction, and Operation, in that order. This means taking all the information you have about the equipment and dividing it into three blocks, then adding a Summary Statement (see Fig. 4–2). Instructors use these blocks to help

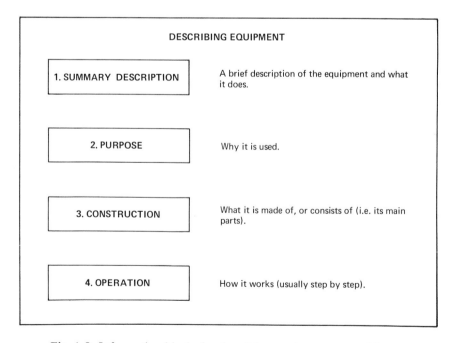

Fig. 4–2. Information blocks for describing equipment or machinery.

them describe tools and equipment. A plumbing instructor describing a drain plunger (see Fig. 4–3) would hold it up and say something like this:

This is a drain plunger used by plumbers and householders to clear clogged drain pipes.	1. & 2. SUMMARY DESCRIPTION & PURPOSE
It is simply a cup-shaped piece of rubber with a 30-inch wooden handle screwed into its base.	3. CONSTRUC-TION
The cup is inverted over the drain hole, and water is run into the sink. Alternate upward and downward pressure on the rubber cup pumps water into and out of the drain, loosening clogged matter in it.	4. OPERATION

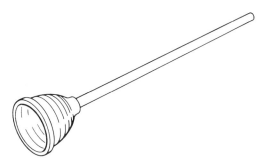

Fig. 4–3. A plumber's drain plunger.

In industry you are likely to be describing much more complex equipment. This is particularly true for the staff at Reece, Minnesota, transit system garage, where a Washtronics Conveyorized Bus Washing System[1] has just been installed. But the approach is just the same:

1. The chief maintenance supervisor describes the purpose, construction, and operation of the whole system to the maintenance foremen.
2. The maintenance foreman in each area (e.g., interior cleaning, conveyor, detergent mixing system, and so on) describes the purpose, construction, and operation of his equipment to his staff. Reg Pawluk, for example, describes the wheel washers like this:

Wheels are washed by one of two automatic wheel washers that operate automatically, moving a short distance with each wheel of the bus.	1. & 2. SUMMARY DESCRIPTION and PURPOSE

[1] References in this chapter to the Washtronics Conveyorized Bus Washing System courtesy of Washtronics Ltd., Winnipeg, Canada.

The two wheel washers are mounted on short tracks, one on each side of the conveyor. Each has a rotating brush and a spray head fed by a water and detergent solution.

> 3. CONSTRUC-
> TION

As the front wheels of the bus reach the wheel washers they engage a roller arm that starts the system, moving each wheel washer carriage along its track while the spray heads and brushes wash the wheels. At the end of the track, the water and detergent switch off and the carriages return to their starting positions.

> 4. OPERATION

When the rear wheels reach the wheel washers, the operation is repeated. At the end of the complete cycle, the wheel washers switch off automatically.

The orderly arrangement of the Operation block helps the listener understand the explanation. Because you are a reader and cannot see the wheel washers or ask Reg any questions, you may refer to the photograph in Fig. 4–4.

Describing a Process or Procedure

When the listener is likely to take part in a process or procedure, a description tends to be more personal. But it still needs an orderly arrangement of information. The blocks are shown in Fig. 4–5.

Maisie Bell supervises the mail services in a manufacturing company. Her description of the collection and delivery routine to a new clerk is relatively simple. Starting with block 1–Summary Description, she says:

> We collect mail from and deliver it to all departments three times a day: at 9.30 A.M., noon, and 3.00 P.M.

Then, in block 2–Purpose, she explains why:

> The first time around is mainly to deliver the morning's incoming mail.
> The noon visit is to pick up and deliver interdepartment mail.
> And the mid-afternoon visit is mainly to pick up the day's outgoing mail.

Maisie then shows the mail delivery cart to the new clerk. Her accompanying words represent block 3–Equipment:

> This is the mail cart we use. The top level has vertical mail compartments for the mail being delivered: one for each department. The lower shelf

Fig. 4–4. Automatic bus wheel washer (courtesy Washtronics Ltd., Winnipeg, Canada).

has two baskets for the mail that is picked up. The red basket is for out-going mail; and the green basket is for interdepartment mail. OK?

The new girl nods her head, so Maisie continues with block 4—Method:

Before going out each time, the mail is picked up from the sorting rack—here—and transferred to the compartments in the mail cart—here.

The route we follow is described on this card. First we take the elevator

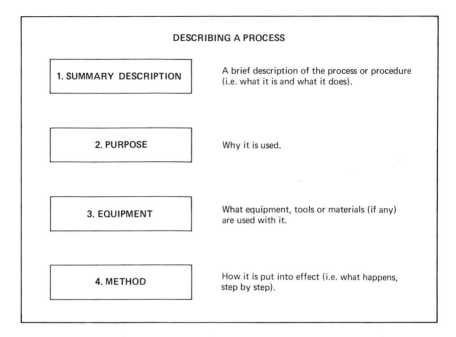

Fig. 4–5. Information blocks for describing a process or procedure.

to the top floor—to the Engineering Department—and then work downward through Production, Purchasing, the offices, and to Shipping in the basement.

At each stop the mail for that department is taken from the cart—here—and placed in the department's IN tray. Then any mail they have ready is collected from the OUT tray and placed in one of the two baskets on the bottom shelf—depending on whether it is interdepartment mail or outgoing mail.

When we get back to the mail room, the two baskets are emptied and the contents are sorted.

At the Reece, Minnesota, transit system garage, Colin Weinstein is describing the new bus interior cleaning and refueling procedure to a group of bus drivers. His words are less personal than Maisie's because the drivers will not be directly involved in the process (the drivers have only to drive their buses through the system). This is what he says:

Starting next Monday, buses will be driven to one of three interior cleaning and refueling bays as soon as they come off the road. From these bays, they will then be driven straight into the automatic wash line.

1. SUMMARY DESCRIPTION

There are three bays, to keep pace with the wash line.
Interior cleaning and refueling takes three minutes, whereas
the Washtronics washing system can accept a fresh bus
every minute.

| 2. PURPOSE |

Each bay contains an automatic exhaust system, manually
operated wand blowguns, and fuel pumps.

| 3. EQUIPMENT |

As soon as the bus stops, the driver opens the front door
and the bellows of the exhaust system advance and en-
velop it. When the exhaust system is switched on it evacu-
ates all loose objects from inside the bus. Simultaneously,
cleaners work with blow guns inside the bus, loosening
sticky objects.

| 4. METHOD |

At the same time a refueling and inspection crew services
the exterior of the bus, checking it mechanically and oiling
and greasing it as required.

WHEN YOU HAVE TO INSTRUCT

An instruction must be given confidently and very clearly, so that
the receiver will feel he can follow directions without making mistakes.
In a description the speaker merely explains what happens. In an
instruction, he tells the listener or reader how to do something.

The four information blocks for an instruction (Fig. 4–6) are the
same as those for a description of a process or procedure. The chief
difference lies in the overall tone—which is crisp and definite—and how
block 4—Method—is handled. It requires the speaker or writer to issue a
series of short, clear statements that sound like commands.

Giving Spoken Instructions

"You" is heard often in spoken instructions. If Maisie Bell had been
instructing the new mail clerk how to deliver and collect mail rather
than describing the process, she would have been more personal and
direct. But the information would have been essentially the same.
Compare this excerpt from her spoken instruction below with her
description on pages 119 and 120.

You follow the route described on this card, first taking the elevator to
the top floor (to the Engineering Department), and working downward
through Production, Purchasing, and the offices, to Shipping in the basement.

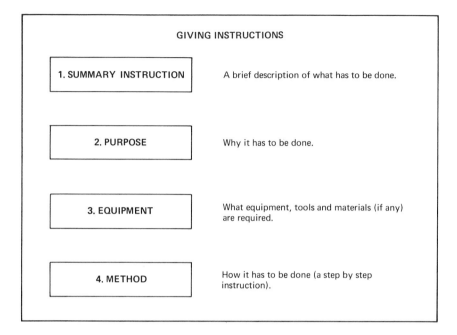

Fig. 4–6. Information blocks for giving instructions.

At each stop you are to place the mail you are delivering in the department's IN tray, and pick up the outgoing mail from the OUT tray. You will place this mail into the red or green basket, depending on whether it has an external or internal destination.

Preparing Written Instructions

Sometimes you may have to write an instruction as well as tell a person what to do. This is what happened to Colin Weinstein. When the Washtronics bus cleaning system was placed in operation, the garage manager asked him both to brief drivers on the new drive-in procedure and to prepare a written instruction for them to carry when they took their buses onto the road.

Colin found it harder to write the instruction than tell the bus drivers personally what to do. He tried using the "you" approach, but found it just did not seem businesslike. So he went to see Gary Watson, the transit garage engineer, who he knew sometimes wrote operating instructions.

"It's really not difficult," Gary explained, "if you remember to write bite-size steps and make each one a command. Short paragraphs help the reader understand what has to be done. He doesn't get confused by having too much to read and do at the same time. If you can give each step a number—1, 2, 3, and so on—then so much the better.

"Every step must also tell the driver to do something. In other words, your instruction must *instruct*. You can do this by using strong verbs that seem to command the reader to act as directed. Here are some:

> *Stop* the bus.
> *Open* the door.
> *Wipe* the window.

"If you can, position these 'action' words at the beginning of each step. The only time you may not want to do so is when you need to 'set the scene' first, like this:

> When the paint is dry, *peel off* the masking tape;
> > or:
> If the base vibrates, *increase* the power.

"What I suggest you do, Colin, is write out your instruction then let me have a look at it."

This is what Colin wrote:

INSTRUCTION TO BUS DRIVERS

1. *Close* all bus windows.
2. *Drive* in through door 4, 5, or 6.
3. *Drive* into the interior cleaning and refueling bay.
4. *Stop* the bus with the front door level with the exhaust system bellows. *Open* the door. *Leave* engine running. *Stay in* or *get out* of bus.
5. After interior cleaning, *drive* the bus to the wash line, guided by the attendant.
6. When the wand switch touches your window, *put* bus drive in neutral. *Leave* engine running. *Stay* in bus.
7. When bus stops moving at end of line (pusher dog disengages), *drive* the clean bus to the parking area.

When Colin showed his instructions to Gary Watson, Gary praised him for using short steps and "tell" words. [The *tell* words are shown in italics in Colin's instruction, above]. Gary said he thought it seemed a little abrupt, so suggested that Colin do something to avoid having curt instructions like "Leave engine running. Stay in bus" (steps 4 and 6).

Gary also thought Colin should write some introductory material to help drivers understand why they should follow this procedure. He suggested using the four information blocks mentioned earlier:

1. SUMMARY INSTRUCTION

2. PURPOSE

3. EQUIPMENT

4. METHOD

Colin's final effort, which he had typed and printed for distribution to the bus drivers, is shown in Fig. 4–7.

DRIVE-IN PROCEDURE EFFECTIVE MONDAY   MAY 8, 19__

Introduction of the Washtronics automated bus-washing system means a change in drive-in procedures. From May 8, bus drivers are to take ① & ② their buses to be cleaned and refueled before parking them. The entire process will take five minutes.

The Washtronics system consists of three interior cleaning and refueling ③ bays, and an automated, conveyorized exterior wash line.

On returning to the garage, every bus driver is to:

1.   Check that all bus windows are firmly closed.

2.   Drive in through door No. 4, 5, or 6.

3.   Enter, or line up for, the interior cleaning and refueling bay directly ahead of him.

4.   Stop bus so that its front door is level with exhaust system bellows, then open door. (Drivers may remain in or step out of their bus during cleaning and refueling, but the engine must be ④ kept running.)

5.   When cleaning is complete, drive bus to the entrance of the wash line, lining up bus as directed by the attendant.

6.   When wand-switch touches driver's window, place bus drive in neutral. (Drivers are to remain in their bus during washing procedure, and are to keep the engine running.)

7.   When the pusher dog disengages the left rear wheel (i.e. the bus stops moving forward), drive your clean bus to the parking area.

Fig. 4–7. Colin Weinstein's written instructions to bus drivers (circled numbers refer to information blocks in Fig. 4–6).

EXERCISES

NOTE: *1. When an exercise calls for you to give a spoken answer, your instructor will tell you who is playing the role of "receiver."*
   2. Some of these exercises contain situations that might be faced by employees as well as by supervisors.

Descriptions and Instructions

Exercise 9.1

Select a process, method, or technique used by the business or industry for which you are being trained. Research information on this process, then describe it to the class, using a visual aid to make your description more interesting. Prepare speaking notes (do not read from them—use them only for reference) and hand them to your instructor when your description is finished.

Exercise 9.2

Select a piece of equipment used during your course (preferably equipment used in the work you are being trained for) and check with your instructor that it is suitable for you to describe. If it is too simple, your instructor may direct you to other or similar equipment; or, if it is too complex, your instructor will probably suggest that you limit your description to only a certain part of the equipment.

1. Using either the equipment itself or a suitable visual aid, describe the equipment to an imaginary audience of high school students who are visiting your college.
2. Assume that a new student transferred to your class has not previously seen the equipment. Instruct him how to use it.
3. Write an instruction on how to use the equipment (or part of it) for a capable worker who has not used this particular equipment previously, but may have used similar types.

Exercise 9.3

Write an instruction for a person who has to do one of the following things (assume this person is not familiar with similar procedures):
Replace a fuse in a car
Clean the filters in a furnace or air conditioner

Replace a needle in a sewing machine
Oil a bicycle
Adjust a bicycle gear
Replace a faucet washer
Replace a door lock
Adjust a thermostat
Replace a lamp switch
Set the timer on a clock radio, alarm clock, or oven clock
Defrost a freezer
Relight a gas or oil burner
Replace the disposable bag in a vacuum cleaner
Adjust the cutting height on a lawn mower

Exercise 9.4

You are Vic Orrison, the dispatcher at Delta Delivery Service (see Exercise 7.13 on page 97).

As a result of this morning's occurrence in which a company van is stolen, write an instruction to all drivers that keys are not to be left in vehicles overnight—instead they are to be brought into your office and hung on the appropriate hook.

Exercise 9.5

You are Rod Stuart, the supervisor of the employee whose car engine ignited in Exercise 7.14 on page 98.

Write a memorandum instructing all employees that while a mechanic is working on a car he must raise the hood and leave it raised until he is finished, even if he is only replacing a bolt on the back bumper, and that no one is to move a car with its hood raised without first receiving your permission.

Replying to Requests

Exercise 9.6

You are the supervisor of the employee who comes to you with a question about the length of his vacation (see exercise 7.2 on page 91). His name is John Phipps.

You know that to qualify for three weeks' vacation an employee must be with the firm from April 1 of one year to March 31 of the next. An employee starting after April 1 would have only a partial holiday the following summer, depending on when he started.

Because you do not know how many days' vacation John is entitled to, you ask the personnel manager. He says John has nine working days. If he wants the full three weeks' vacation (which amounts to fifteen working days) he will have to apply for six days' leave without pay.

1. Write a memorandum to John informing him of the vacation days he is entitled to, and explaining what he must do if he wants three weeks' vacation.
2. Call John in and tell him how many vacation days he is entitled to and how you arrived at the figure of nine working days. (You can assume you would hand him the memorandum at this time.)

Exercise 9.7

Write a memorandum to Stew Johnson, the employee who came to you with a request in Exercise 7.5 (1) on page 92, authorizing him to take paper offcuts smaller than 8 in. $\times$ 6 in. out of the plant. (Assume that this is the authority required by the security guard at the door.) Place a three-month limit on the authorization.

Exercise 9.8

You are the supervisor of Jean Carriere, the employee asking for time off in Exercise 7.6 on page 93. Write a memorandum authorizing Jean's absence without pay from 8.30 a.m. to noon on the Tuesday requested.

10

Communicating
with
Management

When a supervisor communicates with management, he is in roughly the same position as a line employee communicating with his supervisor. Both are communicating upward (see Fig. 4–1, page 111), and both are transmitting the same kind of information: complaints, requests, reports, and so on. But there are two subtle differences:

1. While a line employee communicates mainly about things *he* wants, a supervisor more often communicates about things *his employees* want.
2. While most of the time a line employee communicates orally (face to face) with his supervisor, a supervisor often communicates in writing with management.

Who does "management" include? Basically, anyone in a company who has authority, from the president down to the most junior supervisor or foreman. But management is also rather like society, and has class levels known loosely as "top" (senior), "middle," and "lower" (junior) management. As a supervisor or foreman you are junior management and normally transmit information to and receive it from middle management. In a small company where there is no middle management you communicate directly with senior management.

A junior supervisor attends more meetings, fills in more forms, writes more reports, and knows more about company plans and policies than a line employee. And often his promotion brings with it the end of his union membership: a sharp reminder that he is no longer "one of the guys." (In some union-management contracts, however, line foremen are included in the bargaining unit.)

COMMUNICATING FOR YOURSELF

As a supervisor, you will want to communicate with management for the same reasons that as a line employee you wanted to communicate with your supervisor: to ask questions, offer suggestions, and make requests. But now you will write more than before, and give more information and be more persuasive. Management expects a supervisor to think further ahead—to try to anticipate questions and answer the more important ones *before* they are asked.

The information blocks you will use (see Fig. 4–8) are the same as those recommended for employees in chapter 7. But as a supervisor you

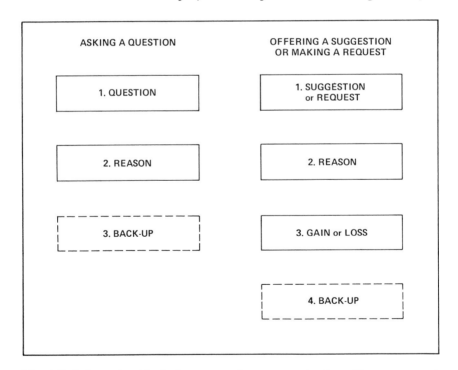

Fig. 4–8. Information blocks for a supervisor communicating with management.

may not always hold as much back-up information in reserve, particularly in written communications.

The difference between the two approaches is shown in Fig. 4–9. The amount of back-up information built into the message depends on what questions you think the reader or listener will ask. Writer A, on the left, has chosen to offer only essential information. Writer B, on the

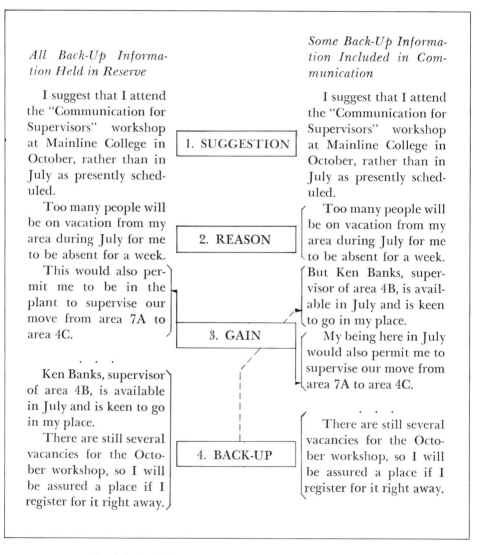

All Back-Up Information Held in Reserve

Some Back-Up Information Included in Communication

I suggest that I attend the "Communication for Supervisors" workshop at Mainline College in October, rather than in July as presently scheduled.

1. SUGGESTION

I suggest that I attend the "Communication for Supervisors" workshop at Mainline College in October, rather than in July as presently scheduled.

Too many people will be on vacation from my area during July for me to be absent for a week.

2. REASON

Too many people will be on vacation from my area during July for me to be absent for a week.

This would also permit me to be in the plant to supervise our move from area 7A to area 4C.

3. GAIN

But Ken Banks, supervisor of area 4B, is available in July and is keen to go in my place.

My being here in July would also permit me to supervise our move from area 7A to area 4C.

. . .

Ken Banks, supervisor of area 4B, is available in July and is keen to go in my place.

There are still several vacancies for the October workshop, so I will be assured a place if I register for it right away.

4. BACK-UP

. . .

There are still several vacancies for the October workshop, so I will be assured a place if I register for it right away.

Fig. 4–9. Building back-up information into the message.

right, has guessed that he will be asked: "Who do you think should go, if you don't?" Both have felt that the last item of back-up information is of lesser importance and probably will not be needed. And both are aware that good communications contain no more information than the reader really needs.

COMMUNICATING FOR YOUR EMPLOYEES

When an employee comes to you with a question you cannot answer, a complaint you cannot settle, or a problem you cannot resolve, you will probably turn to your boss for help. If you want a simple "Yes" or "No" answer to the employee's request, you can state your case in words just as the employee did when he came to you. But in many cases you should make the request in writing.

The rule is simple: if the information you hand to the employee will be referred to again, or quoted, or used as a basis for future decisions, what you or management say must be given to the employee in writing and a copy kept on file. Then if in future there is any doubt as to what was actually said or decided, the words are always available.

Spoken Communications

When Patti Ray asks Maisie Bell if she can have Friday off to go to an out-of-town wedding, Maisie is inclined to say "Yes." But she remembers that the senior administrator asked her earlier in the week to have everyone available for a special job on Friday. So Maisie tells Patti that she will look into it and let her know. Then she goes to see the senior administrator, and says:

One of my mail clerks wants Friday off to go to a wedding. What am I to tell her?	1. & 2: REQUEST & REASON
The wedding is out of town, so it's not a matter of just half a day, or leaving early.	4. BACK-UP

Maisie has used three of the information blocks suggested on page 129 for making a request. She has omitted block 3 (there is no Gain), but she has included block 4 (Back-Up), reasoning that she may as well save time by answering an obvious question before it is asked.

Then when Maisie returns with the administrator's decision (which is "Yes, go ahead") she tells Patti orally that she is free to take the day off. It is a simple arrangement between two persons, so no formal record is necessary.

A spoken answer would also be given to the following question posed by the body shop crew. They have been arguing among themselves about whether or not the company will give an extra day off in place of New Year's Day, which falls on a Saturday. They ask their foreman, but he does not know either. So he asks the body shop manager, mentioning that there has been considerable discussion about it in the shop. The body shop manager says: "Yes, Monday, January the third will be a holiday," and the foreman spreads the good news around the body shop.

But in this case the foreman's spoken answer may be followed by a written announcement. When he informed his boss of the employee's question, the foreman was performing one of his major functions as a supervisor: *to listen to the employees so that he can alert management of items of concern.* The body shop manager realized that similar questions were probably being asked in other departments, and so suggested to the plant manager that a notice announcing the Monday holiday be posted throughout the plant.

Either a spoken or a written request could be made in these circumstances: When Vern, a production machinist, comes in on Wednesday morning, he makes a point of seeing Barry Kingsley, the machine shop supervisor. Vern explains that his wife has been involved in an auto accident and has a broken right arm and a dislocated hip. He urgently needs to use a week of next year's holidays right away so he can stay at home and look after her and the children until things get squared away. It is not a decision Barry can make on his own: company policy requires him to obtain the department manager's approval.

The quickest way for Barry to present Vern's request to the department manager is to go and see him. He starts with block 1 (Request), saying to Mr. Smithson:

> One of my machinists has asked me for a week's leave for urgent family reasons. I'd like to say "Yes" but I need your approval first.

Then, because he knows Mr. Smithson will need more information than this, he goes straight on with block 2 (Reason):

> It's Vern Talbot. His wife was injured in a car accident last night. He needs the time to look after her and the kids.

He follows this with the answer to a question he expects to be asked (blocks 3 & 4 combined—Loss and Back-Up):

> I'll have to find someone to take his place for a week. I could probably bring Harry Schmidt back in from retirement—he's always looking for an extra buck—or I can pull someone off the night shift.

If the department manager gives him the nod, Barry can give Vern an immediate answer, either personally like this:

> Vern—your week's holiday is approved. Just fill out an application in the normal way.

or officially in writing like this:

From: B. Kingsley	Date: 19 February 19__
To: V. Talbot	Subject: Emergency Leave

Your request for emergency leave is approved from Thursday 20 February to Wednesday 26 February, inclusive. This represents five days of your normal leave entitlement.

B. Kingsley

Written Communications

Although it would take a little longer for Barry to write a memorandum to Mr. Smithson outlining Vern Talbot's request, in the long run it might speed up the approval process. It can be typed on a pre-printed memo form, or handwritten onto a carbon-interleaved three-copy memorandum set. Barry started writing his request like this:

1. REQUEST

2. REASON

> Vern Talbot, a machinist in my area, has requested one week's leave for family reasons, starting tomorrow (20 Feb.). May I have your approval to grant his request?
>
> His wife was injured in a traffic accident last night, and he needs the time to look after her and their children until he can make other arrangements.
>
> For a temporary replacement, I'll probably call on

At this point Barry stopped, then crossed out the last eight words. He suddenly realized that this memo would be going on Vern's personal file, and should be *only about him*. Because he planned to carry it in to the manager, he could hold the information about getting a replacement in reserve as a spoken block 4—Back-Up.

Alternatively, Barry can ask Vern to write his own request. Provided there is time, and Vern knows how to write a short memorandum, it is the most efficient method. Vern should address it to Barry, and make it short and to the point. If possible, he should try to have it typed by one of the office typists, as in Fig. 4–10, item (A). Barry can then forward the request to Mr. Smithson, indicating his approval or recommendation by penning a note containing back-up information beneath Vern's, as he has done at (B) in Fig. 4–10.

Because an immediate reply is needed, Barry would probably take the memo in to Mr. Smithson and discuss the subject with him. Mr. Smithson can then write his approval or disapproval right onto Vern's memo, as he has done at (C) in Fig. 4–10. This both speeds up his work and gives Barry a quick answer.

MALTON MANUFACTURERS

INTER - OFFICE MEMORANDUM

From: .... Vern Talbot .... Date: .... 19 February 19____ ....

To: .... Barry Kingsley .... Subject: .... Request for Leave ....

(A)

I urgently request one week's leave, starting tomorrow, 20 February.

My wife has been injured in an auto accident and I need to look after her and our children. I would like to use a week of my vacation time for this purpose.

V. Talbot

> 1. REQUEST

> 2. REASON

(B)

Mr. Smithson —
Vern's request has my approval. I can arrange for a temporary machinist to take his place next week.
B. Kingsley.
19 Feb.

> 3. BACK-UP

(C)

Approved
J.A.S.   Feb 19.

(D)

Vern —
Your leave will be for 5 working days, from Thursday 20 to Wednesday 26 inclusive. I hope Marjorie recovers quickly.
Barry.

Fig. 4–10. A written request. This request from an employee has been approved by his supervisor, passed to the manager for final approval, and returned to the employee.

When Barry tells Vern that his request has been granted, he also gives him his original memo with the two approvals on it, perhaps adding a short note like that at (D). He should, of course, also take the precaution of making a copy for the company's files.

The memorandum and submemos in Fig. 4–10 may seem to be a very formal way to obtain approval for a simple request. Yet a large company with many employees must keep records of everything that happens, otherwise no one would know how much vacation, sick leave, and so on each person has had.

COMMUNICATING AT MEETINGS

You will find a difference between the meetings you attended as a member of the employees' social committee or union and those you attend as a supervisor. While employee meetings (particularly union meetings) tend to follow a semiformal procedure (see chapter 6), company meetings usually discuss points and make decisions without a formal proposal being stated or a formal vote being taken and recorded.

Most meetings will be called by your department manager. Normally they will be attended by all the supervisors in the department, plus other people affected by the topics to be discussed. For example, the company stores supervisor may be invited to attend a production department meeting if one of the topics is streamlining the procedure for obtaining spare parts. Such department meetings may be held regularly (i.e., once a week, once a month, or even every day) or only when the department manager feels they are necessary.

Although it is not always done, an agenda (list of topics) should be drawn up before the meeting by the department manager, who usually acts as chairman. He should prepare a proper agenda for occasional and monthly meetings, and distribute copies to all persons who will attend them. This gives you, as a meeting participant, fair warning that the meeting is scheduled and time to think about the topics to be discussed. A published agenda is not always necessary for daily meetings, although your chairman should at least jot down a list of topics for his own use.

Because department meetings often are the only occasion when all supervisors in your department get together, they can easily become chatty affairs. A certain amount of informal conversation is good, because it helps develop an informal atmosphere in which even shy supervisors are not afraid to say what they think. But the meeting should not become an occasion for exchanging more than one or two of the latest jokes, or a place for doing business that is outside the purpose of the meeting.

One reason that many supervisors dislike attending department meetings is that they last much too long. Their usefulness as a means of communication is lost if they become a boring nuisance rather than a convenient way to exchange information and reach group decisions. Yet if everyone remembers that a person's role is to listen more than he or she talks, meetings can be kept quite short.

Your Role as a Listener

During most of a meeting, other people do the talking while you listen to what is being said. You should be a thoughtful listener (sometimes listening attentively and other times critically), speaking only when you have something useful to say. Whenever you feel like passing a comment, offering an opinion, or making a suggestion, check first that you are not opening your mouth just so your voice can be heard.

Remember, too, that only one person should be speaking at a time. It is poor practice (let alone bad manners) for two persons sitting at one end of the table to hold a private conversation while someone else is speaking. If the meeting chairman does his job properly, he will call on persons to speak in turn. When you have something to say, you should quietly try to catch the chairman's attention so he will call on you to contribute your ideas. This is much better than trying to jump in ahead of everyone else by suddenly blurting out your thoughts.

Your Role as a Speaker

When the chairman calls on you to speak, you will immediately have everyone's attention. Don't rush. Try to speak slowly and carefully, so that you offer your thoughts in logical sequence. If you are merely offering your opinion on a topic that is already being discussed, make your contribution short and effective. Say what you think, and briefly why:

Comment	*Suggestion*
The guys in my area won't take kindly to a shorter work week. They've been watching what happened over at Magentic Manufacturing.	Why not work an extra two hours every Monday in October and November? Then we could have a clear week off between Christmas and New Year.

Sometimes you will go to a meeting knowing you are going to have a lot to say. When foreman John Regan receives the agenda for a department meeting, he notices that one of the topics is "Renovations to Area

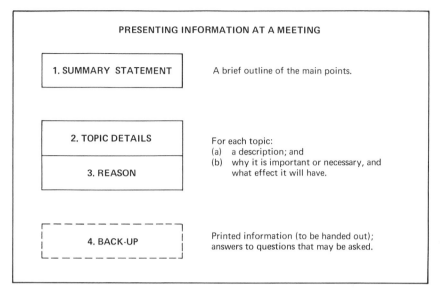

Fig. 4–11. Information blocks for presenting information at a meeting.

4B" (his area). Before the meeting, John lists what alterations, repairs, and redecorating need to be done. Then, because the list is long, he makes copies to hand out.

When the time comes to present his data, John uses the information blocks in Fig. 4–11 to help him arrange the facts clearly. This is what he says:

Renovations I would like done in area 4B fall into three categories: putting up a soundproof wall between my area and area 4A, rebuilding work station 3, and general re-decorating.

1. SUMMARY

The soundproof wall is the most important. Ever since Dave installed his stamping machine (*he nods to Dave, another foreman*) my girls at station 5 have complained of the noise. I've had the lab take sound readings, and at times the noise level is as high as 85 decibels. What I need is a cinder-block wall put up where the frame and ply wall now stands on the north side of the area. (*He passes around a sketch*).

2. & 3. TOPIC DETAILS AND REASONS

(developed separately for each major topic)

Work station 3 needs to be rebuilt to accommodate the cable tester we have on order. A work order to build the components has already gone into the carpenter shop. This must be done before the end of March, when the tester is due.

Patching and painting are long overdue. The scars are still on the wall from when the packing department occupied the area—that's over three years ago.

Items John has prepared for block 4 are:

- A sketch of the proposed soundproof wall (he issued this when he spoke).
- A table of noise level measurements given to him by the laboratory.
- A sketch of the plan for work station 3.
- A list of patching needed, and suggested colors for repainting the area.
- Possibly a cost estimate for all or part of the work.

> 4. BACK-UP

He keeps most of this back-up information to himself, expanding on a specific topic or issuing preprinted notes only if asked for more details. In this way he keeps his presentation down to the essential information needed by those attending the meeting.

Sometimes it is difficult to know how much to say and how much to hold back. You should try to answer your listeners' immediate questions by giving them the essential information they need to understand what you are talking about, and hold in reserve the less important details that their curiosity (which you cannot predict) might prompt them to ask for.

EXERCISES

NOTE: *Your instructor will tell you who is to assume the role of "receiver" when an exercise calls for spoken communication.*

Exercise 10.1

You are the supervisor of Ken Lindquist, the employee requesting permission to use company equipment in the evening (see Exercise 7.7, page 93).

Taking his memorandum of request with you, go to the production manager and ask for his approval.

Exercise 10.2

You are the supervisor of the employees in Exercise 7.9 (page 94):

1. Go to the personnel manager and ask him to arrange for a police patrol in the lane between 8.45 and 9.15 p.m. whenever the company works late.
2. Write a memorandum to the personnel manager requesting that he have the building owners install better lighting outside the building night door and on the building wall skirting the lane.
3. Ask the production manager (who is your boss) to authorize payment of cab fares, from the company night door to the Main Street bus stop, for women working overtime.
4. Suggest to the personnel manager that sandwich and drink machines be installed. Do this first orally, then follow it up with a written request.

Exercise 10.3

You work in a manufacturing company that closes down almost completely for the last two weeks in July and the first week in August. Management wants all but a skeleton staff to take their vacation at the same time. Anyone not taking their vacation at the shutdown time must have a pretty good reason for not doing so.

Your hobby is skiing. Next winter, the Alpine Ski Club you belong to is sponsoring a skiing holiday in Switzerland from December 20 to January 5, and you very much want to go. The all-inclusive price, which includes charter airline flight, accommodation, and meals, is surprisingly low.

You would like to take only one week of your vacation during the plant shutdown, and the remaining two weeks at Christmas. This would mean finding a reason for working in the plant when almost everyone else is away. The alternative would be to take the regular vacation in the summer, plus an extra two weeks' leave without pay at Christmas (which you really cannot afford to do and pay for the trip). In either case, you realize you will have to ask for the time off at Christmas.

You think you can justify staying in the plant during the summer by suggesting that you completely update the production control records. This needs doing, but cannot be attempted when production is in full swing.

1. Go to your department manager and ask if you may save two weeks of your vacation until Christmas.
2. At his suggestion, write a memorandum to him requesting the special vacation dates (he wants to process it through the proper channels).

Exercise 10.4

Ever since you were promoted foreman one year ago, you have been wanting to take a course in supervision. Now an opportunity has occurred.

The Extension Department of your local Community College has advertised a course entitled "Industrial Supervision" in the newspaper. You telephoned for more information, and now you have received a leaflet advertising
the course as "ideal for newly appointed junior managers or senior employees
anticipating promotion."

The course is run as a "supper session" on Mondays from 4 to 8 p.m.
for ten consecutive weeks starting in one month. Some of the details are:

1. The cost is $60, which includes ten suppers.
2. Enrollment is limited to twenty persons.
3. It is a workshop-type course rather than instructional.
4. There are two course leaders, one from the college and one an industrial
   relations manager from Constart (a major local industry).
5. About four hours per week of personal study will be necessary.
6. A Certificate of Attainment will be granted to all who successfully complete the course.

Write a memorandum to your manager (Ken G. Simpkins) asking for
approval to attend and for the company to pay for the course.

Exercise 10.5

The owner of the 130-employee company in which you are a junior
supervisor is Roger Forsythe. He holds a meeting once a month with all his
supervisors, at which both work progress and the employment environment
are discussed.

One of the topics listed on the agenda for tomorrow's meeting is employee parking. This is a continuing problem for employees, who have to pay
ever-higher commercial parking rates in nearby autoparks—if they can find a
vacancy. The company is situated in a densely built-up area with no open
spaces and one-hour parking limits on all nearby streets.

You have some ideas, and you want to present them at the meeting.
You haven't organized them yet, so you jot them down like this:

1. I wonder how many more people live close together, and don't know
   about it. They could form carpools. Maybe we should conduct a survey.
2. People in carpools could share parking costs.
3. Maybe the company should look for a block of spaces in one of the
   two nearby autoparks, then allocate them to employees.
4. Would it be possible for the company to rent a block of spaces, and then
   bill employees who use them? Maybe these spaces should be only for
   employees in carpools. Could we say they must have four persons to a
   car?
5. How do people feel about carpools? How many "don't like" and how
   many "don't mind"? Maybe this could be part of a survey, too.

Before you go to the meeting, you arrange these thoughts into a better
order.

1. Write a "speaking outline" to use at the meeting.
2. When the topic of employee parking comes up, present your ideas to the meeting.

Exercise 10.6

Your ideas (Exercise 10.5) sparked considerable interest and discussion at yesterday's monthly supervisors' meeting. A three-person committee was formed to investigate the availability of parking space in a nearby autopark and to survey employees to find out which employees live close together and who would be willing to travel in carpools. Mr. Forsythe, the company owner, said that if more employees are willing to use carpools, he will certainly rent space in the company's name and will even consider bearing part of the cost.

You are named chairman of the "Employee Parking Committee," with Janet Holstrom and Dennis Lang as the other two members.

You plan to hold your first committee meeting at 1 p.m. in your cubicle in two days. You want to work out how to tackle the problem, decide how the survey of employees is to be done (i.e., by personally approaching everyone or by sending out questionnaires), and determine how to go about looking for a block of parking space. You also want to set a deadline for the project that is early enough for the committee to assemble its information and report its findings at the next company meeting, four weeks from today.

Write a meeting notice and agenda to send to the two other committee members. Also send a copy to Mr. Forsythe.

11

Communicating About Your Work

Every company wants to know what is going on in each of its departments—to "keep a finger on the patient's pulse," so to speak. You, as a junior supervisor, provide this "finger."

Management wants a continual stream of information directed to it. For example: what caused an accident that sent an employee to hospital and stopped production for three hours in the welding shop; what progress has been made on a particular project for one of the company's clients; what was found out during a trip to a foundry to investigate why so many castings are of poor quality; and so on.

Some of this information you will pass on by word of mouth, just as you did when as an employee you told your supervisor what was happening (see page 88). Some information you will relay at department meetings. And the remainder you will probably prepare as short reports.

The word "report" to some people conjures up an image of a very formal document written in precise, dignified language. Let's set the record straight right from the start: Over 95 percent of reports written in business and industry are short informal notes that convey a message in brief, easy-to-read (and write) terms. These are the reports you are most likely to write, and they are the ones described in this chapter.

Nearly all of these reports are written as memorandums from one person to another. A nurse on the night shift in Ward B of a hospital, for example, may want to leave a note to tell the ward supervisor (who works the day shift) that the inhalator has been knocked over during the night and needs to be repaired. Or a chief draftsman may be asked periodically to describe to the plant engineer how his draftsmen are progressing on a large project. Or a plumber installing toilets in a new high-rise apartment block may have to inform the building contractor that some of the holes cut in the floor are too small to accept the size of pipe described for the job, that he has spent extra time enlarging the holes, and that his company will have to charge for the extra work he has done.

These persons each have something to tell somebody:

The nurse wants to *tell* the ward supervisor.
The draftsman has to *describe* progress to the plant engineer.
The plumber wants to *inform* the contractor.

Such telling is, in effect, **reporting** (much as a newspaper writer *reports facts* about a bank holdup he has witnessed).

The reports you are likely to write will nearly always deal with facts, because they tell the reader about something that has happened, or is currently happening. There are four basic types:

1. If they report an event—
   they are known as *Occurrence Reports*.

2. If they report what was done during a field assignment (that is, on a job that was done out of town or away from your normal place of work)—
   they are known as *Field Trip Reports*
   (or simply *Trip Reports*).

3. When they report on job progress (normally of a project that is not yet complete)—
   they are called *Progress Reports*.

4. When they report on the condition of a location, building, or equipment—
   they are known as *Inspection Reports*.

Occasionally you may want to tell what has happened and then suggest what should be done to correct a problem or improve a situation. When this occurs, the reports you write become more detailed because:

5. They report on a problem and recommend a means for solving it—
   such reports are known as *Investigation* or
   Evaluation Reports.

REPORTING AN EVENT

An Occurrence Report uses the same four information blocks that an employee uses to inform his supervisor of something that has happened (see page 89). They are repeated here in Fig. 4–12, and comprise:

1. A **Summary Statement** that mentions very briefly what the occurrence was and its main effects.
2. The **Situation,** which includes all the information the reader needs to fully understand what has happened.
3. The **Event,** which covers only the incident.
4. The **Result,** which mentions factors evolving from the event, and possibly their implications to the reader or to the project.

The length of an Occurrence Report can vary from very short to moderately long, depending partly on the size and effect of the event and partly on the amount of information needed by the reader. It can be a simple one-sentence statement of fact:

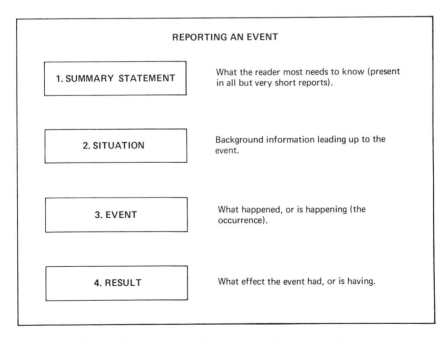

Fig. 4–12. Information blocks for an Occurrence Report.

As Harry Karr was entering the machine shop, he tripped on the steps, fell, and broke an ankle.

Here, the **Situation** is:

As Harry Karr was entering the machine shop

The **Event** is:

he tripped on the steps, (and) *fell,*

The **Result** is:

and broke an ankle.

For most readers such a basic statement of fact would be inadequate. If you were Harry Karr's supervisor and you knew he was supposed to attend a union meeting at 3.00 P.M., you might write a short but more detailed note like this to the union shop steward:

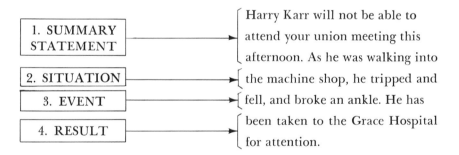

1. SUMMARY STATEMENT	→	Harry Karr will not be able to attend your union meeting this afternoon. As he was walking into
2. SITUATION	→	the machine shop, he tripped and
3. EVENT	→	fell, and broke an ankle. He has
4. RESULT	→	been taken to the Grace Hospital for attention.

Note how the report has been broadened to include a Summary Statement and a more detailed Result. Note also that the phrase "and broke an ankle" can be part of either the Event or the Result.

Now let's look at how much more information the company's industrial relations manager might need. Probably he would want to know the time the accident happened, the names of other people involved, the condition of the steps, more information about Harry Karr, and possibly comments on how Harry's absence will affect the workload. Here is an example:

Harry V. Karr was injured this morning, and will be off work for at least one week.

1. SUMMARY
STATEMENT

The incident occurred at 9.15 A.M. on the steps just inside the machine shop. Harry was carrying a 40-lb box of machine tools which obscured his forward view. There were no obstacles on the steps but they were wet, having been washed 15 minutes earlier.

| 2. SITUATION |

As Harry entered the machine shop his foot slid on the top step and he fell forward, tumbling down the remaining eight steps.

| 3. EVENT |

The company first aid assistant suspected a fracture and arranged for Harry to be taken to the Health Sciences Center, where his injury was diagnosed as a simple fracture just below the left ankle. Although he will probably return to work in a week, his activities will be limited because he will have to walk with crutches.

| 4. RESULT |

An Occurrence Report contains the same three information blocks (Situation–Event–Result) regardless of its length.

REPORTING A FIELD ASSIGNMENT

Whenever you return from a field assignment you should write a brief report on what you saw and did. This applies just as much to a quick visit to a local bakery where you looked at a new bread-slicing machine, as it does to a three-week stay at a lumber mill during which you and a three-man team replaced old wiring and installed a new power control panel. In both cases a written report should be made of your impressions (of the bread-slicing machine) or of the work that was done (at the paper mill). Your employer is bearing the cost of the field assignment and he is entitled to this information. A written report on the work you did is also protection for your employer in case you are transferred to another assignment, are ill for several weeks, or even resign to accept a job elsewhere. The person taking over will need your report to find out what happened previously.

The information blocks for a Trip Report are shown in Fig. 4–13. Their contents are described below.

1. This is one of the few reports in which you may not need to include a **Summary Statement**, or may combine it with the Circumstances.
2. The **Circumstances** are all those pieces of information about the assignment that are not *doing* parts of the job. Generally they include

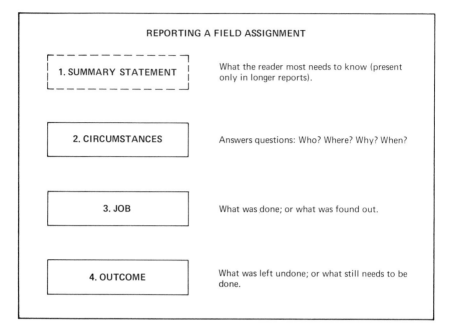

REPORTING A FIELD ASSIGNMENT

1. SUMMARY STATEMENT — What the reader most needs to know (present only in longer reports).

2. CIRCUMSTANCES — Answers questions: Who? Where? Why? When?

3. JOB — What was done; or what was found out.

4. OUTCOME — What was left undone; or what still needs to be done.

Fig. 4–13. Information blocks for a Trip Report.

the names of persons involved, where they went, why they went there (i.e., purpose of trip), and when the trip took place.
For example:

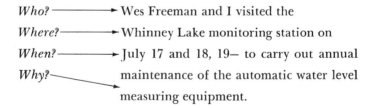

Who? ————————➤ Wes Freeman and I visited the
Where? ———————➤ Whinney Lake monitoring station on
When? ————————➤ July 17 and 18, 19– to carry out annual
Why?————————— maintenance of the automatic water level
measuring equipment.

Additional information that may be included in this block is: the name of the person authorizing the trip, the type of transportation used (such as automobile, scheduled airline, or charter helicopter), and the names of persons contacted at the job site.

3. The **Job** covers all the work done while you were at the job site. It can range from a very short statement describing a routine situation to a long narrative pointing up problems and describing unscheduled work. As a rule of thumb, you should

1. Cover planned or routine work very briefly, if possible referring to an instruction sheet or maintenance procedure rather than mentioning every little item that was done.

2. Cover unusual or unplanned work in more detail, because it will be new to the reader. Tell him what you did, why you did it that way, and what the results were.

3. Cover problems in detail, so that your company
   a. Understands the factors that made the job more difficult than expected;
   b. Can possibly take steps to prevent similar problems from happening during future field assignments.

4. The **Outcome** draws attention to work that could not be completed, and if possible suggests how, when, and by whom it should be done. It can also suggest things that should be done as a result of what was found out during the trip.

A short trip report might be like this:

I went to Modern Bakeries' Main Street plant on October 20 to examine the Rega bread-slicing machine in operation. Mr. George Kenton, Modern Bakeries' production assistant, accompanied me during the demonstration.

> 2. CIRCUM-
> STANCES

The machine is fast, efficient, and extremely safe. It fully lives up to the manufacturer's claims in the attached advertising leaflet. Mr. Kenton said that it regularly slices ____ 16-oz loaves per hour (this is 20 percent faster than our machine), and has had no breakdowns during the seven months it has been in operation. Its positive safety features are a particularly attractive aspect.

> 3. JOB

I am convinced that this is the right machine for our plant, and recommend that we budget funds to buy three next year.

> 4. OUTCOME

REPORTING PROGRESS

Because you are most likely to write a Progress Report for your immediate boss, or to someone else in management, you must constantly remind yourself that he wants answers to three questions:

1. How are you getting on with the job?
2. What problems have you run into, and how are you coping with them?
3. When will you complete the job, and what action are you taking to try to finish it on time?

The simplest way to present this information is in a logical sequence from the past through the present to the future. So once again we have

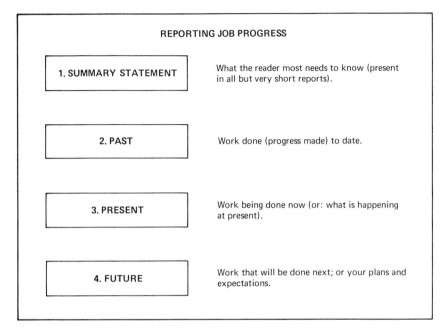

Fig. 4–14. Information blocks for a Progress Report.

three blocks of information, plus a Summary. These are shown in Fig. 4–14 and described below.

1. The **Summary Statement** is an important feature of Progress Reports. Managers are particularly interested in job progress, so tell them what they most want to know in the very first paragraph. Here is an example:

   Although work at the construction site is now two days behind schedule, I expect the crew to finish the job on May 18, the planned completion date.

   Having told your boss you are behind schedule (but immediately set his mind at ease), you can let the rest of your report explain how you arrived at this general statement.

2. The **Past** describes progress made since the job started. If there has been a previous report, the Past may be divided into two segments: (a) a general part describing what has been done since the job started; and (b) a more detailed part telling what has been done since the previous report was written. Its length and depth of topic coverage will depend on the particular situation. If only a general statement of progress is necessary and the project has been running smoothly, then the entry will probably be quite short. For example:

   Since arriving on site on October 17, we have rebuilt the interiors of all six rooms, and have painted two of them.

But if more exact information is required, further details will have to be inserted. These should include facts, such as the quantity of items completed, the number of hours worked, or the amount of material used. If there is an extensive list, you can attach it as a separate sheet and refer to it in the report.

Problems that affect a job and hinder your progress should also be mentioned. This is particularly important where delays have occurred or the project has slipped behind schedule.

3. The **Present** describes what is currently being done. It may be no more than a short paragraph or sentence that says you are tackling a certain aspect of the job:

We are now cutting and installing indoor-outdoor carpet.

It can also describe what you are doing to bring a delayed project back onto schedule:

The crew is working two hours overtime for three evenings this week to recover 18 hours lost time.

4. The **Future** tells the reader what you plan to do next, and often forecasts a job completion date. If the job is running smoothly it can usually be a short statement:

The siding and shingles will be started on Monday so that, weather permitting, we will finish the job by Friday, May 18.

But if you have had problems and have had to make up for lost time, you should tell the reader what your plans are and how you intend to put them into effect. For example:

To meet the scheduled completion date, I plan to wire up the main control panel this week so the government inspector can check the building on May 13 rather than make a special trip to the site at a later date.

A complete progress report appears at Fig. 4–15.

REPORTING AN INSPECTION

Persons who are particularly good at their work are often promoted to the position of inspector so they can check on work done by others. In the building trades, for example, skilled craftsmen may check on work being done at several small construction sites or on a large construction project.

The reports they write combine parts of both the Trip Report and the Progress Report. They are called Inspection Reports and have the

From: Ken Willis,   Date: October 16, 19__
         Highway Inspector

To: R. J. Caminsky   Subject: Progress –
         Highways Engineer   Inspection of Highway 201

This year's check of the surface of highway 201 will take one week
longer than usual. I now expect to finish the job on October 21.

The stretch from St. Cloud to Reece, Minn. was completed on
September 30, on schedule. Breakdown of my panel truck on October
3 caused an unplanned five-day delay, mostly because the wrong
parts were flown in from Detroit. Then a freak snowstorm at
Winona on October 10 prevented road surface inspections until the
snow melted two days later.

I am now at Vincenne, Minn., and this is the supposed completion
date for the project.

I plan to inspect 15 miles a day for the next 75 miles, which
should see the job completed one week from today.   (4)

                              Ken Willis

Fig. 4–15. A Progress Report written as a memorandum. (Circled numbers on
the right refer to information blocks in Fig. 4–14)

five information blocks shown in Fig. 4–16. The purpose of each block
is outlined below.

   1. The **Summary Statement** describes in just a few words the general condition found or the overall impression gained by the inspector. For
   example:

      Installation of the data processing equipment is on schedule, but
      minor deficiencies may prevent switchover on the planned date.

   2. The **Circumstances** are all the bits and pieces of information relating
   to his inspection:

      My visit to the Boris Lake site took place on September 13. It was
      authorized by D. Jarvis, who in a September 8 memo asked me to
      check on installation status.

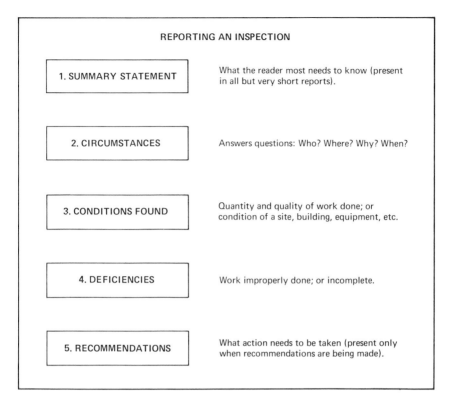

Fig. 4–16. Information blocks for an Inspection Report.

Note the similarity between this and the Circumstances information block for the Trip Report.

3. Under **Conditions Found** are entered details of what the inspector saw or found out. If he is assessing the *quantity* of work done, these could be:

Yards of concrete poured.
Number of doors hung.
Extent of painting completed.
Depth of excavation reached.
Length of cable installed.
Percentage of piles sunk.
. . . and so on.

If, however, he is assessing the *quality* of work done, he would comment on the condition of the work he inspected. For instance:

Wallpaper has been raggedly trimmed and has air bubbles under it

And if he is commenting on both quantity and quality, he would broaden his description to something like this:

Drape tracks have been installed in all rooms of the main floor, but the work has been poorly done. The track in room A3 is not properly centered, and the one in room A6 slopes downward from right to left.

4. **Deficiencies** are all the things the inspector says must be corrected. They are items that during his inspection he noticed either have not been done or have been poorly done. He should list them, using definite words to indicate that the work *must* be done or repaired (i.e., he can use strong expressions such as *is to, shall,* and *must,* but not a weak word such as *should*). Here is an example:

The green and yellow wires to pin B of connection 17 must be re-soldered.

5. **Recommendations** are present only when the inspector has reason to include them. They should not repeat what has already been said under Deficiencies, but may follow naturally from the Deficiencies block:

I recommend that the technicians at Boris Lake be given refresher training in soldering.

Some employers issue printed forms like the one at Fig. 4–17 for their inspectors to use when writing Inspection Reports. This considerably eases their writing burden, because it automatically divides into blocks the information they have to present. But because a form may not offer a special block for the Summary Statement, the inspector has to remember to include it as the first paragraph under Conditions Found. When there are more than two items to mention under Conditions Found and Deficiencies, it is better to list them, as has been done in the sample report.

REPORTING AN INVESTIGATION

An investigation is carried out whenever there is a need to look into a problem or to find a better way of doing things. The range of topics can vary widely. For example, you might:

* Investigate why there has been a big increase in the number of poorly machined parts coming from your area.
* Evaluate compact station wagons to assess which make would be the best replacement for the company's three full-size wagons.
* Consider better ways to store and issue spare parts.

INSPECTION REPORT

LOCATION: ___521 Barclay Bay_____ DATE: __20 August 19___

ITEM(S) BEING INSPECTED: ___Interior Decorating_____

INSPECTOR: __R.B. Dryfus_____ CONTRACTOR: __Phil-Dec Inc._____

CONDITIONS FOUND:

Progress and workmanship are generally good, although some deficiencies need to be corrected.

1. All walls and ceilings painted and satisfactory.

2. All wallpaper hung; satisfactory in kitchen and bathroom, but not in dining room.

3. Trim on door and around windows painted and satisfactory.

4. Tiles installed in bathroom and kitchen; complete.

5. Rubber baseboard messily installed in kitchen and bathroom.

DEFICIENCIES:

1. Carpet to be installed in living room and hall (carpet has been received, but underlay not yet delivered).

2. Wallpaper to be stripped and rehung in dining room.

3. Mess around baseboard in kitchen and bathroom to be cleaned up.

RECOMMENDATIONS:

Because of delays in delivery of underlay, I recommend contractor's invoice be paid (less $120.00) when deficiencies 2 and 3 have been corrected.

Fig. 4–17. An Inspection Report written on a prepared form.

* Look for a better way to pack round products.
* Investigate how rainwater has been seeping into the storage area.

At the end of your investigation you will need to describe what you have found out and recommend what needs to be done. You may present your findings orally, or as a written report prepared in one of three ways:

1. As a memorandum addressed to someone in the company (usually one's department head);
2. As a letter addressed to someone outside the company (often a customer);
3. On plain paper, headed by a title such as "Investigation into Basement Flooding."

An Investigation Report is likely to be the biggest report a junior supervisor will write. It is also the most complex, because it calls for two sets of information blocks. The basic set is similar to those used for Occurrence Reports. The second is an expansion of the middle block of the first set (that is, the Investigation block). Both are shown in Fig. 4–18 and described below.

1. The **Summary Statement** is always necessary and has a very clear purpose: to tell the reader as quickly as possible what the problem is and how it can be overcome. For example:

   The basement flooding we experience each spring is caused by squirrels depositing rubbish in the drainpipes the previous fall. It can be corrected by placing wire-mesh screens over open entries in the gutters.

2. The **Situation** mentions facts or events that led up to the investigation, how it came to be assigned to you, and any other information you think would be useful to the reader:

   Since moving into this building five years ago, the basement has been flooded for about one week every spring and sometimes after particularly heavy rainfalls in the summer. Although a nuisance, damage has never been enough to warrant an expensive investigation and repairs. On July 18, management decided to use the basement for additional storage space. I was assigned by K. Reiter to investigate the cause of the flooding and to suggest a possible remedy.

3. The **Investigation** describes how you went about the investigation, what you found out, what methods can be used to correct the problem, and which method you believe is most suitable. As shown in Fig. 4–18 (b), the **Investigation** comprises the four sub-blocks of information described below.

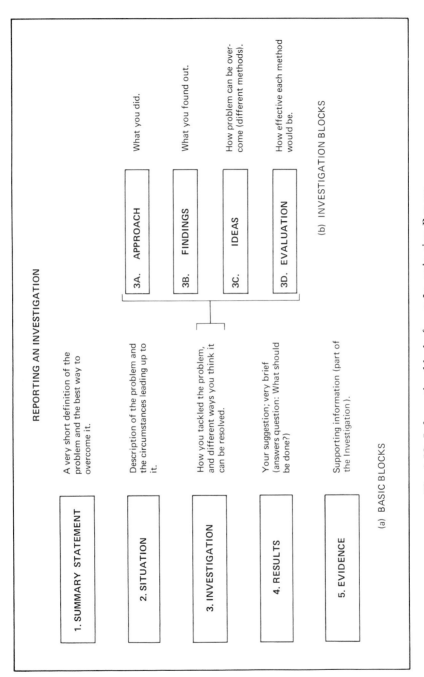

Fig. 4-18. Information blocks for an Investigation Report.

A. The **Approach** describes both what you planned to do and what you actually did:

> Because it had always been assumed that the flooding was caused by a watercourse passing near or under the building, I went first to the city hall to look at plot plans. From these I discovered that no watercourse passes within 300 feet of the building.

> I then turned my attention to the drainage system that empties into the storm sewer, thinking there might be a major crack at a joint or in a pipe. But none was found. This meant that the cause must be above ground.

B. The **Findings** describes what you found out (the cause of the problem, in this case):

> By pouring water from a fire hose into the roof gutter, I repeated heavy rainstorm conditions. This in turn produced a small flow of water onto the basement floor. I then traced the water back to its source behind a closed-in section of the north wall, where I discovered water flowing over the sides of a blocked funnel fed by three drainpipes.

> The funnel was full of nuts, leaves, and similar debris, plus the body of a dead squirrel. Apparently, squirrels have been entering the drainpipes from the gutters, running down the pipes to the funnel, and using the funnel to store food for the winter (see sketch at Attachment 1).

(Division of information into blocks is not always clearcut. In the example above, the first paragraph of the Findings could also be considered part of the Approach.)

C. The **Ideas** section describes possible ways you have thought of to correct the problem:

> There are three ways we can stop squirrels from blocking the pipes:
> 1. Redesign the catch basin in the basement so the three downpipes feed directly into the main sewer without passing through the funnel. Cost: at least $800.
> 2. Cut the drainpipes before they enter the building, and connect them to new drainpipes that would be installed outside the building. These pipes would have to feed directly onto the sidewalk. Cost: about $400.
> 3. Bolt wire-mesh screens over each drain hole in the roof gutters. Cost: about $160.

D. In the **Evaluation** you take a look at all the ideas and comment on their suitability:

> Methods 1 and 2 would be 100 percent effective, but both would have to be approved by the municipality before they could be

done. This approval might be difficult to obtain. Method 3 would be cheap and easy to do, but could result in leaves collecting around the screen and causing water to spill over the edges of the gutters and onto the sidewalk.

4. In the **Results,** you use what has been written earlier to draw a conclusion and suggest what you think should be done:

> Because of its simplicity and low price I suggest that we place a wire screen over each of the three drain holes, as shown in Attachment 2. If this is done, I suggest that the gutters and screens be cleaned of leaves each fall and spring, to prevent water from overflowing onto passers-by.

5. The **Evidence** is a useful place to put drawings, photographs, lists of equipment, calculations, and results of tests so that they do not interrupt the flow of information in your report. They are usually called *Attachments* (in which case they are numbered "1," "2," "3," etc.) or *Appendixes* (in which case they are lettered "A," "B," "C," and so on). Each piece of evidence must be referred to in the report, as has been done at the end of the Findings and in the Results, above. A typical Attachment is shown at Fig. 4–19.

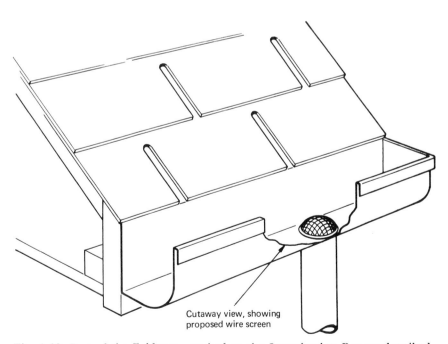

Cutaway view, showing
proposed wire screen

Fig. 4–19. Part of the Evidence attached to the Investigation Report described on these pages.

Not all investigation reports contain every information block. Some are quite short, as in the example at Fig. 4–20, while others can be considerably longer than the two examples shown here.

The Furniture House

From: D.L. Pritchard   **Date:** April 9, 19__

To: K.G. Murray   **Subject:** Rug Damage Complaints:

Mrs. V. Carson

I have investigated Mrs. Carson's complaint and agree she has a case. Damage has been done to her carpet, but it was partly her own fault. ①

I called on Mrs. Carson at suite 1407 - 2022 Dover Road yesterday afternoon. She showed me brown paint marks on her white shag rug, which she claims were made by our furniture repairman when he did a touch-up job on her buffet the day before (Tuesday, April 7). ②

The rug has about a dozen brown marks each about the size of a 25-cent piece clustered in a 3-ft diameter area. Their color is the same as the buffet.

This morning I talked to the repairman, Andy Bowen, who said straight away he knows all about it. Apparently he twice warned Mrs. Carson to keep her cats away from his tools and paints, but she kept insisting they wouldn't be a nuisance. Then while he was working on the buffet, and she was out of the room, one of the cats put a wet paw into the brown paint powder. Andy wiped its paws, but not before it had made several marks on the rug. He says he told Mrs. Carson what had happened, but at the time she seemed not to think much of it. ③B

From my examination I agree the marks could have been made by a cat's painty paw.

It may be difficult to remove the spots, because paint remover cannot be used and normal rug cleaning processes may be only partly effective. ③C
If cleaning will remove the spots, I think we should bear the cost. But if Mrs. Carson pressures us for a new rug, then I think we should ④
hold out for a small cash settlement.

D.L.P.

Fig. 4–20. A short Investigation Report that uses only some of the information blocks in Fig. 4–18.

EXERCISES

Reporting an Occurrence

NOTE: *Your instructor will tell you who plays the role of "receiver"*
when an assignment calls for spoken communication.

Exercise 11.1

You are the supervisor of Gil Wyvern, the employee who caused the
Mobex copier to run all night in exercise 7.12 on page 97. You would prefer
your manager hear about it directly from you rather than from someone else,
so you walk down to his office right away.

1. Tell him what happened.
2. At his request, report it to him in a short memorandum.

Exercise 11.2

You are in charge of a group of women assembling electronic modules.
Twenty type J modules have been assembled, so you suggest to Mary
Winscombe that she get out the test set. You have turned away for less than
a minute when there is a screech, followed by a crash, and you turn around to
see Mary lying on the floor surrounded by broken modules and the test set.

As she struggles to her feet, she gasps: "I got a shock! I was plugging
it in and I got a shock!"

There is a burn on the fingers of her right hand, and a cut on her
arm. You telephone Mrs. Jasper, the personnel manager, who calls a cab to
take Mary to hospital.

"Send one of your girls with her," Mrs. Jasper says, "then send me a
report."

By piecing together information from other persons in the group, you
gradually find out what probably happened.

"I think Mary was holding onto one of the terminals of the test set as
she plugged it in," was Colleen's opinion.

"That shouldn't make any difference," you say.

"It would, if the set was switched on."

You examine the test set. Sure enough, the ON-OFF switch is set to
ON. "Even then . . ." you start to say.

"If she also touched the metal container on the electrical outlet," Har-
riett interrupts, "wouldn't that make a circuit?"

You agree it probably could. You also realize the test set will have to go
for a safety check before it is used again.

When the modules have been picked up, you find that thirteen of the twenty are damaged and will have to be repaired or rebuilt.

Write an Occurrence Report describing the accident and how it probably happened. Prepare it as a memorandum addressed to Mrs. Jasper.

Reporting a Field Assignment

Exercise 11.3

As part of your training course, you may be sent to visit a company near your school or college that employs persons with the training you will have when your course is finished. Such a visit is often called "familiarization," and may be as short as one hour or as long as two weeks (or, in some cases, even longer).

1. If a company visit is arranged for you, on your return write a trip report describing what you saw and did. For a short visit your report should cover mainly what you saw and what your impressions were. For a longer visit your report should also cover what practical experience you obtained while at the company. In both cases, include a comment on what could be done in future to make familiarization visits more useful to trainees. Address the trip report (which should be written as a memorandum) to your instructor.
2. If your familiarization visit is a long one, mail a progress report to your instructor halfway through it or on a preselected date.

Before going on the familiarization visit you should ask your instructor what special things you should be looking for or learning. Knowing this beforehand will give purpose to your visit and help you write a better report.

Exercise 11.4

You work for Wilding's Motors, Inc., a large automotive dealership which also sells and rents boats, camping equipment, and camping trailers. The company has offices and automotive centers in several cities, and shortly will be opening a new business operation at Ransome Lake—a popular holiday resort. It has acquired a choice piece of land between the waterfront and the highway, and will be operating an automobile service station on one side and a marina on the other. It will also rent camping trailers and equipment. These new facilities will open in four months, when you will be transferred there.

Two days ago, you were asked by your department manager (Carl Bjornson) to go to Ransome Lake to check on water depths beside the marina. He wants to know whether there is sufficient water to bring in a larger boat than originally planned. He suggests you also take Mel Davidson who is to be transferred there but has not previously seen the site.

Yesterday you drove to Ransome Lake, leaving the city at 7 a.m. and arriving at 9.45 a.m., pulling a light trailer and boat with a 10hp motor behind you. Mel helped you launch the boat beside the public dock, then he drove the car round to Wilding's Motors' construction site while you drove the boat a few yards out from shore.

You drove straight in to the Marina, noting that construction of the boat mooring docks was complete, and tied up between docks 5 and 6. You then pulled out a sketch of the docks and marked twelve locations at which you would measure water depth (see sketch). At positions A to H you decided to measure the water depth both at the edge and 3 ft. out from the shore. At positions I to L you would measure depth 30 ft. out from the shoreline.

You walked along the water's edge to take the first measurements at positions A to H and recorded them in the table below. You then jumped into the boat and tried unsuccessfully to start the motor. It would not start because long weeds were wrapped around the propellor. (You noticed only then that there were a lot of weeds just out from the water's edge.) When the weeds had been unwrapped, you took the readings 3 ft. out at positions A to H, and 30 ft. out at positions I to L. You also charted an area of extensive weed growth, and mentally noted that the weeds would have to be cleared before boats could use the marina.

Table of Water Depths

Position	Shore	3 ft. out	Position	Shore	3 ft. out	Position	30 ft. out
A	8 in.	11 in.	E	14 in.	19 in.	I	33 in.
B	7 in.	13 in.	F	15 in.	19 in.	J	47 in.
C	9 in.	16 in.	G	17 in.	22 in.	K	68 in.
D	11 in.	17 in.	H	20 in.	26 in.	L	71 in.

While taking your measurements you noticed that the launch ramp had been finished, so suggested to Mel that he back the car and trailer to the ramp so you could load the boat back onto the trailer.

"No way!" he said. "Whoever asphalted the approach road (at M on the map) didn't break the curb (at N). The trailer wheels are too small to pull over it."

So you drove the boat back to the public dock and loaded the boat there. Then you and Mel ate, and drove away at 3:45 p.m., expecting to be home by 6:30.

But you were unlucky. At 5:15 p.m. a trailer wheel went flat and you pulled hastily to the side. You didn't have a replacement with you, so had to jack up the trailer, remove the wheel, and drive into the nearest town (Biladou) to find a spare. Again you were unlucky, so you and Mel decided to drive

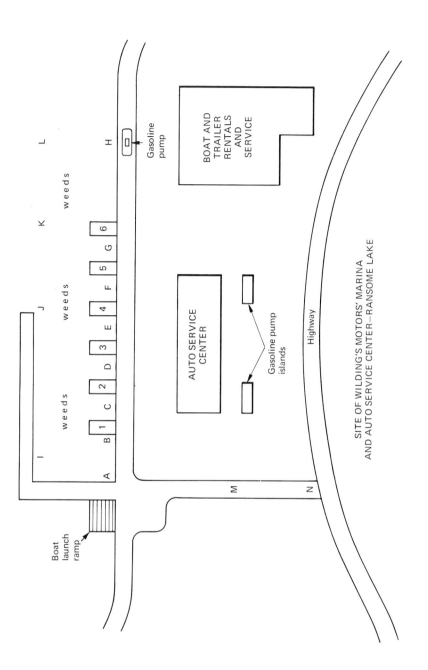

SITE OF WILDING'S MOTORS' MARINA
AND AUTO SERVICE CENTER—RANSOME LAKE

home and pick up a wheel from company stock. You arrived home at 10:45 p.m.

On the way, Mel asked if your water depth measurements were satisfactory.

"In places," you replied. "Some dredging will be necessary right along the front, probably to about 6 ft. out from the shore. And there are a lot of weeds—they'll have to be cleared every two months or so. And, of course, there's that curb at the entrance to the approach road—it will have to go."

Today Mel has driven back alone to fetch the boat and trailer.

1. When Mr. Bjornson comes in at 11 a.m., tell him what happened and why Mel is not there.
2. Write a trip report covering your visit to Ransome Lake.

Reporting Progress

Exercise 11.5

Management has decided to set up a small lunchroom in the area of the company where you work. Because it is in her department, your manager (Ms. Kim Watson) is responsible for seeing that the lunchroom is built and properly installed. She in turn has told you to keep an eye on what is going on and to let her know of progress from time to time. So far this has meant going into her office and telling her.

But today she asks you to give her a written report of progress. Tomorrow there is to be a union-management meeting, and she has to give the industrial relations manager this information because he expects to be asked for it.

You know from previous visits that all the partitions have been erected and the area has been painted. The carpenter is making the counter and cupboards for the small food serving area, and you ask him when they will be finished. He says: "In one week. The plumber will be here this afternoon to connect the sink to the water supply and the drains. And the painter will be here on Friday. They'll both be finished in one day."

You go down to stores and check the situation on tables and chairs that have been ordered: all the tables are there, but only half of the fifty chairs. You check the delivery slip and note that the remaining chairs have been back-ordered and should be delivered in two days.

You also telephone the vending company to enquire when the sandwich, drink, and cigarette machines will be installed. Mr. Cariotti tells you that your company's equipment is scheduled to be brought in three weeks from today. You ask if it can be brought in sooner.

"Definitely not," he says. "It's being shipped directly from the factory in Chicago. Your units are dated for production two weeks from today. Don't worry," he adds, "they're always on time. You can bank on it."

Write a progress report addressed to the industrial relations manager (Mr. K. L. Vincent), with a copy to Ms. Watson.

Exercise 11.6

You are in charge of a group of eight persons assembling components into modules for a manufacturing contract held by your company. This aspect of the job will last about six weeks. This morning your department manager (Ms. Isabel Cross) telephones you to say she is going to a meeting with the government department involved with the contract and would like a short description of your group's progress to take with her. You write her a memorandum based on the following information:

1. Work started three weeks ago today, so you are exactly halfway through the project.
2. There are three different modules, known as J, M, and TA. The contract requires you to make 1000 modules in six weeks:
   500 of module J
   400 of module M
   100 of module TA
3. J and M are relatively simple modules; TA is quite complex.
4. Work started immediately on modules M and TA. At the end of three weeks 300 module Ms have been built, tested, and packed; 50 module TAs have also been built, but could not be tested because a special test set from Seattle did not arrive until this morning.
5. Work on module J could not start immediately because a major component (the bypass filter) was not shipped in time by the supplier (Dally Electronics, Paramus, N.J.). The filters arrived a week ago today. Since then, 70 modules have been built, tested, and packed.
6. You expect to finish the remaining 100 module Ms in four working days.
7. You expect to finish assembling the remaining 50 module TAs in two weeks, and to have tested all of them by then.
8. You expect to assemble and test the remaining 430 module Js in three weeks exactly.

NOTE: Isabel Cross needs to know if you are on schedule at the contract halfway point and, if not, what percentage of the 1000 modules have been completely finished (i.e., assembled, tested, and packed).

Reporting an Inspection

Exercise 11.7

Assume that the administration of your college has asked for a report on the condition of parking lots serving staff and students. The project has been assigned to your instructor, who asks you to examine a specific part of the parking lot and then submit an inspection report to him.

During your inspection you should examine the condition of:

Surface

Curbs

Grass, fences, flower beds, etc. surrounding the lot

Parking lines painted on the surface

Signs and instructions

Approach roads

Separate your report into three parts: comments on the condition of the lot, comments on deficiencies (items that are missing); and recommendations for repair work you believe needs doing.

Exercise 11.8

New office equipment has been ordered for your department. Your department manager (Ms. Alice Kenny) tells you that the whole shipment has come in and is awaiting inspection in the company's stores department. She gives you a copy of the purchase order and asks you to check the items against it.

"Look for equipment condition as well," she cautions.

The purchase order lists:

4 desks

1 secretary's desk

4 office chairs with arms

1 secretary's chair

2 gray filing cabinets (four-drawer)

1 Vancourt electric typewriter

5 trash cans

1 coat tree

1 metal bookshelf (three shelves)

You find that the equipment has been piled just inside the door, so ask the storekeeper to help you move the larger items onto the floor where you can more easily examine them.

A quick count tells you that all five desks and chairs are there, and so are the two filing cabinets, the coat tree, and the bookshelf. One of the desks has a 12-inch scratch on its top, which could have been made before delivery or when the desks were moved onto the floor. (The latter is possible, you discover later, because the foot is missing from a leg of one of the other desks, leaving a sharp bare metal edge; the desk also rocks noticeably without its foot.)

The keys are inside the top of four of the desks, but missing from the fifth.

The typewriter is crated and has a notice on it: KEEP TYPEWRITER IN SEALED CRATE FOR VANCOURT SERVICEMAN TO OPEN.

You find five trash cans under one of the desks.

Although both filing cabinets have been supplied and both are gray, they are not a pair: one is dark gray and the other is light gray.

There is no other damage to the equipment, but the bookshelf is missing two of the twelve L-shaped brackets required to hold up its shelves.

You are just leaving when you notice that all the chairs are identical. This means that a fifth office chair has been supplied instead of a stenographer's chair.

Write an inspection report addressed to Ms. Kenny (assume you attach the purchase order to it).

Reporting an Investigation

Exercise 11.9

Your company owns a large station wagon which it uses as a general runabout vehicle and for making local deliveries and pickups. It seldom has to carry very heavy goods, or anything measuring more than 2 ft. × 2 ft. × 2 ft. But a series of breakdowns followed by expensive repairs, plus the wagon's high running costs, have prompted management to consider buying a new subcompact station wagon.

Your department manager (R. McIntosh) has assigned a small investigation project to you.

"There are two parts to it, really," he says. "Which would be the best model to buy? And which would be cheapest—buying or leasing?"

He suggests you take a look around—make a comparison—then write a little investigation report he can take to the next management meeting. You ask some questions:

Just how much does the company want to spend?
> (He is not sure, but suggests a practical limit of $5000 for outright purchase.)

How long would the company keep the wagon, before trading it in?
> (Going on past performance only, about five years; but for a smaller wagon, maybe only three years.)

What options?
> (Automatic transmission; AM/FM radio; heavy-duty suspension; radial tires)

What about annual mileage?
> (In previous years: 16,000 miles a year)

Later, you find that the sale or trade-in value of the existing station wagon is $550, about one-third of its mileage is for out-of-town trips, and it travels about 1200 miles a year on trails and rough country roads.

1. Telephone a local auto dealer and request the specifications, price, and availability of a suitable subcompact wagon.
2. Write to another dealer and ask for the same information.

3. Visit a leasing company and inquire about leasing a similar size wagon. (Be sure to obtain all costs and details of a leasing contract.)

4. Analyze the information you have obtained, then write an investigation report addressed to Mr. McIntosh that discusses the various alternatives, draws conclusions, and makes a recommendation.

5. With your report in your hand, go to Mr. McIntosh and brief him on the results of your investigation, then give him your report.

6. Assume that the company accepts your recommendation, but changes its needs slightly: rather than an AM/FM radio, an AM radio plus 8-channel tape deck is wanted (the difference in price is an extra $40). Write a letter ordering one of the station wagons. Stipulate the options required, including sky-blue exterior, azure interior, and delivery in two months. (You may include other options, provided a price has been obtained for them.)

12

Communicating
for Your Company

When an employee deals directly with a company's customers (see chapter 8) or with other businesses, a supervisor is normally standing in the background ready to offer assistance, give direction, and make decisions. An employee's communicating is mostly of the "front line" type—spoken briefly and with the intent to get the job done. A supervisor's communicating more often involves problem solving. It takes longer, and frequently requires a written explanation or report to provide a visible record of what was said or agreed.

COMMUNICATING WITH THE COMPANY'S CUSTOMERS

You are most likely to communicate with your company's customers when they

1. Ask a question or request something be done
2. Want to know how their job is coming along
3. Have a complaint

Replying to Requests

Customers usually make requests by telephone or come in to see you. This means that your reply has to be immediate, which gives you very little time to organize it into information blocks. Nevertheless, it is important to know what the information blocks are, for this may help you to *think* in information-block format.

Because your answer has to come quickly, the information blocks for a spoken reply are very simple (see Fig. 4–21). But before you use them, you must first find out exactly what the questioner is asking. Remember that the person talking to you may not know about the pyramid approach or how to use information blocks, so his request may seem a bit muddled. If it is, ask a question or two of your own to find out exactly what he wants.

For example, what is a customer leading up to when he asks:

You people do industrial air conditioners? Or only commercial?

He may want you to give him a quotation on installing an air conditioner in a manufacturing plant. But you don't know this. He could just as easily be asking you to send someone in to repair a home air conditioner that is leaking. So you must try to find out by careful questioning:

1. What he wants done
2. How soon he wants it done
3. Where he wants it done

Then you can reply with a **Summary Statement** like this:

We can install your air conditioner starting next Tuesday if it has already been delivered, or in ten weeks if it still has to be ordered.

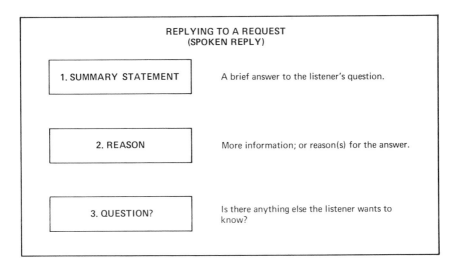

Fig. 4–21. Information blocks for a spoken reply to a request.

Having briefly answered his implied question, you should follow it with more information (this is the **Reason** block in Fig. 4–21):

> The ten weeks' delivery applies only to the Vancourt line. Other manufacturers are quoting 15 to 20 weeks for delivery.

Then you can ask if he has further **Questions,** either directly or by suggesting the next step:

> Can I show you some air conditioners?
>   or:
> What size unit were you thinking of?
>   or:
> Would you like me to call on you tomorrow morning, to look at your plant and go over your requirements with you?

The information blocks are increased by one when the answer has to be written. This **Reference** block (see Fig. 4–22) simply draws attention to the inquirer's letter or spoken request, so that your answer can be linked with it.

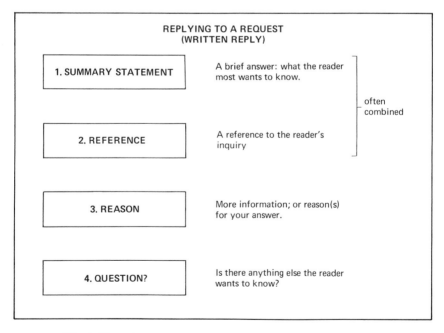

Fig. 4–22. Information blocks for a written reply to a request.

Montrose Gas Company

Box 301   Montrose, Ohio   45287

July 23, 19__

Ms. G. Linklater
2020 Plessis Road
St. Ardans, Ohio   44237

Dear Ms. Linklater:

      We would like to do the work requested in your letter of
July 18, but regret that at present we cannot accept any new customers. ① & ②

      The current shortage of natural gas means we have had to re-
fuse many orders from potential gas users who, like you, want to
convert their oil-burning furnaces to natural gas. We hope in time ③
the supply situation will improve, and will keep your letter on file
for when it does.

      Thank you for your enquiry.

                        Yours sincerely

                        Wanda Simpson

                        Wanda Simpson
                        Customer Sales

Fig. 4–23. A written reply to a request. (Circled numbers refer to information blocks in Fig. 4–22.)

In short letters, the Reference may be combined with the Summary Statement:

A Model 701 amplifier has been shipped to you by rail express, as requested in your May 14 telephone call.

Note that the Reference mentions both the date of the request and how it was made (by letter, telegram, or telephone).

A written reply to a request is shown in Fig. 4–23, in which block 4 (Question?) is omitted. If included, it might have been something like this:

> If you have further questions, please call me at 489-9039.

Reporting on Work Done (Progress)

Sometimes a customer will ask how a job you are doing for him is coming along. Or, if there have been problems or delays, you may prefer to take the initiative and tell him before he inquires. Such progress reports require the same information blocks used to report progress to your company (see page 150). These information blocks are shown in Fig. 4–24.

If you are *speaking* to a customer, your report can be packaged like this:

1. In the **Summary Statement** you tell him what the situation is now, and the date the job will be finished (apart from price, this is probably what he most wants to know):

   > Your water-level recorder has been repaired, but still requires calibration. It should be ready next Wednesday.

2. In the **Past** you highlight the most important features of work done so far:

   > We traced the main fault to a stripped drive shaft, which has been replaced.

3. In the **Present** you tell him what you are doing now:

   > Because the drive shaft is a major component, I'm having the recorder recalibrated.

4. In the **Future** you tell him what else will be done, and possibly predict how long it will take:

   > I'll have a calibration chart made up and send it to you with the recorder.

5. In **Back-up,** you hold in reserve information the customer might ask for. This could range from a simple question about the warranty or the cost of the repair job to a technical question about calibration accu-

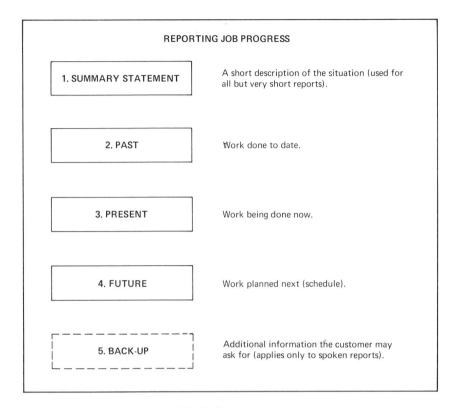

Fig. 4–24. Information blocks for reporting progress to a customer.

racy. The former you might be able to answer immediately, but the latter would probably require some research before you could offer a proper answer.

How the first four information blocks are used to shape a *written* report on progress to a customer is shown in Fig. 4–25. The circled numbers beside the letter refer to the information blocks in Fig. 4–24.

Replying to Complaints

Some of the most difficult situations that a supervisor has to deal with concern customers who have complaints, particularly if the customer is angry. No matter how angry or rude a customer may be, you must not lose your control. This applies not only to you as a supervisor but also to everyone in the company—from the general manager down to the newest employee.

Westwin Testlabs

3067 East 47th Street
Vienna, Oklahoma, 73246

January 21, 19__

Mr. R.G. Spelchake
Manager
Admiral Chemicals
Reece, Minn. 55747

Dear Mr. Spelchake:

We have analyzed 27 of the samples you sent to us with your letter on December 22, and expect to finish the remaining 13 by February 1. ①

To date, we have found 14 samples that conform to the specifications for group 1 described in your letter, and 8 samples that can be classified as belonging to group 2. ②

The remaining 5 samples are also being base tested to find out whether they contain impurities that prevent proper classification. ③

We will ship the samples in two batches. The first, which will be mailed on February 1, will contain all the samples classified as groups 1 and 2. The remainder will be mailed one week later, when base tests are complete. ④

Sincerely

Vince Hendrix

Vince Hendrix
Lab Supervisor

Fig. 4–25. A letter describing progress to a customer.

As a supervisor you cannot escape the problem. Although an employee can politely direct an angry customer to you, you cannot pass the problem along. You have to deal with it.

Dealing with an angry customer calls for tact and diplomacy. Sometimes it helps to understand why some people are unreasonably angry, and even rude, when the cause does not seem to warrant it. A mature person who knows his complaint is justified may be angry at first, but will quickly calm down when he sees he is getting some action. (A warning: this kind of person readily recognizes if he is being given only "lip service," and his annoyance then increases.) This is the type of person you are most likely to deal with. A less mature person who has a complaint but does not know how to handle either it or himself, may use anger and abuse as an axe that he swings wildly in the hope of making his point. He uses a lot of noise to cover up for his lack of confidence. He may even deliberately provoke you (sometimes with abusive language, and sometimes much more subtly) into responding angrily. He then uses your anger as a weapon to show what a poor company he is dealing with.

Dealing with a mature customer is no problem. Handling the less mature person can be extremely difficult. Aggrieved customers have the potential capability to turn other customers away from doing business with your company, particularly if they feel they have been treated badly by an employee (even though the "bad" treatment may be imagined rather than real).

The best advice is to do much the same as you would with an employee who comes to you with a "beef"; that is, be ready to *listen* (see chapter 9 page 114). Make sure the customer knows you are: (1) concerned that he has a complaint, and (2) interested in him and in trying to set things right. Give him time to work off some steam, then when he has calmed down ask questions to make sure you have understood him correctly.

If the customer has telephoned you, tell him you will look into the problem and call him back within, say, half an hour. This will give you time to give him a proper answer. But be sure you do call him back within the time you have stated; if you don't, you will only add to his annoyance. If he has come in to see you, make sure he has somewhere to sit while you excuse yourself to look into the problem. It is wise to do your checking out of his sight; but it should be done quickly so he is not kept waiting too long.

Try to model your answer around the information blocks in Fig. 4–26. You will find your task much easier when you agree with a customer that he has a complaint and tell him the company will do something about it, than if you have to tell him the company does not believe his

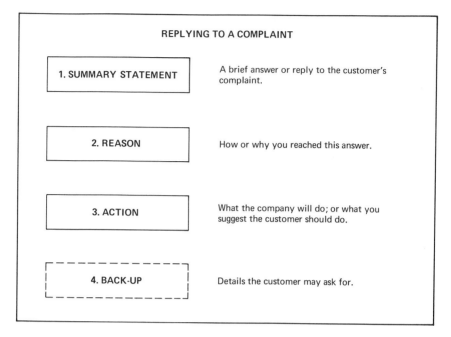

Fig. 4–26. Information blocks for replying to a complaint.

complaint is valid. A customer will readily accept the first reply, but probably will strongly resist the second one. In both cases, the tone of your reply must be polite and respectful. If the customer insists on carrying his case further, and names an executive of the company he wants to see, you can do no more than suggest politely that he do so.

The information blocks should contain:

1. A short **Summary Statement** in which you either tell him his complaint is warranted and what is going to be done to correct it, or that he does not have a justifiable complaint. If the latter is the case, you should politely express regret that you cannot meet his request (even though there may be great temptation to "put a rude customer down"). The two approaches are shown in Fig. 4–27.

2. The **Reason** is simply why you agree or disagree with the customer. If you agree, there is usually less to say than if you disagree. A dissatisfied customer wants to know not only your answer but also on what basis you are giving him that answer. He wants evidence, and unless your evidence is sound he will have even more reason for believing he still has a complaint.

Agreeing with a Customer's Complaint		Disagreeing with a Customer's Complaint
We checked your castings, Mr. Walters. You're quite right; they are defective and we'll replace them.	**1. SUMMARY STATEMENT**	I'm sorry, Mr. Davis, but we can't do warranty repairs on your minicalculator.
They are all from the same batch, made last May. The fault shows up under ultrasonic testing; there is no visible sign of it.	**2. REASON**	I agree, it shouldn't have failed after only two months. But once the seal is broken, the warranty is void. It says that right on the warranty. There's no way we can tell what someone else has done inside it: maybe a lot of work is needed.
I suggest you let us test all the castings we shipped to you under order 2707. We'll replace any that show the same fault.	**3. ACTION**	What I suggest you do is send it in for an estimate. If not too many parts have to be replaced, we'll still supply them under the warranty—just charge you for the labor. Fair enough?

Fig. 4–27. Spoken replies to a complaint.

3. If you agree with the customer, then the **Action** block says what the company will do to correct the situation and suggests action that the customer should take (see Fig. 4–27). If you disagree, the Action block may:

1. Go part way toward meeting the customer by offering a partial settlement, as "good will";
2. Suggest alternative action that the customer can take, such as going elsewhere for service; or
3. Simply offer nothing—neither suggestions nor assistance.

If nothing had been offered in the "Disagree" (right-hand) situation in Fig. 4–27, the Action block might have been like this:

I'm sorry, Mr. Davis. There's nothing I can do to help you.

4. **Back-Up** is information kept in reserve in case the customer asks for it. For the defective castings problem in Fig. 4–27, it might be details of the paperwork needed to exchange the castings, or comments on the possibility of a similar fault occurring in more recent batches. For the minicalculator problem, it might be the hourly rate charged for labor, or more information on the company's warranty policy.

A written answer to a complaint uses the first three information blocks in Fig. 4–26, but also includes a reference to the date the customer lodged his complaint and whether he did so by letter, telephone call, or visit. Information that normally would be held in the Back-Up block for a spoken reply may be built into the Reason or Action block for a written reply.

A typical letter replying to a complaint appears in Fig. 4–28. The circumstances leading up to this letter are described in the memorandum in Fig. 4–20 (page 160).

COMMUNICATING WITH OTHER BUSINESSES

Businesses with which you, as a supervisor, are likely to communicate fall into two categories: those your company sells its products or services to, and those it buys parts, materials, and services from. Because the former are customers, they fall into the group discussed earlier in this section. For the latter, the positions are reversed: *you* are now the customer. How efficiently you buy parts, materials, and services will directly affect the cost of the service your company supplies or products it manufactures.

Your main reasons for communicating with another company will be to

1. Request information
2. Place an order

The Furniture House

Winston, Illinois 61323

April 11, 19__

Mrs. V. Carson
1407-2022 Dover Road
Winston, Ill. 61323

Dear Mrs. Carson:

Although we might agree to share the cost of cleaning your white rug, I regret we cannot replace it.

Mr. Pritchard tells me that his examination of your rug on April 7, and discussions with both you and our repairman, indicate the marks on your rug probably are small splotches of furniture paint from the repairman's kit. (A chemical analysis would prove this conclusively.) But their cause cannot readily be attributed to the repairman, since he placed protective covering beneath his kit and around your buffet where he was working. Apparently, one of your cats dipped a paw into the paint and then wandered off the cover and onto the rug.

I suggest that you call Mr. Phillips at Colony Cleaners and ask him for an estimate for cleaning the rug. If you will then kindly telephone me again, I will be happy to come to some arrangement with you for sharing the cleaning costs. ③

I hope this will prove satisfactory.

Sincerely

Ken G. Murray
Manager, Customer Services

Fig. 4-28. A written reply to a complaint. (Circled numbers refer to information blocks in Fig. 4-26.)

3. Get faster action
4. Complain

Much of this communicating can be done by telephone when the other company is nearby; only when you need a permanent record of the communication (such as a written order for parts) is the communication written. But the reverse is more true when the other company is far away: then most communications are written and only the very urgent ones are telephoned.

Requesting Information

It is wise to group the parts of your request into information blocks before making an enquiry. The information blocks in this case are the same as those you would use to place an order. They are illustrated in Fig. 4–29, and described in the captions to the *left* of the blocks. They contain:

1. A **Summary Statement** that says in general terms what you want to find out. For a spoken enquiry:

   I'm looking for information on factory-built storage shelves and bins.

2. **Details** that describe specific features (such as make, size, weight, strength, color, and construction), quantities, prices, and so on:

   They need to be of steel construction, 12 feet high, and have adjustable shelves that can accept cartons up to 40 inches high, wide, and deep.

   I need descriptive literature, prices, and delivery times.

3. **Instructions** on who the information is to be sent to, by what date it is needed and, sometimes, how it is to be sent (i.e., by post, air express, or personal delivery). For example:

   Can you mail this information to me by June 20? I'm at Arkright Industries, 1100 Arden Avenue, Reece, Minnesota. Address it to the attention of Don Bale.

or

   Can you send one of your salesmen around before the end of the week? I'm at Arkright Industries, 1100 Arden Avenue. Tell him to ask for Don Bale.

   The Instructions block can be omitted from conversation in which the information is supplied immediately.

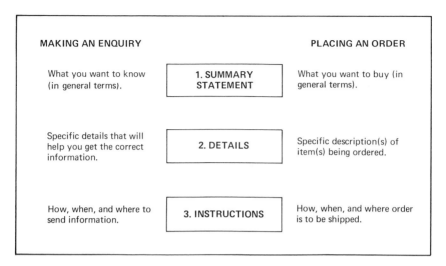

Fig. 4-29. Information blocks to request information or place an order.

In a spoken conversation there are two persons taking part, so a request might run something like this (circled numbers refer to information blocks in Fig. 4-29):

Person Requesting	*Person Answering*
This is Lynne Thompson calling, Purchasing Agent for Daly Electronics in Denver.	
	Yes, Ms. Thompson.
(1) We want to order spare parts for an old Hektik Model 700 amplifier. But first we need a circuit diagram and parts list. Can you send me one?	
	I think so. What year was it made?
(2) No idea. The only information I have is that it's a model 700, series E, serial number 2160.	
	700 . . . series E . . . 2160 . . .
(3) Can you airmail it to me? That's Lynne Thompson, Box 181, Station C, Denver.	
	OK, I'll do that.
Thank you!	

A written request would follow essentially the same pattern:

Dear Mr. Corinth:

I need advice on how to adjust the pressure control in our Vancourt water level meters.   **1. SUMMARY STATEMENT**

We use models 201 and 206A, and with both have difficulty in obtaining exact readings during flood conditions. Ideally, we would like to adjust the pressure control at the top end of the scale to give readings with ±2 percent accuracy at depths of 10 to 15 ft.   **2. DETAILS**

Please send this information to me by February 15 so that my field technicians can make adjustments before the spring thaw.   **3. INSTRUCTIONS**

Sincerely,

David K. Wallace

Placing an Order

Although materials and parts may sometimes be ordered by telephone to speed delivery, the spoken order should always be followed by a written order. A written order is visible authorization for the supplying company to ship goods or supply services, and eventually to invoice your company for them.

Written orders are usually prepared on a preprinted form known as a Purchase Order (see Fig. 4–30). They vary in shape, size, and content, although most contain spaces for you to enter:

1. Name and address of supplying company
2. Name and address of person or office to whom goods are to be shipped
3. Date the order is made out
4. Details of the goods required—specifically:
   a. Quantity (number required of each item)
   b. Description (full name and details)
   c. Price (for each, a dozen, a gross, or a hundred, etc; plus the price for the total number ordered)
5. Date the goods are required
6. How the goods are to be shipped (rail, air, post, etc.)
7. Purchasing terms (e.g., whether a discount applies; or net if paid in 30 days; etc.)
8. Number of invoices to be supplied
9. Your signature (or that of the company's purchasing agent)

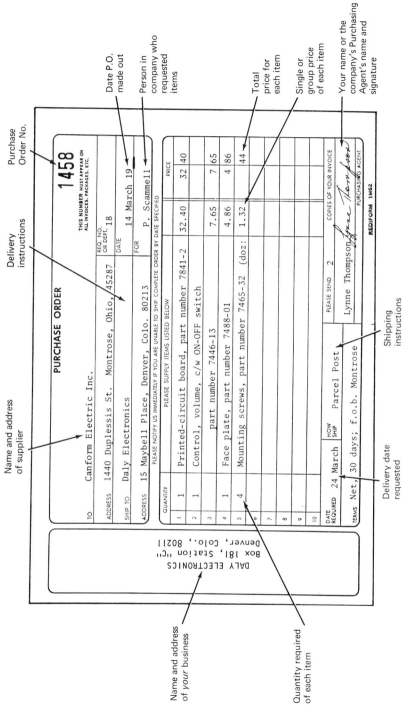

Fig. 4–30. A typical Purchase Order. This is a Rediform off-the-shelf type sold in pads, which may be purchased from stationery stores (form illustration by permission of Moore Business Forms).

If the company you work for is very small, it possibly may not use Purchase Orders. If this is the case your order will have to go out as a letter, using the information blocks in Fig. 4–29. These are described briefly in the captions to the *right* of the three blocks, and in more detail below.

1. The **Summary Statement** describes in general terms what you want to buy:

   Please supply a Series 80 automic sorter at $665 FOB our plant, plus federal and state taxes.[1]

2. **Details** clearly describe the item or service. They must be exact to avoid any possibility that the wrong goods will be supplied. They should cover factors such as size, weight, speed, type of thread or fitting, finish (e.g., cadmium plate, anodized, lacquer), color, quantity, price, and warranty. The example started in block 1 might continue like this:

   The sorter must have 16 bins each able to hold 200 sheets of $8\frac{1}{2} \times$ 14 in. 20-lb. bond paper, and come complete with parts for attaching it to a Model 410H copier.

3. **Instructions** concern delivery and invoicing. These can include how, where, and when the goods are to be delivered, to whom they should be addressed, and the number of invoices required. For example:

   The sorter is to be delivered by 28 February, then installed and tested by one of your technicians within three days of delivery. Installation and testing are included in the price. We require two copies of your invoice.

Because letter orders contain so many unrelated pieces of information, it is sometimes difficult to keep them from becoming fragmented, as has happened in block 3 above.

A letter order containing numerous items should be prepared as two sheets. The first contains the letter without the Details block, as in Fig. 4–31. Details are then typed onto the second sheet, which is called an *Attachment* and looks rather like the Details section of a Purchase Order. It should be stapled to the letter.

When an order is urgent, you may need to telephone it to the supplier right away, and then follow it with a confirming purchase order or letter (when this is done, the words "Confirmation Only" are stamped on the purchase order so it will not be thought to be a new order, in

---

[1] FOB is the point to which the supplier pays shipping costs, and beyond which the purchaser pays them.

H. L. Winman and Associates

475 Reston Avenue-Cleveland, Ohio 44104

April 14, 19___

Mr. Carl Kaminsky
Chief, Materials Supply Section
Plum-Rad Distributors
147 Winona Street
Winston, Ill.   61323

Dear Mr. Kaminsky:

　　Please supply the plumbing items listed on the attached sheet for a total price of $836.75, tax included.　　①

　　The goods are to be shipped collect by rail express, f.o.b. Winston, Ill., for delivery by May 6, 19___, to:

> 284 Main Street
> Reece, Minnesota
> Attention:　Mr. Dan V. Carling　②

　　Please acknowledge receipt of this order, and also inform me by Telex on the day that the goods are shipped.　　③

Yours sincerely,

Paul Richardson
Supervisor
Plumbing Installations

Fig. 4–31. A letter order referring to a separate Details section (not shown).

which case a duplicate set of goods would be sent out). The information in a telephone order is identical to that in a written order:

This is Bevco Construction calling. Will you please send us the following supplies against purchase order number 21675:

> 1. SUMMARY STATEMENT

Item one—two dozen one-pound tubes of AJ-70 bitumastic compound.
Item two—ten gallons exterior latex primer—white.
Item three—twelve gallons Velvetura exterior latex paint—daffodil; color number 3181.

> 2. DETAILS

This is an urgent order, so could you put it on the 4 P.M. coach to Davyridge? Send it prepaid—we'll pay the shipping costs. Address it to Cal Martin, Bevco Construction, and mark it "Hold for pickup." I'll put a confirming order into today's mail. OK? Thank you!

> 3. INSTRUC-
> TIONS

The price of each item and invoicing details have not been included in this telephone order because they are standard items for which the prices are already known. They are not, however, omitted from the confirming order.

Demanding Action

The need to demand action happens more often than most businesses like to admit. Lynne Thompson of Daly Electronics placed an order with Canform Electric, Inc. on March 14 (see Fig. 4–30), expecting delivery in ten days. But after fourteen days nothing had been received. So she telephoned the supplier to find out what had happened to the order.

Information Blocks

Canform? Oh, good morning. This is Lynne Thompson of Daly Electronics in Denver. I'm calling about an overdue order.

①

The purchase order number is 1458, and it was dated March 14. Delivery was scheduled for March 24—that's four days ago. The goods were to be shipped parcel post.

②

Will you look into it? Then call me back between 1 and 3 P.M. Ohio time. Thank you!

③

The information blocks Lynne has used apply to any situation where you have to ask or demand something be done (see Fig. 4–32). Each block contains:

1. **Summary Statement.** A short opening remark in which you state in general terms why you are calling or writing.
2. **Circumstances.** Information the listener or reader needs to identify the job, order, or project: what he must know if he is to check up for you and take action.
3. **Action.** What you want done, ranging from a mild request that the supplier look into the problem to a strong demand that he cancel the order.

A written demand for action may be used when there is no urgency, if your company needs written proof that it has demanded action, or if the circumstances are too complex to handle easily by telephone. For example:

Although the quality of image reproduced by your office copier is excellent, we find that the time it takes your service department to respond to service calls is too slow.

> 1. SUMMARY STATEMENT

The copier is the model 808, and it is rented on a yearly basis under Purchase Order 34827 dated November 15, 19___. During the past two months, each time our copier has broken down I have kept a record of the time it takes for your serviceman to arrive from the time I called your

> 2. CIRCUM-STANCES

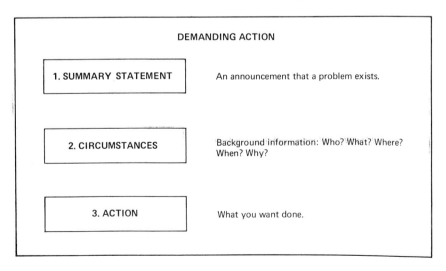

Fig. 4–32. Information blocks for demanding action.

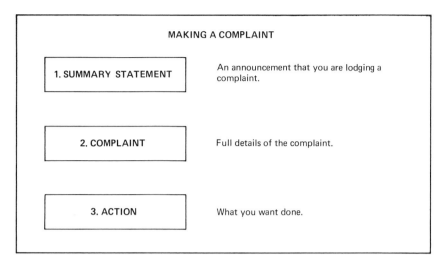

Fig. 4–33. Information blocks for a letter of complaint.

service department. The average was 1¼ days, with the shortest time being 4 hours and the longest 2½ days.

Because we require same-day copying of manufacturing changes, we must have four-hour maximum response time to service calls. Please inform me whether or not you can meet this requirement. ┌─────────────┐ 3. ACTION └─────────────┘

Complaining

To be effective, complaints must be strongly worded (but without strong language) and supported by conclusive evidence that the complaint is justified. They should never suggest or imply that further action will be taken, because this makes them sound weak. And they must never threaten, unless you definitely intend to carry out the threat. For example, before you write "Unless this fault is corrected we will stop doing business with your firm," you must first be sure that it is practical to take your business elsewhere, and that you really would do so. Otherwise your threat will be hollow and your reader will know it.

The information blocks for lodging a complaint are shown in Fig. 4–33. They are similar to those demanding action; indeed, the letter on page 189 could be classed as either a demand or a complaint. Information carried in these blocks comprises:

1. In the **Summary Statement,** a brief comment that you have a complaint and expect something to be done about it. For example:

I believe we have been overcharged for labor on invoice 2731, and request an adjustment.

2. In the **Complaint** block: (a) background information to help the reader or listener identify the situation, job, or project; and (b) a thorough, unbiased (fair, reasonable, impartial) description of the complaint. For example:

> This invoice refers to the November 15 overhaul of our model 284 press. Your serviceman, Harry Wickstead, checked into our plant at 8:15 A.M. and out again at 2:20 P.M. This is shown as 6 hours' labor on your invoice.
>
> I timed his repair work on November 15 and noted that he finished working on the press at 12:15 P.M. The remainder of his time was spent in the cafeteria chatting with employees in other departments.

3. In the **Action** block, a clear statement describing exactly what you want done. It can repeat in greater detail what you have already said in block 1:

> Please reduce the labor charge by 2 hours, and request your serviceman not to distract our employees from their work during future visits.

A complaint can much more effectively demonstrate that you have a strong case by offering a reasoned argument than by screaming something like this at the reader:

> If your noisy, talkative serviceman would only quit wasting both his and our employees' time with his endless stream of chit-chat, maybe both he and we could get more work done!

Complaints that may have financial or legal implications should always be written, so that a record exists of the dialogue between you and the other company. Most minor complaints, however, can be resolved by a quick telephone call. A telephoned or face-to-face complaint is often shorter, but still organized around the same information blocks. The one below is the original complaint that led to the reply in Fig. 4–27 (page 179):

Information Blocks

Mr. Schmidt? This is Chuck Walters at Arnold Manufacturing. Look—there's something wrong with the castings you've been sending us recently. Is there any way we can test them before we start machining?

The problem started in June—that's when I first noticed the reject rate going up. Now we're throwing out at least 20 percent of the castings. The trouble is, a machinist can put in two or three hours work before a casting breaks down. You'll replace the castings, I know, but there's no way I can recover my machinists' lost time.   ②

Can you do two things for me? Check up and correct the fault at your end, and tell me how to test the castings I've got before my guys start working on them. I'm sending six castings back to you so you can see what's wrong.   ③

Inferior products, poor service, and improperly filled orders can be extremely annoying, particularly if you are under pressure to get a job out quickly. They justly warrant a critical complaint and a strong demand for corrective action. But they do not justify a display of anger. Anger interferes with good communication and slows rather than speeds the action you want.

EXERCISES

NOTE: *1. Your instructor will inform you who will play the role of "receiver" when an exercise calls for spoken communication.*
        2. Additional exercises requiring you to deal with other business appear at the end of Chapter 13. They are:
           Requesting information—Exercises 13.9 and 13.14
           Placing an order—Exercises 13.2, 13.10, and 13.16
           Demanding faster action—Exercise 13.3
           Complaining—Exercises 13.11, 13.13, and 13.17

Communicating with Customers

Exercise 12.1

When Mrs. Freda Wilshire telephoned you earlier this morning she wanted to know why it was taking so long to have her television set repaired. You told her it was done several days ago and you thought it had already been delivered. You promised to check on it and call back.

From your inquiries you discover:

1. The set was finished four days ago.

2. It was delivered to the caretaker of the block in which Mrs. Wilshire lives because she was out of town.

Telephone Mrs. Wilshire and tell her this.

Exercise 12.2

Mrs. Wilshire (Exercise 12.1) says the television set has not been delivered. She is obviously quite annoyed, because she neither lives in an apartment block nor has been out of town. Embarrassed, you tell her you will check further.

Your checking reveals that the company driver mislaid Mrs. Wilshire's address, so looked it up in a telephone book. You find he confused Mrs. Freda Wilshire's name with that of an "F. Wilshire," not realizing that your customer was listed under "Geo. Wilshire" (her husband's name).

You and the driver go to the apartment block where he delivered the TV set, but the caretaker won't part with it until he has talked to his Mrs. Wilshire, who will not return for two days.

Visit Mrs. Freda Wilshire and explain what has happened. You may tell her you are lending her a TV set until hers is returned.

Exercise 12.3

Three days later you have retrieved Mrs. Wilshire's television set and it has been returned to her.

Write a courtesy letter of apology to her (she lives at 212 Bourbon Street).

Exercise 12.4

Your company has a contract to supply and install gas-fired heating systems in sixty new homes being built by Marginal Houses, Inc. of 208 Neptune Street. All the homes are in a new development known as Scarsdale Heights. The contract calls for you to install ten systems a month over a six-month period.

Three months have elapsed but you have installed only eighteen heating systems. There have been two problems: (1) you have had difficulty in getting furnaces—you received only twenty initially, and now the manufacturers cannot positively guarantee to increase deliveries to the fourteen units you require a month; (2) the houses have been ready in two batches of ten each instead of two or three a week, which was the arrangement you made with Marginal to permit you to have a steady workload.

Telephone Jim Dentsch, Marginal's construction manager, and tell him what progress you have made, what the problems have been and may yet be, and try to predict a completion date.

Exercise 12.5

It is now six weeks later (see Exercise 12.4) and your installers are working considerable overtime. You have received a further twenty furnaces, but manufacturers now claim that a four-week strike of metalworkers has put them far behind schedule. It will be at least another six weeks before the remaining twenty units will be delivered. This is one week after the completion date in your contract with Marginal Builders Inc.

Because of good weather, Marginal has speeded up its construction and now fifty-four houses have been finished. The remaining six will be ready in two more weeks. Jim Dentsch, Marginal's construction manager, has been growing very impatient with your company's inability to keep up with his company's construction rate.

Write a letter to Henry G. Marginal, president of Marginal Builders, Inc., reporting progress, explaining the problem, and requesting a four-week extension of the contract completion date.

Exercise 12.6

You are the supervisor of Reg Danyluk, the employee who delivered an outboard motor to Mr. Terry in Exercise 8.5 (page 108), and who Mrs. Terry now accuses of damaging her husband's car. Eventually Reg suggests that Mrs. Terry speak to you.

Cope with Mrs. Terry's shrill accusations that Reg damaged her husband's car and that either he or your company must pay to have it repaired.

Exercise 12.7

You are a foreman working for A. S. Mills and Company, the contractor building a service station and marina at Ransome Lake (see Exercise 11.4, page 162). The work is being done for Wilding's Motors, 2015 Watson Avenue, Ventnor—a city some 160 miles from the lake.

You can hear Ernie's Dredging Service chugging noisily and clearing weeds from the water behind the building. Ernie is dumping weeds into a truck that has been backed right up to the new gasoline pump, which was installed yesterday.

When Ernie White and Jack Larkin (the truck driver) come in for their coffee break, the talk turns to the previous night's ballgame.

Suddenly, Ernie jumps up. "Hey! What's going on?" he yells, and runs out of the building. You scramble up and follow him.

As you round the corner of the building you see the dump truck's box tipped high in the air. Immediately there is a slithering sound and a full load of weed, stones, and wet grit pours out, much of it crunching onto the new gasoline pump. Ernie comes running up.

"Why didn't you lock your cab?" he shouts at Jack. "Or at least take the keys out of the ignition?"

Ernie turns to you. "It was kids," he says. "I saw them—two of them—they were already out of the cab and running. I couldn't get to the cab in time to stop it."

You ruefully survey the mess.

"Can't remove this with a machine," says Ernie. "We'd damage the fuel lines. We'll have to do it by hand."

Three hours later, tired, sore, and gritty, you examine the gasoline pump. It is twisted, all its glass is broken, and it has been partly torn from its base. There is no doubt it will have to be replaced.

1. Telephone Mr. Wilding in Ventnor and tell him what happened.
2. Write him a letter describing the occurrence and suggesting he order a replacement gasoline pump. (You may assume that Ernie's insurance company will pay for it.)

Communicating with Other Businesses

Exercise 12.8

You are the supervisor of the employee in Exercise 7.12 (page 97). After the employee tells you what has happened, you go down to the copier and note the copy counter readings before and after the incident. They are:

Before:	121,087
After:	126,213

You deduct the 20 copies the employee intended to make, then calculate that the machine counted off 5106 extra copies during the night.

Write to the Mobex Copier Company, 2807 Barton Boulevard, telling them what happened to their copier and requesting credit for the number of copies run off accidentally.

Exercise 12.9

The department in which you are supervisor is to be redecorated. Your manager suggests you also replace the twenty-two rather old-fashioned light-ing fixtures with something more modern. He gives you a free hand to make your own selection, but says you must limit the cost to $500.

You know immediately the type of fixture you want: it is of Danish make, and you have seen it in the Mod-Art Import House at 414 Logan Avenue.

1. Telephone Mod-Art and ask the manager if he can sell you twenty-two fixtures, what the price will be, and how soon he can supply them.

He regretfully explains he has only two fixtures in stock, it will take three months to bring in the number you want from Denmark, and the best price he can give you is $27.95 each. But he suggests an alternative source of supply: European Wholesalers at 1400 Atlantic Road, Wells, Connecticut.

2. Write to European Wholesalers and make the same inquiry, this time saying that you need the fixtures in one month and asking for a firm price quotation.

Exercise 12.10

European Wholesalers' reply (see Exercise 12.9) says:
We can supply you with 22 Model 80B "Spiroform" light fixtures at $19.70 each, FOB Wells, Connecticut. Delivery will take three weeks from receipt of your order. Taxes not included.
Prepare a purchase order (either letter or form) ordering the light fixtures. Say you want delivery four weeks from today. Assume that state tax of 8 percent will have to be added to the price.

Exercise 12.11

It is now six weeks later and you still have not received the light fixtures (see Exercise 12.10). Telephone European Wholesalers and demand action.

Exercise 12.12

The light fixtures arrived today (see Exercise 12.10), nine weeks after they were ordered. You open the cartons and find that three of the plastic shades are noticeably discolored and the plastic is twisted slightly out of shape, probably from exposure to heat. Complain to the manager at European Wholesalers, requesting three replacements.

1. Complain by telephone.
2. Complain in a letter.

Exercise 12.13

You are the supervisor of the employee in Exercise 7.11 (page 96). Write a letter of complaint to Morgantown Auto Repair, claiming the cost of additional repair work that had to be carried out in Brandon because the work done in Morgantown was faulty. You are writing this letter because the employee was traveling on company business when the incident occurred. Assume that you attach copies of both work orders to your letter.

V

COMMUNICATING WHEN YOU GO INTO BUSINESS FOR YOURSELF

13

Communicating with Customers and Other Companies

Every day, people go into business for themselves. They seldom have previous management experience, more often being skilled tradesmen who would rather work for themselves than for someone else. Their venture into business ownership gives them the independence they want, but also plenty of headaches. Each has to be laborer, manager, salesman, accountant, purchasing agent, clerk, and, if the business is large enough, employer. He must also be an efficient organizer, so that his business makes enough money to justify his "going it alone."

Going full time into business for oneself can be an adventure—a challenge to build up a thriving concern. Many who do so trip and stumble along the way, learning from their mistakes all that managing a business entails. Caution causes others to build their businesses slowly, using weekends and evenings to do private work while they continue to be fully employed during the day. For both, sound interpersonal relations are important: they may be extremely capable workers, but as small-business owners they must be equally efficient communicators. For without good relations with customers and suppliers, a business will founder.

Much of the communicating done by the owner of a small business is the same as that done by employees and supervisors in a large business. There still are customers to deal with, suppliers to order material and parts from, and sometimes employees to give instructions to. But there is no management to pass information on to, because you, as owner of the business, are management.

COMMUNICATING WITH YOUR CUSTOMERS

To own even a very small business means communicating with customers on at least some of the following occasions:

* When you want to inform them of the products or services you sell
* When you need to quote a price for a job
* When you need to bill them for goods you have delivered or work you have done
* When something unpredictable happens or something goes wrong

Describing Your Products and Services

No business can exist unless potential customers are told that the business is there and what products or services it sells. A large well-established business keeps its name before customers' eyes through expensive advertising. A small well-established business depends partly on advertising but largely on reputation and word-of-mouth recommendation. A small but newly established business has yet to carve a name in the community, and has little if any cash available for advertising. It depends heavily on word-of-mouth recommendation, particularly if it sells a specialized service, and to some extent on small advertisements placed in the classified columns of local newspapers.

A new business should have a short, interesting description of itself and its products or services that its owner can give to potential customers. The description does not have to be an expensive production. Indeed, it is better if it is not, otherwise it may convey the impression that the company's products are expensive. A single $8\frac{1}{2} \times 11$ in. sheet, neatly printed in one color, should suffice. The words it contains should clearly and interestingly inform the reader what the company sells.

Harry King is a carpenter who, after working for a general contractor for eleven years, has decided to go into business for himself. He is a very capable person whose skills are not limited to carpentry, so he is able to do a fairly wide range of work. Harry already has a small number of customers who have hired him occasionally over the years to build recreation rooms, remodel kitchens, and do general repairs in his spare time. Among them is Chuck Wainwright, who retired at age 55 by selling a small engineering consulting business he had built up. It is to Chuck that Harry turns when he needs advice about running his own business.

When Harry tells Chuck he is planning to quit his job and go full time into jobbing carpentry, Chuck suggests that Harry print a leaflet describing exactly what kind of work he does, which he can mail to both existing and potential customers. Harry cautiously agrees "it's a good idea," but doubts whether he can do the writing.

"All right," says Chuck, "you go away and make a list of all the things you do now for people, and also things you don't do yet but would do if someone asked you. Then bring it back to me."

Three days later Harry returns with his list, which is shown in Fig. 5–1.

Chuck explains that they will build up Harry's description of services from this list, using the information blocks in Fig. 5–2, which are made up of:

1. A **Summary Statement** which announces Harry's business and explains very briefly the kind of work he does.
2. A **Service-Products** block that describes the full range of work that Harry can do. It can be written either as paragraphs (which would suit a consulting business or a description of a single product) or as a series of short points. Where several services are offered, a list is better.
3. An **Invitation** block which contains Harry's address and telephone number, plus any other information a customer might be interested in, such as evidence of Harry's credentials (where he worked before, what certificates he has earned or papers he carries, and possibly his affiliation with trade associations).

Chuck uses Harry's list to build up block 2. He questions Harry to find out what jobs he did particularly well or liked especially, and lists these as his "specialties." The remainder he groups under a separate heading to show that Harry has a broad capability. Then, with Harry's help, he writes blocks 1 and 3. The completed description is taken to a jobbing printer, who for $35 prints 2000 copies of the leaflet shown at Fig. 5–3.

Quoting a Price for a Job

Estimating the cost of doing a job for a customer means calculating the cost of labor, overhead (operating expenses), materials, and parts; including a small contingency for error; adding on your profit; and possibly adding in sales tax. But the way you present this final price to the customer is equally important. If it is not exactly clear what your quotation

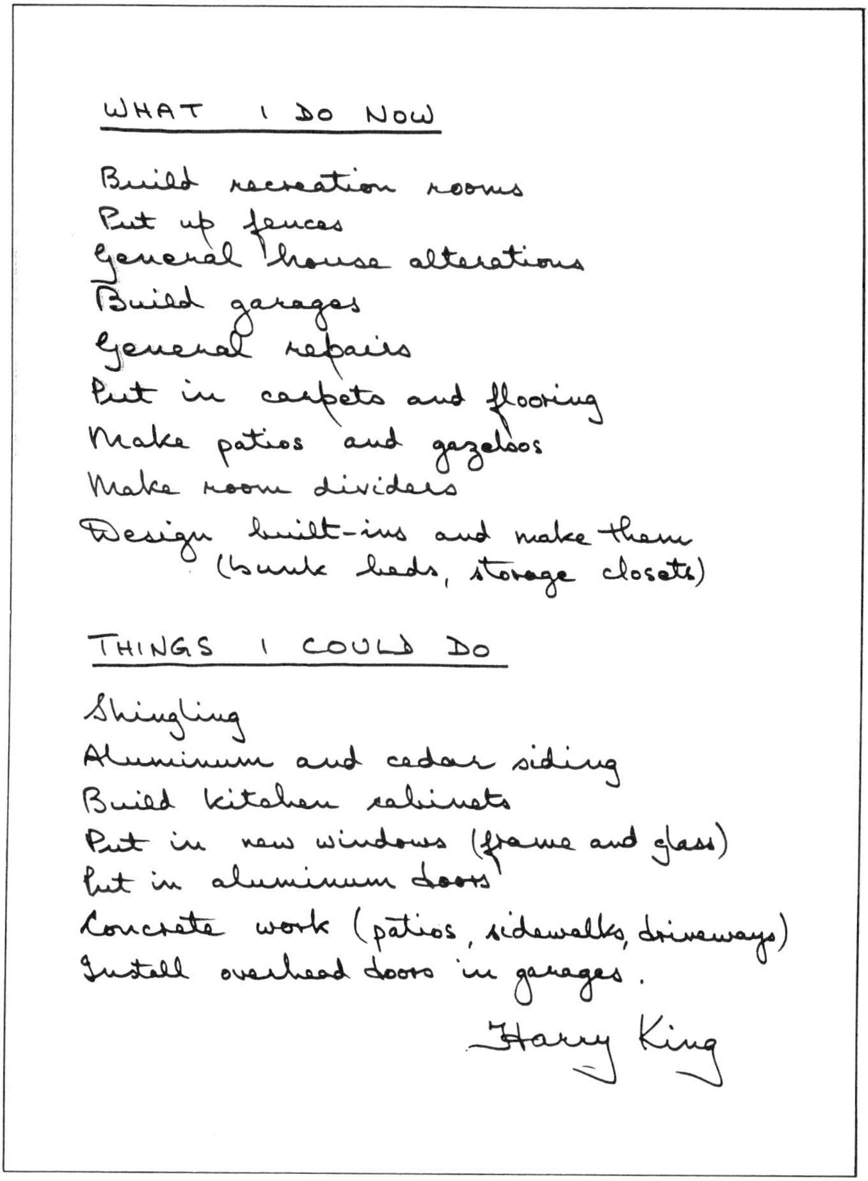

WHAT I DO NOW

Build recreation rooms
Put up fences
General house alterations
Build garages
General repairs
Put in carpets and flooring
Make patios and gazeboos
Make room dividers
Design built-ins and make them
    (bunk beds, storage closets)

THINGS I COULD DO

Shingling
Aluminum and cedar siding
Build kitchen cabinets
Put in new windows (frame and glass)
Put in aluminum doors
Concrete work (patios, sidewalks, driveways)
Install overhead doors in garages.

                              Harry King

Fig. 5–1. Harry King's list of work he can do.

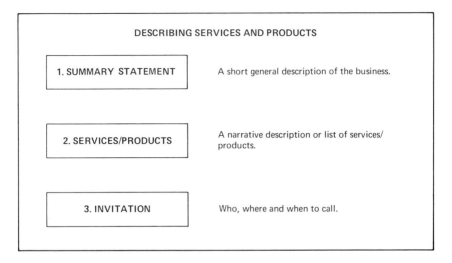

Fig. 5–2. Information blocks for describing a business.

covers, you may do the job only to find that the customer expected something different, or more work than you intended. The argument that then ensues can result in hard feelings, and probably expense to you. You may lose a valued customer, who also may influence potential customers not to deal with you.

A vacationing student knocked on my door early last summer, and asked if I wanted some painting done. His timing was excellent. I hate painting, and both my garage and fence were dropping curls of flaky white paint into the flowerbeds.

We agreed on a price of $85, and he did a good job. But when I handed him his $85, he hesitantly mentioned that he had said $95, not $85. Well, we talked about it. And then we settled on $90. But neither of us was really happy about it. I'm sure he felt, just as I did, that he had been done out of five bucks. And the pity is, it was an honest misunderstanding.

No businessman can afford a misunderstanding like this—it is bad for customer relations. What my painter friend should have done was to write the price on a small sheet of paper (or better still two sheets—so we could each have one), and include with it a brief statement describing the job.

Before carpenter Harry King decided to go into business for himself, he did odd carpentry work in his spare time. On one of his first jobs he was called in by Chuck Wainwright, who asked him to quote on a kitchen rebuilding project. Chuck and his wife showed Harry what they wanted done, and Chuck also gave him a sketch of a new cupboard Harry would

Call On

HARRY KING

For Expert

RESIDENTIAL CARPENTRY SERVICE

Harry King offers a specialty construction, alteration and repair service for the homeowners of Reece, Minn.

- Exterior and interior house repairs and alterations.
- Recreation rooms, garages, room dividers, storage cupboards, kitchen cabinets, and built-ins.
- All types of flooring installations (hardwood, carpet, tile, cushionfloor)
- Shingling; aluminum and cedar siding
- Aluminum doors and windows, overhead garage doors
- Gazebos, sheds, fences
- Concrete work (driveways, sidewalks, patios, steps)

All work fully guaranteed

Estimates free **No obligation**

HARRY KING

(Carpenter)

550 Wellington St.
Reece, Minn.
Tel. 786-2112

(Member, Reece Junior Chamber of Commerce)

Fig. 5–3. Harry King's printed description of services.

have to build. Harry then went away to do his calculations, and later wrote this note for Chuck:

Mr. Wainwright —

Cost of refinishing your kitchen to your requirements . . . . $647.50.

H. King

20 March 19__

Harry thought he had protected himself by submitting his price like this. But what he had really done was leave himself wide open for a future hassle. He had not said what he meant by "refinishing," or outlined what Chuck Wainwright's "requirements" were (Chuck could easily change them); he had not made it clear whether he or Chuck would be supplying the materials for the job (a counter top, sink unit, floor covering, paint, and wallpaper were needed); and he had not explained whether federal or state taxes were included in the price.

If Harry *assumed* that Chuck would be supplying all the materials, and Chuck *assumed* that Harry would be supplying everything but the paint and wallpaper (thinking that Harry understood he was to supply the counter top, sink, and floor covering), Harry would lose all his profit on the job, and maybe more.

Fortunately for Harry, Chuck telephoned him and suggested that he more accurately describe what his price covered. He even gave him a few pointers on how to write a quotation. Briefly, this is what he told Harry to do:

To write a quotation, divide your letter into three compartments, or information blocks. [*Illustrated in Fig. 5-4*] Use them for any size job. For a simple quotation, such as repairs to a concrete sidewalk, everything can be said in one paragraph, or maybe two. For a slightly larger job, like the one you are quoting for me, three paragraphs are better. And for the really big jobs, such as modifications to a plant wiring system, each compartment becomes a section heading with many paragraphs in each section.

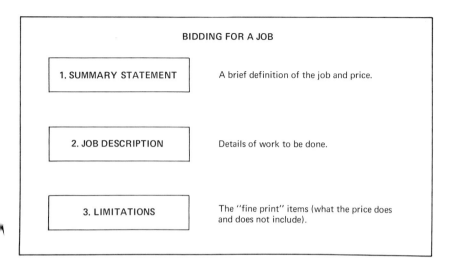

Fig. 5–4. Information blocks for a price quotation.

So Harry went away and carefully composed a longer letter, which is shown in Fig. 5–5.

Chuck noticed right away that Harry's letter was not well-written. It was unimpressive because it did not sound businesslike. The last sentence in paragraph 2 was vague (it did not say who was to supply materials and dispose of rubbish), and in the final sentence Harry sounded almost defeatist—as though he did not even hope to receive a reply.

But Chuck also realized it was unlikely that anyone had ever shown Harry how to write a proper quotation. By now he knew Harry and felt reasonably sure his workmanship would be good, so he told him to go ahead with the job. At the same time he decided to take Harry aside and show him how to write a more businesslike quotation.

Chuck pointed out to Harry that he might have discarded Harry's quotation if he had also asked other carpenters to bid on the kitchen renovation job. If their prices had been close, but someone else's letter had been better written and more businesslike, he probably would have chosen that carpenter *because the quality of his letter would seem to indicate he could do a better-quality job.* He agreed with Harry that this was an unfair way to select a carpenter, but to many people in a similar situation it might be the only evidence they have of how a contractor does business.

So while Harry cut and sawed and glued and painted in Mrs. Wain-

3 May 19___

Dear Mr. Wainwright –

Here is the price for the job you asked me about: $647.50.

Price quoted is for counter and cupboards built like you described, and putting in the Corlon floor your wife wants, all labor on carpentry, painting and plumbing. Materials to be supplied and rubbish to be disposed of.

The lowest price I can do all this for is $647.50, as I said before. Includes tax. Cupboard built to your drawing.

Hoping you will let me know of your decision.

Yours truly

Harry King

Fig. 5–5. Harry King's second attempt at writing a quotation.

wright's kitchen, Chuck jotted down some notes to explain more clearly to Harry how a quotation should be written. He started by describing what information should go into each of the information blocks he had suggested that Harry should use:

1. **Summary Statement.** Normally this is no more than a brief statement that generally describes the job, followed by the total price for doing the work:

   We can install indoor-outdoor carpet throughout the first floor of the Raulston Building for $2,420 (tax not included).

2. **Job Description.** The brief details in the Summary Statement need to be followed by a clear description of what the quotation covers, including accurate definitions of materials that will be used. It is not enough, for example, to refer to materials as being "high-grade" or "top-quality"; the make, color, style, model number, etc., should be quoted. Only in this way can both the person giving the quotation and the buyer be protected from creating or gaining a false impression of the quality of materials that will be used. In the carpet installation project, the Job Description paragraph might read like this:

   The carpeting will be Picadilly style 2746, rubber-backed, pattern Pansy in blue and green. It will be installed from the foot of the east entrance door to all walls of the foyer, in all four business offices, and inside both elevators.

   If several things are to be done, or there are variations in the types of materials that will be used for different parts of the job, it is probably better to use a main paragraph and several subparagraphs:

   The carpeting will be Picadilly style 2746, rubber-backed, installed as follows:
   a. In the foyer, from the foot of the east entrance door to all four walls, and inside both elevators, pattern Pansy in blue and green.
   b. In the offices of Mexicana Distributors, Inc., pattern Rochester in mauve and yellow.
   c. In the offices of Walston Oil Company, solid pattern No. 147 (sea blue).
   d. In the vacant offices in the northwest section of the floor, pattern Pansy in rose and amber.
   e. In the offices of Montrose Trust, pattern Hawthorne in black and ivory.

3. **Limitations.** The final paragraph or section of a quotation should cover small items which, if not mentioned, might result in a misunderstanding. Typical items might be:

   * Who is to supply parts and materials.

* Whose responsibility it is to prepare the area before work starts (for example, if heavy equipment has to be moved).
* When the work can be done, possibly including the amount of lead time (notice) required, how long the job will take, and any special working times such as evenings and weekends.
* The extent that garbage, old materials, and construction debris will be cleaned up and removed from the site. (A plumber installing a new hot water tank, for instance, does not have to cart away or even move the old tank out of the house if he has not said that he will do so.)

The Limitations paragraph for the carpet installation job might be like this:

> The work will be done on five successive evenings, April 10 to 14, between 5 P.M. and midnight. We will supply the new carpet and all materials, remove and dispose of the existing (worn) carpet, and clean up after each evening's work. But we would require you to arrange for individual offices to be opened, and for the building to be locked up at midnight.

By the time Harry had finished renovating the Wainwright's kitchen to Mrs. Wainwright's satisfaction, Chuck had written a sample quotation for the job, which he gave to Harry as a model for future quotations he would write. It is included here in Fig. 5–6, just as Chuck wrote it.

Billing the Customer after the Job is Done

For a small-business owner, a job is not complete when the work is finished. Some paperwork has yet to be done if he is to be paid. This paperwork usually comprises two forms:

1. An **Invoice,** which bills the customer for the service or goods as soon as the work has been done or the goods have been delivered.

2. A **Statement of Account** (commonly called a statement), which is sent monthly to customers who, by the end of the month, have not yet paid all of the amount they owe.

An invoice can be prepared on either plain paper or a prepared form. Plain paper is the simplest to use where a service has been provided. It should contain:

1. Your (or your company's) name and address
2. The date
3. The name and address of the person or company buying the service

```
                         H. King (Carpenter)
                         550 Wellington Street
                         Reece, Minnesota 55747


                         8 May 19__



Mr. C. Wainwright
271 Blaydon Street
Reece, Minn. 55747

Dear Mr. Wainwright:

    My price for refinishing your kitchen is $647.50, taxes in-
cluded.

    This estimate is based on your verbal instructions and a
sketch.  It covers:

    1.  Removing the existing counter top and sink, and install-
        ing a new molded arborite top (design A274) and 24" x 22"
        single-basin stainless steel sink.

    2.  Building and installing storage cupboards over the stove
        and refrigerator, dimensioned according to your sketch.

    3.  Installing Corlon flooring, pattern 2786.

    4.  Painting all cupboards, the ceiling, and three walls,
        and hanging paper on the fourth (south) wall.

    The price I have quoted includes all materials (except paint
and wallpaper), cost of plumbing alterations, removal of old sink
and counter top to your garbage area, and general clean up.  I can
start the work any time after 12 May, providing you give me one
week's notice.

                         Yours sincerely


                         H. King
                         H. King
```

Fig. 5–6. Chuck Wainwright's revision of Harry King's quotation.

4. A very brief description of the service provided, and the date(s) on which the work was done
5. A reference to the original quotation (if there was one)
6. The full price

Harry King, for example, billed Chuck Wainwright, as shown in Fig. 5–7, for the kitchen renovation work described on page 209. If no quotation had been prepared, or Harry had simply quoted labor at $7.50 per hour with parts and materials extra, then a more detailed invoice would have had to be written. This is shown in Fig. 5–8.

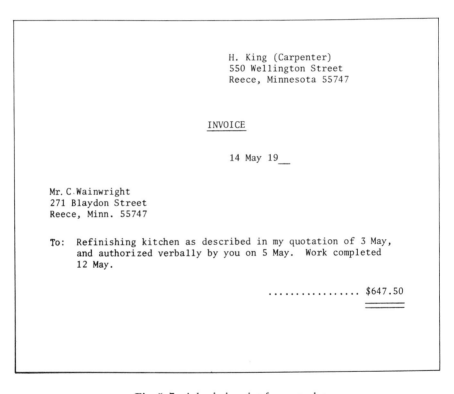

Fig. 5–7. A basic invoice for a service.

Most established businesses use an invoice form of their own design with the company's name printed on it. But new or very small businesses need not go to this expense. They can buy pads of preprinted invoice forms in duplicate or triplicate sets from a stationer, and then rubber-stamp the company's name, or their own name, on them.

Forms generally have spaces in which to insert:

1. Your (or your company's) name and address
2. Name and address of the person or company buying goods or services from you
3. Name and address of the person to whom goods have been shipped or for whom work has been done
4. Method of shipment of goods (i.e. rail, bus, air express, freight) or the route used
5. Current date

```
                              H. King (Carpenter)
                              550 Wellington Street
                              Reece, Minnesota 55747


                        INVOICE


                        14 May 19__


Mr. C. Wainwright
271 Blaydon St
Reece, Minn. 55747


To:  Refinishing Kitchen as authorized verbally by you on 5 May:

        Labor:      48 hrs. @ $7.50/hr.                    $360.00

        Materials:  Arborite, Design A274 (see receipt)      49.10
                    Stainless Steel sink, 24" x 22"          32.40
                    Lumber, screws & glue (see receipt)      53.90
                    Corlon flooring, pattern 2786,
                       18 sq. yd. @ $5.95/yd               107.10

        Sub-contract - Plumbing (see receipt)               45.00
                                                         ─────────
                                                          $647.50
                                                         ═════════

Job Completed 12 May
```

Fig. 5–8. A detailed invoice prepared on plain paper.

6. Customer's purchase order number, or reference to his letter of authorization (if either has been used)
7. Terms under which the goods have been sold (e.g., net 30 days)
8. Point to which you prepay shipping delivery costs (this is known as the FOB point and may be your city, the customer's city or plant, or any point in between.)
9. Details of the items and services supplied, in four columns:
   a. Quantity of each item delivered
   b. Description of item or service
   c. Price of a single item or group of items, plus the unit by which it is being measured (i.e., each, ounces, dozen, etc.)
   d. Total price for each item or service

A completed invoice, referring both to a service and to goods supplied, is shown at Fig. 5–9. The form here is an off-the-shelf type you can purchase in pads from a stationer.

Although a statement can be prepared on a special form, the new business owner can just as easily use his normal correspondence paper and cut off the bottom of the sheet. The statement contains the word "Statement" across the top, the date, the name and address of the customer, and the amount the customer still has to pay. A statement is simply a reminder to a customer that he has not paid his account. One prepared by Harry King for the work he did for Chuck Wainwright is at Fig. 5–10. Harry would continue sending out monthly statements like this until Chuck fully paid him.

Dealing with Customers' Inquiries and Complaints

As the owner of a small business you will have to deal with customers' problems, inquiries, and complaints just as you would if you were working for a large business. The only difference is that as a small-business owner all the problem situations come your way and have to be dealt with by you. The techniques, however, are the same as those discussed in Chapter 12, pages 170 to 180.

COMMUNICATING WITH OTHER BUSINESSES

The communicating that you as a small-business owner do with other firms and those who work for you is essentially the same as the communicating done by a supervisor in a large company. The only really noticeable difference is that you cannot hand over sticky problems to someone higher up the management tree. To some people this is a matter of concern: they feel uncomfortable without that back-up. To others it is a freedom to be enjoyed, because they are no longer accountable to anyone for their decisions and actions.

How you go about inquiring, ordering, hastening delivery, and

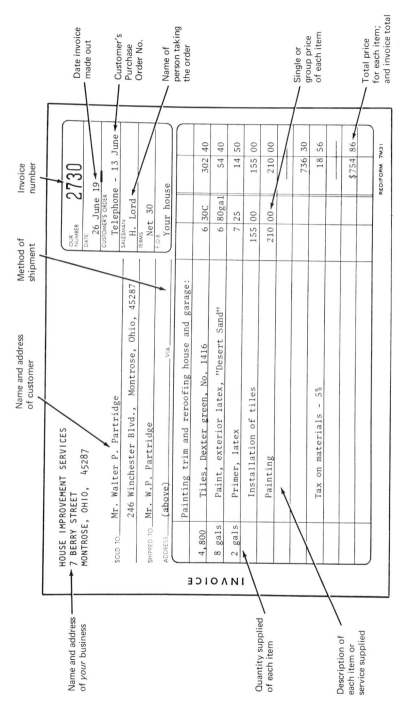

Fig. 5-9. An invoice for services and goods typed onto a form. (Form illustration by permission of Moore Business Forms.)

Name and address of *your* business

Name and address of customer

Method of shipment

Invoice number

Date invoice made out

Customer's Purchase Order No.

Name of person taking the order

Single or group price of each item

Total price for each item; and invoice total

Quantity supplied of each item

Description of each item or service supplied

HOUSE IMPROVEMENT SERVICES
7 BERRY STREET
MONTROSE, OHIO, 45287

SOLD TO Mr. Walter P. Partridge

246 Winchester Blvd., Montrose, Ohio, 45287

SHIPPED TO Mr. W.P. Partridge

ADDRESS (above)   VIA

INVOICE

OUR NUMBER **2730**

DATE 26 June 19

CUSTOMER'S ORDER Telephone - 13 June

SALESMAN H. Lord

TERMS Net 30

F.O.B. Your house

	Painting trim and reroofing house and garage:			
4,800	Tiles, Dexter green, No. 1416	6	30C	302 40
8 gals	Paint, exterior latex, "Desert Sand"	6	80gal	54 40
2 gals	Primer, latex	7	25	14 50
	Installation of tiles	155	00	155 00
	Painting	210	00	210 00
				736 30
	Tax on materials - 5%			18 56
				$754 86

REDIFORM 7M31

213

```
                                   H. King (Carpenter)
                                   550 Wellington Street
                                   Reece, Minnesota  55747


                        STATEMENT


                                   31 May 19__



  Mr. C. Wainright
  271 Blaydon St.
  Reece, Minn.  55747



  To account rendered....................................$647.50
```

Fig. 5–10. A monthly statement of account.

complaining is exactly the same as described in Chapter 12 on pages 182
to 192. But in some cases your ordering of supplies will be simplified because, rather than raise a purchase order for materials, you can drive
down to the wholesaler or building materials supplier and buy what you
need. If the materials are in turn to be billed to one of your customers,
you should obtain a written invoice that describes the items rather than
a cash register receipt. This can prevent problems if a customer later
disagrees with the cost of materials. (Because a cash register receipt does
not describe what was purchased, it can be difficult to prove that the
items you bought were only for that customer.) Each customer's materials
should be entered on a separate invoice.

Telephone orders are acceptable for purchases of off-the-shelf items
from local suppliers, because it is simple to correct an error if the wrong
goods are supplied. But if you are ordering items to be cut, built,
assembled, or manufactured, or if you are ordering off-the-shelf items from
an out-of-town supplier, you should always follow up a telephone order
with written confirmation. The confirmation can be either a letter order
or a printed purchase order like those shown on pages 185 and 187.

THE PAPERWORK NEEDED FOR COMMUNICATING

Some of the forms and materials you will need to communicate with customers and suppliers if you go into business for yourself are illustrated in Fig. 5–11. This is a basic list that offers reasonable economy, yet gives your operations a businesslike appearance. The rubber stamp is used to imprint your name and address on the kraft (brown) envelopes, purchase orders, and invoices.

Even greater economy can be achieved by buying plain white correspondence envelopes and rubber-stamping your name and address on them. Alternatively, better appearance at greater cost could be gained by printing your own purchase orders and invoices.

All correspondence and quotations should be typed (and, if possible, so should invoices, statements, and purchase orders). This means you will need a typewriter, or the services of someone living nearby who does typing at home.

The typing should look businesslike so that customers will not gain the impression that your business is sloppily run. Always remember that the impression conveyed by the appearance of your correspondence can go a long way toward convincing a hesitant customer that you do good work.

EXERCISES

NOTE: 1. *These exercises concern communications that evolve from setting up and running four small businesses.*

       2. *Where an exercise calls for a spoken communication, your instructor will tell you who is playing the role of the "receiver."*

Running a Home Maintenance Service

Exercise 13.1

Assume there is a 3½-month break in the middle of your course. You need to have a job for the summer, but would prefer to be self-employed than employed by someone else. So you and Bev Carmichael (another student) decide to set up a "home service" business: You will do any work that home-owners in the city need done, from painting fences and planting flowerbeds to cleaning basements and washing out garbage cans.

Paperwork Needed Initially by the
Small-Business Owner

Name and Description   *How to Obtain*

BUSINESS LETTERHEADS

Preprinted sheets with   From a jobbing printer.
your (or your company's)   An initial purchase of
name, address, telephone   1000 sheets will go a long
number, and possibly the   way. Use standard paper
nature of your business   so you can easily match
printed at the top. Stan-   envelopes to it.
dard size is 8½ × 11 in.
Second-page sheets can be
unprinted or contain just
your or company's name
at top left; they must be
same paper as first-page
sheet.

ENVELOPES

For normal correspon-   From the same jobbing
dence, 9 × 4 in. white,   printer. Paper should
preprinted at top left with   match stationery. An ini-
your (or your company's)   tial purchase of 500 should
name and address.   suffice.

For mailing larger mate-   From any stationery sup-
rials, kraft (brown) envel-   plier. Small quantities of
opes of varying sizes.   standard sizes should do
                                initially.

VISITING CARDS

Contain your name, name   From any printer. About
of your business, address,   200 should be sufficient.
and telephone number.   Suggest one-color simple
                                printing for economy.

PURCHASE ORDERS

Preprinted in pads, in   Most stationers stock them.
duplicate or triplicate sets.

INVOICES

Preprinted in pads, in   Most stationers stock them.
duplicate or triplicate sets.

RUBBER STAMP AND INK PAD

Stamp contains your (or   Order from stationery sup-
your company's) name and   plier.
address.

Fig. 5–11. Basic paperwork needed for communicating with
customers and suppliers.

So that homeowners will know about your service, you decide to print an advertising leaflet and distribute it as widely as possible. But to make the leaflet you must first decide what kind of work you will do and services you will offer.

1. Hold a think-tank session with Bev Carmichael and together draw up a list of
   a. Work you are most able to do.
   b. Work you would be willing to do, or services you could also provide.
2. Using the list as a source of information, devise your advertising leaflet. Use your own names, addresses, and telephone numbers, but give your "enterprise" a name.

Exercise 13.2

You and Bev Carmichael have decided to go into business for yourselves as described in the previous exercise. Assume that

1. Bev has an import compact truck you can use to get around.
2. Your work, initially at least, will comprise mostly lawncutting and trimming, garden-digging, hedge-trimming, fence-painting, rain-gutter-clearing, and general cleanup.
3. You have about $350 cash between you for buying equipment, but could borrow up to $500 more from the bank.

For this exercise:

a. Draw up a list of equipment and material you will need.
b. Obtain comparative prices, if possible from three separate suppliers.
c. Write a letter-form purchase order for the items you need. Request delivery in one week.

Exercise 13.3

It is ten days later. Your supplier has delivered all the equipment you ordered except for the lawnmower(s). You have telephoned twice, and each time have been assured the lawnmower(s) "will be right out."

You decide to drive down to the supplier, inquire what is going on, and ask for immediate delivery (you will pick up the lawnmower(s) right now). When you arrive there, you ask for the sales manager. Tell him what you want.

Exercise 13.4

The sales manager in Exercise 13.3 apologizes, but says there are no lawnmowers in stock. His supplier has shipped a whole truckload to him and "they'll be here any day now."

You and Bev look around some more, then find that Argus Sales has several lawnmowers in stock of the kind you want, but at a slightly higher price.

Write a letter to the first company canceling the part of your order referring to lawnmower(s). Use the company's failure to meet the delivery requirements stated in your purchase order as a reason for taking this action.

Exercise 13.5

You and Bev Carmichael are offering the services described in Exercise 13.1 to local householders.

A phone call from Mrs. Fiona Walsh takes you to her home at 226 Newberry Street. She explains she is a widow living alone and there are a whole lot of things she would like done. She shows you:

1. A coal storage area in the basement, no longer used because she now has a gas-fired furnace. She wants the coal-hole thoroughly scrubbed out so she can use it for storage. It has about 200 lb. of coal in it, which will have to be carried to the garbage disposal area.
2. Two flowerbeds at the back of the house filled with rotting apples which were not plucked from four trees last fall. They need to be cleaned out to remove the sour smell.
3. Her television antenna, which is perched at a crazy angle on a 20-ft. pole atop the bungalow's roof. It needs to be straightened.
4. Stacks and stacks of newspapers and magazines in the basement. She wants them thrown out.
5. A screened porch in which the wire mesh was long ago punched full of holes. She would like it repaired so she can sit on the porch this summer.

"Well," she says. "That should do for a start. Give me a chance to see what kind of a job you do. What would you charge me for doing those five things?"

You tell her you'll have to work out a price and bring it back tomorrow.

"Better itemize it," she comments. "Then maybe I can choose what I want done—in case it costs too much."

You and Bev kick around prices, and finally decide on $25 for job 1, $15 for job 2, $15 for job 4, and $40 for job 5. All these prices are for labor only. You'll need strong garbage bags for job 2 ($3) and screen wire for job 5 ($28). You have neither the equipment nor know-how to tackle job 3.

Prepare a price quotation for Mrs. Walsh.

Exercise 13.6

Two days after distributing your advertising leaflet (see Exercise 13.1), you and Bev are called by Mr. Hugh Beamish to see him at his ten-room residence at 308 Guernsey Drive.

"All right, you two," he says. "I've got a proposition for you. If you can give me a good price, I'll give you a contract for the summer to do the outside maintenance around here. Previous years I've used a contracting service —but they're pricing themselves right out of the picture."

Mr. Beamish walks around the fairly large premises with you. He says he has a weak heart, so can't do anything strenuous. So he would want you to:

1. Turn over the earth in the flowerbeds almost right away, then keep it hoed and raked at regular intervals.
2. Plant about ten dozen annuals (small plants he will purchase from a grower).
3. Keep the flowerbeds clear of weeds.
4. Cut the grass at regular intervals and trim the lawn edges.
5. Apply weed killer to the grass. (He thinks twice during the season should be sufficient.)
6. Trim evergreen bushes that grow around the front door, and a hedge between him and his neighbor on the south side of the property.

As well as doing regular garden maintenance like this, he would like you to keep the interior of his garage clean and tidy, clear leaves and debris from the gutters of the house and garage, and generally keep the property clean (e.g., pick up bits of paper and leaves that blow onto it).

You ask him how frequently he would want all these things done. He replies that the contractor came in every Tuesday morning to do garden maintenance.

"The other jobs—well, you work out when they should be done," he adds. "But don't be unreasonable like the contractor. He started pushing his power mower around here at 8 a.m.—woke me up every Tuesday!"

He suggests you work out the cost, then let him have a proposal based on a regular price per month. That way, both you and he will know where you stand. He would like it in two days so you can start work at the beginning of the next month.

Write a letter-form proposal to Mr. Beamish. Assume that the cost of weed killer for item 5 is not included in your price.

Exercise 13.7

Mr. Beamish accepts your proposal in Exercise 13.6. Prepare the invoice you will send him at the end of the first month.

Exercise 13.8

After three months the contract period in Exercise 13.6 is nearly over. Mr. Beamish has seemed pleased with the service you have given him, and not too happy about having to go back to using the previous contractor.

You and Bev discuss continuing your service in a limited way right through the year as a means for gaining additional income when you go back to school in the fall.

Write a proposal to Mr. Beamish suggesting you continue garden maintenance for the next twelve months, possibly changing from grass-cutting to snow-clearing as the seasons change. Describe what you propose to do and offer him a monthly price (which may vary according to the season).

Running a Typing-Duplicating Service

Exercise 13.9

Assume you are considering opening a typing and duplicating service in a large office block. It would be a small business operated initially only by yourself, with the possibility of bringing in a second person if the volume of business is sufficient to warrant it. (For this exercise you must also assume you know how to type, or will work with someone who can type; you need not know how to operate duplicating equipment, because this can be learned quickly.) But before going any further you want to find out three things:

1. The availability of a small office of about 1800 sq. ft. in a business building. Ideally, it should be on the main floor or in the lower half of the building, and visible from the elevator doors. You need to know the rental per month.
2. The type and cost of equipment you will need.
3. Whether you should own or rent the equipment.

Make the following inquiries:

a. Write to Kingston and Walsh, Inc., owners of three office buildings in the major business area, and inquire whether they have any suitable vacancies or shortly will have offices available. Their address is 313 Main Street. The buildings are known as Polo Towers, Regency Building, and Connaught Complex. Tell them you want a one-year lease, with an option to extend the lease two more years.
b. Telephone Davy Office Equipment Suppliers and ask for literature and prices on electric typewriters with a 16-inch typing line and elite type (that is, a machine that can type on paper 16 inches wide, and type 12 letters to the inch).
c. Visit Maritime Leaseholds and ask what the leasing terms will be for:
   A Vancourt Model 370 typewriter priced at $610.
   A Dandy Duplicator priced at $360.
   You want to know the length of the lease, cost per month, and any special provisions in their lease agreement.

Exercise 13.10

You are going into the business you were considering in Exercise 13.9. Write a purchase order for the following items (you are buying all the equipment, not leasing it):

1. A Vancourt Model 370 typewriter. It must have an 18-inch carriage with a 16-inch typing line. You want it to have a carbon-type ribbon. Type size must be elite and the type face you want is known as "Carillon." The machine's price is $610.
2. A dozen carbon typewriter ribbons, Vancourt type 717, at $1.65 each.
3. Typing paper—3000 sheets of 16-lb. bond at $4.90 per 1000 sheets. Paper size should be 8½ × 11 in. You also need 1000 sheets 8½ × 14 in. ($5.65 per 1000) and 500 sheets 10 × 17 in. ($1.10 per 100 sheets).
4. Carbon paper—one box of 8½ × 11 in. Vancourt 270 black at $5.05, and one box of 8½ × 14 in. Vancourt 275 black at $7.10.
5. Two bottles of Vancourt white correction fluid at $1.35 per bottle.
6. Two types of envelopes: 9 × 4 in. white wove, 500 to a box, at $10.25 per box; and 200 kraft envelopes, 9 × 12 in., at $2.10 per 100. The white envelopes should be similar in appearance to the typing paper.

Order these items from Davy Office Equipment Suppliers, 244 Wilson Street. Request delivery in one week and quote terms as "net 30." Assume tax has not been included in the above prices.

Give your typing-duplicating service a name and ask for delivery to be made to room 304 Connaught Complex, 400 Main Street. Prepare the order either as a letter or on a preprinted purchase order form (your instructor will tell you which is required).

Exercise 13.11

You bring in two types of duplicating equipment for your typing-copying business (see Exercise 13.9): an offset printing machine for large orders (which you buy) and an office copier for small copying orders (which you rent).

The copier is a Vancourt Model 770, and it has consistently given you trouble. It has been plagued with "paper jams" that twist, turn, and tear the printed copies instead of delivering them. In the two months you have been in operation, you have called in the serviceman eleven times (from Davy Office Equipment Suppliers, 244 Wilson Street).

You are annoyed not only because the machine keeps breaking down but also because the response to your calls for service often is very slow (sometimes it is two days before the serviceman arrives). These continual breakdowns are extremely bad for your business because they are causing you to fail to meet delivery times you promise your customers.

You have been seriously considering changing to a different make of copier supplied by another company. Although you would prefer the Vancourt 770 because its speed and price are right, a less-suitable machine that works would be a better deal than the one you now have.

Write to Davy Office Equipment Suppliers to complain about their machine and the poor service you have had. Tell them you will give them a week to correct the problem.

Exercise 13.12

After you have done several cash typing and printing jobs for Mansask Insurance Corporation, the company's office manager drops in to see you. His name is Fred J. Dalziell, and his office is in room 1216 of the Connaught Complex, 400 Main Street. (Your business is in room 304 of the same building.)

Mr. Dalziell tells you he is happy with the quality of work you do, and plans to use your service more often. But he finds a cash basis inconvenient and so asks you to consider billing him monthly. You agree, and two days later he sends you a purchase order confirming the arrangement. Work is to be charged from the beginning of next month.

At the end of one month you look back at the list of work you did for Mansask Insurance Corporation, which comprises:

1. Typing a 20-page document "Changes in Fire Insurance Coverage." The typing charge was $22.50. You made six copies (charge: $12). Date done: the 3rd.
2. On the 8th you printed 2000 copies of a record card, 5 × 8 in. Charge: $31.
3. On the 10th you typed a six-page Agreement Document (cost $7.50), and then on the 17th printed 300 copies, which you asembled and stapled into sets. Charge for printing and assembly: $47.
4. From the 12th to the 19th you typed a 54-page Table of Insurance Rates (hundreds of columns of figures) on large paper. The charge for typing this tedious job was $108.
5. From the 26th to 28th you photographed the Tables of Insurance Rates, then printed, collated, and stapled 165 sets. The charge: $190.

Prepare an invoice for this month's work, referring to Mansask's purchase order No. M3047 and quoting terms as "net 30 days." The invoice may be written either on your company's letterhead or on a preprinted form (your instructor will tell you which is required).

Exercise 13.13

During the following month Mr. Dalziell of Mansask Insurance Corporation (see Exercise 13.12) gives you a particularly heavy workload, much of it printing of forms. At the same time you also receive a lot of work from other companies in the building. Because you have taken in more work than you can handle, you telephone around until you find a jobbing printer who can do some for you at a competitive price. His name is Dave Garland, and his shop is at 22 Kerrymoor Street.

One of the jobs you send him is a card that has to be printed "tumble" (that is, with the information on the back printed upside down). When he sent the job down, Mr. Dalziell telephoned to warn you this *must* be done, and you carefully repeated the instructions to Garland. The cost of this particular printing job is $56.50.

A week after the job has been delivered, Mr. Dalziell appears in your office, waving one of the cards about and complaining bitterly that he'd asked you to print it tumble, and now they needed to use the cards right away and all of them are the wrong way up.

1. Respond to his complaint.
2. Complain to Dave Garland, who did the printing for you.
3. Write a letter to Garland, asking for a refund of the $56.50 you have already paid him (he demanded cash and would not hand over the printed work until he had it).

Tuning Small Automobile Engines

Exercise 13.14

Because you are handy at repairing and tuning up small automobile engines (particularly subcompact imports from Europe), you have built up a small but profitable sideline business. Most of the work is done in the evenings and on weekends.

One evening you are visited by Prof. J. Watson, who asks you to install a special exhaust kit on his "Omniwagen." He shows you an article in a magazine called *Driving Enthusiast* that describes the increased performance that can be gained with it. He asks if you can do the job (you say "Yes" because you are interested in seeing how effective the kit is), and then suggests you give him a price for the job and let him know when you can take his car in. You take down some details:

1. His car is a two-year-old Omniwagen model 180L.
2. The magazine article states that the kits can be ordered from Import

Distributors, 1075 Bay Street, Boston. The kit is identified only as "Special Exhaust Kit."

3. The article also says that installation time is about seven hours.

Write to Import Distributors and ask for a leaflet describing the kit, its price, and how soon it can be delivered.

Exercise 13.15

Import Distributors sends you a leaflet (see Exercise 13.14), says the price is $76.50 FOB Boston, the kit's weight is 42 lb., shipping costs to your area would be $8.70, and kits can be delivered from stock. (The kit is still described only as Special Exhaust Kit.)

Write a letter to Watson quoting a price for the job (assume you charge $7.50 per hour for labor). Tell him it will take you three evenings to do the job.

His address is 208 Varsity Valley Drive (he lives about thirty miles out of town).

Exercise 13.16

Prof. Watson telephones you to say that he accepts the price you quoted (Exercise 13.15), and for you to order the kit. He would like to bring the car in on a Monday so he can have it for the following weekend.

Write a letter ordering the kit to Import Distributors (for their address, see Exercise 13.14). Assume you send a check for $85.20 with the order.

Exercise 13.17

The exhaust kit described in Exercises 13.14 to 13.16 has arrived and Watson has left his car with you.

On Monday evening, following the instructions provided with the kit, you remove the existing exhaust system. You have great difficulty in disconnecting it from the engine, and one of the bolts shears. But this is of no great concern because it is to be replaced by hardware supplied with the kit. The gasket between the engine and the exhaust system also is damaged and cannot be re-used.

Late in the evening you try joining the new exhaust system to the engine, but it will not fit. You study the instructions carefully and note that there seem to be small differences between Prof. Watson's engine and the diagrams in the instructions. Only then do you realize that Import Distributors have sent you a kit for the *180S* Omniwagen, instead of the *180L*.

On Tuesday morning telephone the sales manager at Import Distributors long distance, tell him they have sent the wrong kit, and ask him to send a kit for the 180L by the fastest possible method.

Exercise 13.18

The Sales Manager (Exercise 13.17) says: "Sorry, we're right out! That article in *Driving Enthusiast* sparked more orders than we could handle. It'll be ten days before the next shipment comes in from Europe. I'll send you a kit as soon as I can."

You try telephoning Prof. Watson, but his wife tells you he is away at a conference until Thursday. Write him a letter explaining what has happened and that it will be at least two weeks before he can have his car.

Exercise 13.19

You are working on another car on Wednesday evening when you hear footsteps. It is Prof. Watson.

"Just passing by with a friend," he says. "I've been out of town—I'm on my way home right now. Thought I'd drop in and see how you are getting on."

Tell him.

Exercise 13.20

You were lucky: Import Distributors shipment came in early and you received the proper kit nine days after your inquiry. Prof. Watson is very happy with his car's performance, and drives away with a smile on his face; he says: "Send me a bill."

Write the invoice you would send him.

Doing Small Construction Jobs

Exercise 13.21

Mr. George Kowalchuk calls you in to give him an estimate on a bar he wants built in his recreation room. The work involves building the bar (he shows you a dimensioned sketch he has drawn up), installing a small sink with hot and cold faucets, doing some plumbing alterations, and installing decorative lighting over and around the bar.

George claims to have many connections, so he is getting all the lighting fixtures from a wholesaler "real cheap." And his cousin, who is in the glass business, is getting a plate-glass mirror to go behind the bar. "All you have to do," George says, "is put them up."

You ask him what kind of lighting fixtures they will be (and how many), and the size of sink he wants. Then you go away to do your calculations:

1. You will do all the carpentry and painting yourself, which you estimate will take 18 hours @ $12 per hour (total labor = $216).
2. You will have to bring in an electrician and a plumber to help you. When you show them the plans, the electrician says he will do the work for $65, and the plumber for $45 plus materials. You add 15 percent contingency to their prices, which gives you a total for subcontract work of:

$$\$65 + \$45 = \$110 + 15\% = \$126.50$$

3. Materials will comprise:

Lumber	$84.00
Vinyl	16.50
Arborite	12.00
Paint	13.00
Brackets, screws, etc.	8.00
Pipe, etc., for plumbing	28.00
Stainless steel sink	
(14″ × 11″ with faucets)	41.00

4. Local taxes will be 10 percent extra.

Write a price quotation for Mr. Kowalchuk. His address is 212 Botany Crescent.

Exercise 13.22

Kowalchuk accepted your price quotation (prepared in Exercise 13.21) and you completed the job for him yesterday evening.

While you were in the house, Mrs. Kowalchuk asked if you could build a table between the automatic washer and dryer in her laundry area, using some old lumber her husband had in the garage. You said you could, but it would cost an additional $36 (i.e., 3 hours' labor). So she asked her husband, and he said for you to go ahead and use whatever lumber you wanted. This job also has been done.

Write an invoice billing Mr. Kowalchuk for building and installing the bar, and for building the table in the laundry area.

14

Communicating
as an Employer

If your business grows large enough, you may need to hire one or possibly more persons to help you. As an employer, you must communicate your ideas and plans, and how you want things done, to your employees.

DEVELOPING GOOD EMPLOYER-EMPLOYEE RELATIONS

The relationship you develop between yourself and your employees can have a marked effect on the quality of products or services you sell. And this effect will be evident to your customers. Employees who know they are understood and appreciated, and who in turn can understand you, your methods, and your reasons for doing things a certain way, will develop a loyalty that will be reflected in the way they represent themselves and you to outsiders.

The methods outlined for a supervisor for a large company to develop good communication between himself and line employees (see page 110) can be used equally well by a small-business owner. But there are two additional factors to consider:

1. You cannot take difficult problems to higher management: when a decision is needed, you must make it.

2. The employees' view of an employer is different from their view of a supervisor (who, after all, is still an employee like them).

Employees may more easily communicate with you as a junior supervisor than with you as "the boss." A lot will depend on how you draw them into your confidence and make them feel part of your company.

HIRING

Being "the boss" means you will have to do all the hiring. Chapter 5 described techniques prospective employees should use during an interview. As an employer, you also should use interviewing techniques if you are to learn as much as possible from the applicants you talk to. You want to create an atmosphere that will help them relax sufficiently so you see the real person, rather than an "interview image."

A properly run interview has three stages, with the applicant present only during the middle one. They are:

1. Preparing for the interview.
2. Holding the interview.
3. Selecting the right person for the job.

Too often, a busy small-business owner goes through only the second stage—and then only part of it. The first applicant may appear at his door before he has had time to think about the type of person he wants, so he lets "gut reaction" affect his decision. Or he is overly influenced by the easy manner and good appearance of an early applicant, and makes a snap decision to hire him. He does not have to hold any more interviews and, for better or worse, he has a new employee. (He will never know that Fred Windsor, who looked in later in the day but was told that the job was filled, would have been a much better person to hire.)

Preparing to Interview

This means deciding on the *type* of person you want. It is no good hiring a likeable, talkative hunting-fishing-mountain climbing enthusiast for a job that will keep him sitting at a desk. Or a quiet, shy, security-minded father of three for a job that calls for considerable travel and calling on many customers every day. Both would be square pegs holding round-hole jobs. Neither would be very happy at his work, and certainly would not do as well as someone better suited temperamentally.

Some of the questions you should consider before interviewing anyone are:

1. Do you need someone who already has experience, or would you prefer to train him yourself (let him learn on the job)?
2. Will the new employee have to work with you or other employees, or will he be pretty well on his own? Some people need other people around them, while others like to work on their own.
3. What level of education does the job call for? You obviously would not hire someone with only an eighth-grade education to run the office and keep the accounts for your business. But you might be tempted to hire a personable college graduate who desperately needs a job to be a packer. On a very short-term basis he might be suitable, but as a long-term employee he would quickly become dissatisfied because the work neither challenges his intelligence nor offers him an interesting future.
4. How much activity does the job call for? Physically active persons need work that lets them move around a lot (so they can be actively doing things). Less active persons are often happier if they can remain at one place most of the working day. (Harder to identify is an applicant's need for mental activity: a mentally active person needs work that will keep his mind busy. Some desk jobs fall into this category.)
5. Does the job entail selling? Or meeting customers? If it does, you will need someone who gets on well with people and is reasonably comfortable talking to persons of almost any educational level and background.

Preparation also includes jotting down a few sample questions so that you cover roughly the same ground with every person you interview. This does not mean holding a series of stereotyped interviews, each like the one before it, but rather having certain topics you want to discuss with each applicant.

Your questions should invite applicants to give more than single-word answers. If you ask:

Did you like working at Western Steel?
or
Who did you work for at Modern Bakeries?

they are likely to reply with simple answers, from which you learn very little. Questions that force an applicant to say more, however, also help to get him talking. An applicant would find it difficult to answer these questions with a single word:

> What did you like most about working at Western Steel?
> or
> Why did you leave Modern Bakeries?

Even if he answers the first question with "The pay," you can make him continue his answer by simply saying: "For example?"

Holding the Interview

Your principal role during an interview (after you have encouraged the applicant to talk) should be to listen. Let the conversation drift into all kinds of avenues if this will help the applicant relax. If he has lived in Australia for a year, then by all means let him talk about his experiences, because in doing so he will be showing you the kind of person he is. But on the other hand, do not let a particularly talkative applicant prevent you from covering some of the topics you want to cover. And never make the unforgivable error of doing so much talking about *your* work, *your* company, and *your* interests that the applicant has little chance to tell you about himself.

For more information on interviewing, refer to "The Interview's Parts" (page 52), which describes an interview from the applicant's viewpoint.

Selecting Your New Employee

Although you will probably form an opinion of an applicant's suitability during the interview, you should never make a decision until all the interviews have been held. During and immediately after each interview jot down notes on the applicant's strong and weak points, and his suitability for the job. Then look at the next applicant with fresh eyes, trying not to compare him favorably or unfavorably with previous applicants.

Sometimes there is only one obvious choice, which makes it easy to pick the person you want. More often, there are two or three who could fill the job, which means that you must weigh the strong and weak points of each, perhaps selecting one factor as the most important to help you reach a decision. And occasionally there are no really suitable applicants, in which case you may have to lower your sights and select someone with fewer capabilities than you wanted. Whenever the decision is difficult, perhaps the best advice is to say to yourself: "Which of the better applicants would I most enjoy working with?"

A particularly difficult factor to overcome is the "halo effect." This is the aura given off by an applicant who seems on the surface to be so ideally suitable that serious faults may not be noticeable. An applicant with a personable manner may smooth-talk his way into a job before you discover that he really knows very little about the practical aspects of the work, or he is simply a lazy bum. This is where a careful review of notes you made of each person's strong and weak points may show other applicants to be better choices even though they have less personal charm.

Communicating the results of an interview to all applicants should be done as soon as you have made your selection. It is common practice to telephone the successful applicant and then to follow the call with a letter confirming the agreed wage and starting date.

Dear Henry:

As I explained to you by telephone this morning, I am hiring you to take over assembly work from October 1, at a starting rate of $4.85 per hour.

Sincerely,

Carl Griffiths

Although this letter may seem to repeat what has already been discussed, it can prevent an unfortunate misunderstanding from developing early in the employer-employee relationship if either you or the successful applicant misinterprets something said in a telephone conversation.

And don't forget the unsuccessful applicants. It is only fair to let them know as early as possible that they were not successful. This can be done by telephone or letter. Most small employers (and some large ones) omit this important step in the communication process, which leaves applicants wondering where they stand until the passage of time gradually conveys the message—a message a thoughtless prospective employer should have conveyed to them.

FIRING

Being "the boss" means you will also have to do all the firing. As a supervisor, the need to fire someone might have been your suggestion, but at least it was not your final decision. As an employer, not only is the decision yours, but you also have to put it into effect.

It is easier to lay off someone because of a cutback in work (the employee has probably seen it coming and is partly prepared for it) than to fire someone because he does poor work or is too slow.

Because no one really likes firing an employee, there is a tendency to forget the pyramid method and lead gently up to the bad news. Although the news is not good, it should still be placed up front, as shown in Fig. 5–12. The three information blocks are:

1. A **Summary Statement** that introduces the message right away:

> I'm sorry, John, but I have bad news for you:
> I'll be letting you go at the end of the week.

2. The **Reason** why you are letting the employee go:

> Two factors force me to do this: Your inability to get up in the morning—I must have someone here when I go out on early calls—and your lack of experience. You're all right for general carpentry, but you don't know nearly enough about cabinet making.

It helps if you can soften the blow by adding something like this:

> This is no reflection on you, personally, John. You have a lot of good qualities, but I guess they don't quite match up with what I need.

3. Some **Advice** on how you are handling the release with, perhaps, a comment on whether or not the employee can take time off to look for another job:

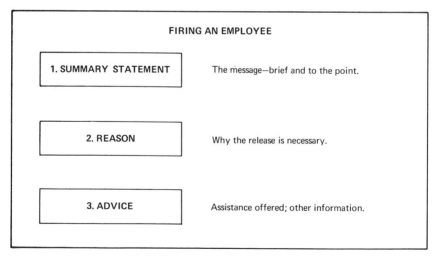

Fig. 5–12. Information blocks for firing an employee.

Your final pay check will have five extra days' pay for earned holiday time. And if you need an afternoon to go job hunting, just let me know ahead of time.

Generally, in industry, an employee cannot be fired suddenly because of misdemeanors he has not previously been warned about. This unwritten rule also applies to you as a small-business owner. You should warn an employee both verbally and in writing if his work, attendance, or attitude is not satisfactory. This gives him the chance to improve. If he does not, then you have good reason for taking the final step.

EXERCISES

NOTE: Exercise 13.1 on page 215 must be done before this exercise is attempted.

Exercise 14.1

You and Bev Carmichael have accumulated more work and customers for your homeowner service business than you expected (see Exercises 13.1 to 13.8 on pages 215 to 220), so you decide to bring in two assistants.

1. Prepare an advertisement to place on your school notice board.
2. List three standard questions you would ask of each applicant, and place them in downward order of importance.
3. Explain briefly why you would ask these questions.

Exercise 14.2

Assume you have finished your training course, and you have been running a small business of your own for a year (it may be either a full-time or a part-time business). You have more work than you can handle alone, so you decide to hire someone to help you.

1. List the type of work this person will do, and his or her duties.
2. Prepare a four-line advertisement for the job opening, to insert in the classified columns of your newspaper.
3. List three questions you would want to ask each applicant.
4. Rate these questions in downward order of importance, and explain briefly why you would ask each question.

VI

THE STYLE
AND SHAPE
OF WRITTEN
COMMUNICATIONS

15

Writing for a Reader

Whenever you write, you convey a message. Yet many people forget that the message they write is going to be read by someone who probably does not know the subject as well as they do. In other words, they write from their point of view rather than from the reader's. Because this is also true of speakers and listeners, many of the suggestions in chapters 15 and 16 apply just as much to spoken communications.

PERSONALIZING YOUR WRITING

Knowing who your reader is can affect what you say and how you say it. So before writing you should ask yourself:

1. *Who will read my message?*

   This does not mean knowing exactly *who* the person is; rather, it means knowing the *type* of person he is (is he a customer? a parts manager? salesman? shipper? clerk? production supervisor?).

2. *How familiar is he with my subject?*

   This will give you a starting point. If the topic is likely to be entirely new to the reader, you will need to give him background information and explain more to make sure he understands why you are writing. But if he already has some knowledge of the subject, you need only refer to previous correspondence or an order number, for example, before jumping directly into the topic. (Perhaps you have written to each other about the subject before, or you are inquiring about some work that is being done for you, or an order for parts that has been only partly delivered.)

3. *What tone should I use?*

Do you need to be firm and direct because you are telling him something and expecting him to take action (that is, complaining, instructing, or demanding)? Or do you need to be persuasive and convincing because you are selling him something and hoping he will take action (that is, asking or requesting)?

The answers to these questions will give direction and purpose to your efforts and help you write more easily. They will help you "see" the person you are writing to, rather than just a company or organization. And if you use personal words like "I" and "you," readers will feel that a real person rather than an impersonal organization is writing to them.

Compare the naturalness of the three paragraphs in the left-hand column below with the coldness of the same messages in the right-hand column.

Examples of Warm (Personalized) Writing	*Examples of Cold (Impersonal) Writing*
I'm sorry, but we cannot change the design of your cabinets as requested in your May 17 letter because we have already cut the lumber.	With reference to your May 17 letter requesting that the design of the cabinets be changed, it is not possible to do so at this late date because the lumber has already been cut.
I have today shipped three-quarters of the parts you ordered on PO 1563. The remainder have been back-ordered and I expect to ship them on August 10.	Three-quarters of the parts ordered on PO 1563 have been shipped today. The remainder have been back-ordered and should be shipped on August 10.
A defective meter probably caused the unusually high electricity consumption reading recorded by our meter reader at your residence on January 26. I have arranged to have your defective meter replaced and I will adjust your bill.	The unusually high electricity consumption recorded by the meter reader on January 26 at 286 Rossmere Road most likely was caused by a defective meter. The meter will be replaced and the bill will be adjusted.

You may have been told in school not to use the word "I" too often, and never to use it as the first word of a letter. But times have changed. Now it is quite acceptable to start a letter with the word "I" (in grammatical terms it is called "the first person") and to sprinkle it throughout your writing. Notice how much it is used in the left-hand column on the previous page, compared to the right-hand column.

You can make your readers feel good by using the word "you." Every reader likes to feel he or she is being personally addressed. This is especially true if you are writing about something that particularly concerns or affects the reader.

Another way to personalize your writing is to use words that you normally use, not words other people use. A fairly common error made by beginning writers is to look at letters written by other people. But they are not really able to judge whether such letters convey messages efficiently. Neither can they recognize when writing contains wordy, old-fashioned expressions considered outdated in modern business.

There is a marked trend today toward writing simpler letters, memorandums, and reports. Expressions such as these are outdated:

> We have for acknowledgement your letter of . . .
> You are hereby advised that . . .
> We respectfully beg to inform you . . .

When you first see a sentence written like this, it may seem to be important-sounding:

> It is a matter of concern to this writer that receipt of your application may be so delayed that the likelihood of your being able to qualify for this year's certification will be jeopardized.

But what does it really say? The writer knows, but he has hidden the message by being too wordy. To him, it probably seems dignified. He has yet to learn that removing unnecessary words and using personal pronouns ("I" and "you") can quickly change it to this meaningful message:

> I am concerned that your application may not be received in time for you to qualify for certification this year.

It is the simplicity of the second sentence that we should strive for.

PLACING THE MESSAGE UP FRONT

Chapter 3 explains that the most efficient way to communicate written and spoken information is to position the essential details right up front. This is the **Main Message** or **Summary Statement,** and it is used in practically every example in Parts II through V.

Summary Statements can be easily visualized if you consider every message to be two main blocks of information. The first block is small and the second block is large, as shown in Fig. 6–1.

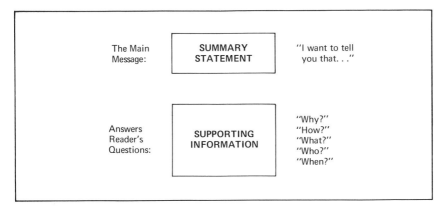

Fig. 6–1. Forming the message into two blocks of information.

The small block is the Summary Statement. It is the continuation of the sentence in Chapter 3 which starts **I want to tell you that . . .** and which, when complete, carries the Main Message in very few words.

The large block contains all the other information that the reader will want (or need) to know. Exactly how much you include depends on what you think the reader will ask after he has read the Summary Statement. You try to ask yourself the questions he is likely to ask, then answer them.

Suppose, for example, you write this as your Summary Statement in the first block:

There was a breakdown at 3.15 P.M., when a sprocket broke off a drive wheel on the assembly line.

From your knowledge of the reader, you must try to answer the questions he would now ask. Most likely they would be:

Why are you telling me this?
What do you want me to do?

To answer these questions, your large block might contain something like this:

This means we will not be able to complete and ship Johnson Brothers' order today. Will you please telephone them to say their order will be one day late.

In practice, the large block is broken into two or three smaller blocks, each a logical compartment of information. These can be seen in the numerous sets of information blocks illustrated in previous chapters.

Even when transmitting bad news you should still try to use a direct approach. It is a mistake to think you must lead up to bad news with a gentle buildup, so that the reader is ready for it when he reaches it. If you were the reader, wouldn't you prefer to receive the most important information (good or bad) right away?

16

Squeezing More Mileage from the Words You Use

CHOOSING WORDS THAT CONVEY IMAGES

Writing is difficult enough without using words that do not work as hard as they should, or are not necessary. Because most of us are mentally lazy, we tend to write words that come easily to mind rather than dig for just the right words to say exactly what we mean.

A single word that clearly describes an action can carry a mental picture right into the reader's (or listener's) mind. These are verbs, such as *dig, climb, twist, shake,* and *tighten.* Each of these words creates a little image which depicts the action the word describes.

If we choose good image-producing words, our sentences convey a series of clearly defined pictures. But if we are lazy and use only general words, we may create out-of-focus pictures that convey only a general impression.

Typical out-of-focus verbs are *put, got,* and *went.* In day-to-day conversation we use these verbs a lot:

The technician *put* the cannister on the shelf.

While in Meridian they *got* two Christmas trees.

The jeep *went* into the ditch.

Out-of-focus words like these are acceptable in casual conversation when we are offering only a general impression rather than specific details—and also when we know that our listeners can ask questions if the words we use are not clear.

A reader, however, usually cannot ask questions. For him, written words must tell stories. Out-of-focus words like *put, got,* and *went* need to be replaced with verbs that describe action:

The technician $\left\{\begin{array}{l} \text{laid} \\ \text{stood} \\ \text{placed} \\ \text{dropped} \\ \text{threw} \end{array}\right\}$ the cannister on the shelf.

While in Meridian they $\left\{\begin{array}{l} \text{bought} \\ \text{borrowed} \\ \text{rented} \\ \text{chopped down} \\ \text{dug up} \\ \text{were given} \end{array}\right\}$ two Christmas trees.

The jeep $\left\{\begin{array}{l} \text{slid} \\ \text{skidded} \\ \text{bounced} \\ \text{was driven} \end{array}\right\}$ into the ditch.

Using descriptive verbs results in colorful writing that is also economical. If you write:

> Our hot water tank was leaking so I **got** a new one from the gas company.

you will have to write a second sentence to explain what you mean by "got":

> This time I decided to rent one for $1.95 a month. Now I won't ever have to buy another hot water tank. *(38 words)*

But if you replace "got" with the more descriptive word "rented" (which you had to use anyway in the second sentence above), you will not only write less but also produce a smoother-reading paragraph:

> Our hot water tank was leaking so I **rented** a new one from the gas company for $1.95 a month. Now I won't ever have to buy another hot water tank. *(31 words)*

Choosing just the right words applies to nouns as well as verbs. A properly selected noun can do much to convey a clear picture. If I refer to "a building," I create only a general image. "A house" would be better because it at least classifies the building as a place where people live, rather than an office, garage, or warehouse. But it is still out of focus compared to image-producing nouns like *bungalow, cottage,* or *duplex.*

Here are more examples of nouns that do not convey clear images:

Out-of-focus Words	In-focus Words
people	men, women, adults, teenagers
vehicle	sedan, truck, station wagon, panel truck, jeep, bus
equipment	drill, analyzer, test set, hoist, bulldozer
road	highway, lane, expressway, street
picture	painting, photograph, sketch, drawing

There may be occasions when you want to use an out-of-focus noun to show you are talking about persons or things generally. But when you are singling out a particular kind of person or object, then you should try to find a better, more descriptive word.

You can also insert extra words to tell more about the verbs and nouns you use. For example:

carefully stood	a *noisy* typewriter
carelessly threw	a *battered* truck
quickly chopped down	a *twisted* post
slid *slowly*	a *subcompact* car
skidded *sideways*	an *ivy-covered* cottage

The left-hand list contains the in-focus verbs which should be used in place of "put," "got," and "went." They are drawn into even sharper focus by attaching action-describing **adverbs** to them (these are the words in italics). The nouns on the right are given extra color by attaching descriptive **adjectives** to them; these also are in italics.

If you wish, you can use more than one adverb or adjective at a time:

skidded *slowly sideways*
a *noisy old* typewriter
a *foreign subcompact* car

But, first, a few words of caution:

1. Too many adverbs and adjectives make day-to-day writing seem much too wordy. Indeed, adverbs and adjectives should be used only when verbs and nouns need extra color to convey the correct image to the reader.
2. Adding adverbs and adjectives to words that are out of focus in the first place does not make the out-of-focus words much clearer. For example:

   The technician *carelessly put* the cannister on the shelf.

   While in Meridian they *quickly got* two Christmas trees.

   The jeep *went slowly* into the ditch.

3. Adding extra words like "very," "really," and "actually" adds wordiness rather than more emphasis.

   The technician *very* carelessly threw the cannister on the shelf.

   While in Meridian they *actually* chopped down two Christmas trees.

   The jeep slid *really* slowly into the ditch.

   The rule should be: if the word you insert does not add *color* to your writing, then leave it out.
4. Digging up the right word does not mean searching through a dictionary trying to find special words to use. Chances are that the words you find may be too big and awkward, and seem out of place. That is exactly how Brian Kemp, a junior accountant at Waco Industries, started writing about "superannuation" and "remuneration" in his memorandums and letters. It was not long before the office manager called him in and gently explained that it is better to use simpler words that everybody understands; words like *pension, pay, wages,* or *salary.*

The fund of words you draw on for both writing and speaking should be part of your vocabulary, which can be built up slowly through reading and trying to use descriptive words every time you write or speak. It takes practice, but in time descriptive rather than general words automatically come to mind when you need them.

ASSEMBLING WORDS INTO SHARP SENTENCES

Whereas words alone create images, when assembled into sentences they convey messages. If they are arranged properly, the message is clear. But if they are arranged badly, the message may be misunderstood.

The three general hints outlined below will help you write better sentences.

Keep Sentences Simple

Experienced writers in industry do not write complex sentences. They realize that their writing must be quickly understood, so they present only one thought at a time. They also keep their sentences short, limiting them whenever possible to no more than twenty words. On the other hand, they avoid stringing too many very short sentences together because this would seem annoyingly jerky to the reader.

Make Sure Every Sentence is Complete

This simply means that every sentence must make sense even if it is lifted out of its paragraph and read on its own. Sometimes a writer lets a sentence depend too much on the sentence before it, as has happened to the second of these three sentences:

> When I tried to remove the lid, it would not loosen. Being wrongly threaded. I had to tighten a clamp around the lid and twist the whole jar counterclockwise to unscrew it.

If the second sentence is lifted out and allowed to stand alone, it is obviously incomplete:

> Being wrongly threaded.

To make it complete, it needs a **subject** up front. This can be either the name of the item being referred to (in this case, "the lid") or a pronoun that clearly refers to it (for example, "it"). So the sentence becomes:

> *The lid was* wrongly threaded.
> or
> *It was* wrongly threaded.

Alternatively, the phrase can be altered slightly by changing "being" to "because it," and then joined to the sentence ahead of or behind it:

> When I tried to remove the lid, it would not loosen *because it was wrongly threaded.*
> or
> *Because it was wrongly threaded,* I had to tighten a clamp around the lid and twist the whole jar counterclockwise to unscrew it.

Many people write incomplete sentences like this without knowing they are doing so. But their readers notice something is wrong, even if they cannot quite place a finger on it.

If you think back to your middle school days, you will probably remember an English teacher saying over and over again: "Every sentence must have three parts: a subject, a verb, and an object." This rule still holds true today, even with the short cuts taken by modern writers. (I discount fiction writers, who in carrying their stories forward, often break far more rules—and get away with it—than you and I are permitted to do.) In nongrammatical terms this simply means making sure your sentences say *who did what* or *what did what*. Like this:

WHO (or WHAT)		DID		WHAT
Subject	—	*Verb*	—	*Object*

Here are some examples:

Subject	Verb	Object
(Who or What)	*(Did or Doing)*	*(What)*
The lid	was	wrongly threaded
Three instruments	were	missing
I	have	the keys
Mr. Peterson	could not find	it
It	is	heavy

This, of course, is oversimplified. We do not write only simple little sentences. But even in longer, more complex sentences these three parts still should be evident:

> Ice on the runway posed a formidable problem for the airline pilot.
>
> *(Ice . . . posed . . . a problem)*

> No matter how busy we are, this particular customer always demands immediate attention.
>
> *(This customer . . . demands . . . attention)*

> During the antenna overhaul Mr. Harker, who was assisted by Len Vigan and Kevin Wilson, recorded in his diary the number of times they each climbed to the top of the tower.
>
> *(Mr. Harker . . . recorded . . . the number)*

End on a Strong Word

The most important part of a sentence is the last word, or sometimes the last phrase. Readers expect an important word to be there, which means you must avoid ending with weak words such as "only," "approximately," or "at least." For example, the following sentences are weak because they end poorly:

> The accountant wants you to hand in last week's expense account only.
>
> There should be a dozen connectors at least.
>
> Odometer readings are to be recorded every hour approximately.

This weakness can easily be corrected by making sure the last word is a **noun** rather than an adjective or adverb. Simply rearranging the sentences achieves the desired effect and gives them much greater strength:

> The accountant wants you to hand in only last week's expense account.
>
> There should be at least a dozen connectors.
>
> Odometer readings are to be recorded approximately every hour.

BUILDING STRONG PARAGRAPHS

Earlier chapters continually urged you to begin everything you say with a Summary Statement. A Summary Statement tells the listener or reader right away what he most needs to know. The remainder of the report, letter, or memorandum then provides details that answer questions the Summary Statement brings to mind.

You can also apply this technique to paragraph writing. The first sentence of the paragraph becomes the Summary Statement, and the remaining sentences offer more information about the subject.

This idea is not new. The Summary Statement in a paragraph is the "topic sentence" that English teachers talk about. But whereas they say that a topic sentence can exist anywhere in a paragraph—at the beginning, middle, or end—unless you are writing a very long letter or report you would be wise to position all topic sentences right up front. Here are two examples, in which the topic sentences are in italics:

> *Many automobiles were damaged by the hailstorm.* The center of the storm traveled almost directly east along Moray street, affecting 3200 automobiles parked up to half a mile away. Hail pellets as large as 1⅜ in. in diameter bounced off roofs, hoods, trunk lids and fenders, causing numerous small indentations. The cost to the public insurance corporation amounted to $928,000, or an average of $290 per vehicle.
>
> *The army's tests on winter roads highlight the danger of driving at certain speeds on frozen lakes.* Each truck pass causes waves beneath the surface

to extend outward from the road. If the waves bounce off a beach within 300 yards, they return and work on the underside of the ice, gradually weakening it. Truck speeds between 7 and 20 miles per hour are particularly dangerous. Lower or higher speeds have less effect.

In both these paragraphs the topic sentence summarizes what the paragraph is about, and following sentences fill in the details. Everything in the first paragraph relates to the effect that the storm had on automobiles. Everything in the second paragraph describes how the passage of traffic can cause waves to weaken the ice. But only one topic is discussed in each paragraph.

This is the secret to good paragraph writing: make sure every sentence is part of or related to the same subject. The insertion of just one unrelated sentence can destroy a paragraph's unity, which in turn will upset the reader because he will wonder why it is there. Notice how the fourth (new) sentence in the paragraph below seems out of place because it has nothing to do with the subject mentioned in the topic sentence:

> *The army's tests on winter roads highlight the danger of driving at certain speeds on frozen lakes.* Each truck pass causes waves beneath the surface to extend outward from the road. If the waves bounce off a beach within 300 yards, they return and work on the underside of the ice, gradually weakening it. Some of the trucks were not fitted with snow tires, having just come from exercises in Nevada. Truck speeds between 7 and 20 miles per hour are particularly dangerous. Lower or higher speeds have less effect.

How long should your paragraphs be? Generally, no longer than eight to ten lines of typing, or five to six sentences. But neither should they be too short. A person writing a series of very short paragraphs, each containing only one or two sentences, does not properly develop his topic. Both he and the writer of king-size paragraphs will annoy readers—one because he creates a "bitty" effect, the other because he offers too much information to digest all at once. Ideally, there should be a good mix of paragraph lengths. If some paragraphs are medium-long and some are medium-short, the reader will appreciate the variety.

17

Using
a Businesslike
Format

The appearance of the letters you write will contribute much to the first impression readers gain of you. If they are nicely centered on the page, and contain all the parts in the correct places that readers expect, your letters will convey that you are efficient and businesslike. This impression will also apply to the company you work for.

The standard parts of a letter are shown in Fig. 6–2. This is a conservative format that is widely used, often with minor variations.

An alternative format used by some modern businesses is at Fig. 6–3. From a typist's viewpoint it is very convenient to use because *every* typing line starts at the left-hand margin.

For your personal correspondence, the more conservative arrangement is recommended (Fig. 6–2), particularly when a letter is handwritten.

Many of the communications you are likely to write in industry will be **memorandums**. Memorandums are informal letters written from one person to another within the same company. They are easier and quicker to write than letters because they do not have as many parts. (Compare the letter formats in Fig. 6–2 and 6–3 with the memorandum format in Fig. 6–4.)

Larger companies print their own memorandum forms, usually some variation in arrangement of the preprinted information in the form at Fig. 6–4. Smaller firms buy carbon-interleaved memo sets from stationery supply houses. These contain a space for the "receiver" to write his reply and then return the form to the originator (first tearing off a copy for his own files). They are, however, comparatively expensive.

249

A cheaper and simpler small memorandum form can also be purchased in pads from stationers. It is particularly suitable for hand-writing short memos. An example is shown at Fig. 6–5.

This format is suitable for both business and personal correspondence. Comments on numbered items are:

1. Try to line up your address, the date, and the signature block (at the bottom of the page) so they all start at the page center. If you are using preprinted business letter paper, this will apply only to the date and the signature block.

2. Always try to personalize your letters by inserting the reader's name here and in the salutation (3). If you don't know his name, insert a title that best describes the person you are writing to in a firm (e.g., *Sales Manager, Chief Accountant*).

3. This is the **Salutation.** If you know your reader well you can use "Dear Hank" instead of the more formal "Dear Mr. Shear." If you don't know his name, insert "Dear Sir" or "Gentlemen."

4. The **Subject Line** is a useful way to tell your reader right away what your letter is about. It must be worded carefully so that it conveys the purpose of your letter. ("Repair Order 2711," for example, would not be sufficiently informative.)

5. Try to space your letter so that the **Body** is roughly in the center of the sheet. Leave a blank line between each paragraph. Either indent the first line of each paragraph (as shown) or start every paragraph flush with the left-hand margin.

6. Type or print your name beneath your signature so that your reader will spell it correctly when he replies to you. Use the form you would like him to use (i.e., *D. B. Bosworth* or *Donald B. Bosworth*).

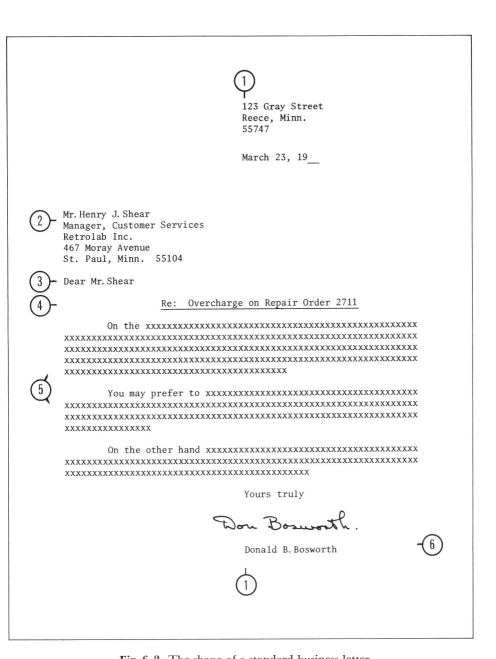

123 Gray Street
Reece, Minn.
55747

March 23, 19__

Mr. Henry J. Shear
Manager, Customer Services
Retrolab Inc.
467 Moray Avenue
St. Paul, Minn. 55104

Dear Mr. Shear

Re: Overcharge on Repair Order 2711

On the xxxxxxxxxxxxxxxxxxxxxxxxxxxxxxxxxxxxxxxxxxxxxxxxxx
xxxxxxxxxxxxxxxxxxxxxxxxxxxxxxxxxxxxxxxxxxxxxxxxxxxxxxxxxxxxx
xxxxxxxxxxxxxxxxxxxxxxxxxxxxxxxxxxxxxxxxxxxxxxxxxxxxxxxxxxxxx
xxxxxxxxxxxxxxxxxxxxxxxxxxxxxxxxxxxxxxxxxxxxxxxxxxxxxxxxxxxxx
xxxxxxxxxxxxxxxxxxxxxxxxxxxxxxxxxxxxxxx

You may prefer to xxxxxxxxxxxxxxxxxxxxxxxxxxxxxxxxxxxxxxxxx
xxxxxxxxxxxxxxxxxxxxxxxxxxxxxxxxxxxxxxxxxxxxxxxxxxxxxxxxxxxxx
xxxxxxxxxxxxxxxxxxxxxxxxxxxxxxxxxxxxxxxxxxxxxxxxxxxxxxxxxxxxx
xxxxxxxxxxxxxxx

On the other hand xxxxxxxxxxxxxxxxxxxxxxxxxxxxxxxxxxxxxxxxx
xxxxxxxxxxxxxxxxxxxxxxxxxxxxxxxxxxxxxxxxxxxxxxxxxxxxxxxxxxxxx
xxxxxxxxxxxxxxxxxxxxxxxxxxxxxxxxxxxxxxxxxxx

Yours truly

Don Bosworth.

Donald B. Bosworth

Fig. 6–2. The shape of a standard business letter.

This format is more suitable for business correspondence typed onto a preprinted business letterhead than for personal correspondence. Specific comments on lettered items are:

(A) *Every* line in the letter must start at the left-hand margin.

(B) It is a good idea to personalize business letters by inserting the reader's name here and in the salutation (C). If you don't know him by name, use a title that best describes the person you want to receive your letter (e.g., *Manager, Industrial Relations; Supply Supervisor*). An even more formal inside address and salutation would use an underlined attention line between the address and the salutation:

> Wilding's Motors, Inc.
> 20 Craven Road
> Weekaskasing Falls, Wis. 53144
>
> Attention: Mr. A. McGuire
>
> Dear Sir:

(C) This is the **Salutation**. If you know your reader well you can use "Dear Andy" instead of the moderately formal "Dear Mr. McGuire." If you don't know his name, or are using a formal inside address and an attention line, insert "Dear Sir" or "Gentlemen."

(D) The **Subject Line** must contain information that shows the purpose of your letter; it is always underlined.

(E) Try to space your letter so that the **Body** is roughly in the center of the sheet. Leave a blank line between paragraphs.

(F) Type your name and job title, so your reader can reply directly to you and spell your name correctly. Show your name in the form you would like your reader to use in his reply.

(G) The first initials are yours, and are in capital letters; the second are those of the person who types the letter, and are in lower-case letters.

H. L. Winman and Associates

PROFESSIONAL CONSULTING ENGINEERS
475 Reston Avenue-Cleveland, Ohio, 44104

14 September 19__

(B)- Mr. Andy McGuire
Wilding's Motors Inc.
20 Craven Road
Weekaskasing Falls, Wis. 53144

(C)- Dear Mr. McGuire

(D)- Re: Servicing of Survey Vehicles

This summer xxxxxxxxxxxxxxxxxxxxxxxxxxxxxxxxxxxxxxxxxxxxxxxxxxxxx
xxxxxxxxxxxxxxxxxxxxxxxxxxxxxxxxxxxxxxxxxxxxxxxxxxxxxxxxxxxxxxxxxx
xxxxxxxxxxxxxxxxxxxxxxxxxxxxxxxxxxxxxxxxxxxxxxxxxxxxxxxxxxxxxxxxxx
xxxxxxxxxxxxxxxxxxxxxxxxxxxxxxxxxxxxxxxxxxxxxxxxxxxxxxxxxxxxxxxxxx
xxxxxxxxxxxxxxxxxxxxxxxxxxxxxxxxxxxxxx

(E)- We need xxxxxxxxxxxxxxxxxxxxxxxxxxxxxxxxxxxxxxxxxxxxxxxxxxxxxxxx
xxxxxxxxxxxxxxxxxxxxxxxxxxxxxxxxxxxxxxxxxxxxxxxxxxxxxxxxxxxxxxxxxx
xxxxxxxxxxxxxxxxxxxxxxxxxxxxxxxxxxxxxxxxxxxxxxxxxxxxxxxxxxxxxxxxxx
xxxxxxxxxxx

If you can xxxxxxxxxxxxxxxxxxxxxxxxxxxxxxxxxxxxxxxxxxxxxxxxxxxxxx
xxxxxxxxxxxxxxxxxxxxxxxxxxxxxxxxxxxxxxxxxxxxxxxxxxxxxxxxxxxxxxxxxx
xxxxxxxxxxxxxxxxxxxxxxxxxxxxxxxxxxxxxxxxxxxxxxx

Sincerely

John Pauls

(F)- John Pauls
Maintenance Supervisor

(G)- JP:ir

Fig. 6–3. An alternative shape for a business letter.

Notes on Fig. 6–4: Memorandum Format

A memorandum is normally sent between persons within the same organization, and is typed or handwritten on a prepared form. If a form is not available, you can create your own by using these headings:

From:
To:
Date:
Subject: (or **Reference:**)

These rules for writing memorandums are keyed to the circled numbers in the example:

(1) Insert your own name and initials, either formally as shown or informally as "Jake Rendale." Omit *Mr.* or *Ms.*, and job titles (such as *Supply Supervisor, Maintenance Technician*), both here and at (2).

(2) Insert the name of the person you are sending information to. If the memorandum is for more than one person, list their names and start the body of the memorandum lower on the page; like this:

> **To:** P. D. Morris
> K. J. Kaminsky
> A. R. Cuthbert
> G. L. Davidson

(3) Insert the date, spelling out the month. (Never use numerals for the months, otherwise the day and month may be read wrongly; e.g., 7/6 can be interpreted to mean either July 6 or 7 June.) Months may be abbreviated to the first three letters, so that *September* is written as *Sep*.

(4) The **Subject** entry is equivalent to the subject line of a letter. Make sure it is informative, so that it *tells the reader what the memorandum is about*. "Painting" or "Areas 4A and 5C" would not be descriptive enough; "Painting of areas 4A and 5C" is better. By inserting the word "Schedule," Jake Rendale has narrowed the content of his letter to one topic, which he indicates clearly in the subject line.

(5) Start right in with the body of your message. There is no need for a salutation like: "Dear Mr. Morris" or "Dear Pete."

(6) Write the message in just the same way you would write a letter. Don't make the mistake of thinking that "memorandum" means you can write short points that are just disconnected jottings. Short points are fine when you have a list of items to offer. At all other times write properly formed sentences and paragraphs.

(7) When you come to the end of your memorandum, just stop. There is no need for "Yours sincerely" or a typed entry of your name and job title. Simply sign or initial the memorandum.

THE RONING GROUP   INTER - OFFICE MEMORANDUM

(1) **From:** ___ J. K. Rendale _____   **Date:** __ June 7, 19__ _____ (3)
(2) **To:** ___ P. D. Morris _____   **Subject:** __ Schedule for painting ___ (4)
                                              areas 4A and 5C

(5) Next week xxxxxxxxxxxxxxxxxxxxxxxxxxxxxxxxxxxxxxxxxxxxxxxxxxxxxxxxxxxxxxxxxxxx
xxxxxxxxxxxxxxxxxxxxxxxxxxxxxxxxxxxxxxxxxxxxxxxxxxxxxxxxxxxxxxxxxxxxxxxxxxxxxxxx
xxxxxxxxxxxxxxxxxxxxxxxxxxxxxxxxxxxxxxxxxxxxxxx

Will you please arrange xxxxxxxxxxxxxxxxxxxxxxxxxxxxxxxxxxxxxxxxxxxxxxxxxxxxxxxxx
xxxxxxxxxxxxxxxxxxxxxxxxxxxxxxxxxxxxxxxxxxxxxxxxxxxxxxxxxxxxxxxxxxxxxxxxxxxxxxxx
(6) xxxxxxxxxxxxxxxxxxxxxxxxxxxxxxxxxxxxxxxxxxxxxxxxxxxxxxxxxxxxxxxxxxxxxxxxxxxxxxxx
xxxxxxxxxxxxxxxxxxxxxxxxxxxxxxxx

              1. xxxxxxxxxxxxxxxxxxxxxxxxxxxxxx
              2. xxxxxxxxxxxxxxxxxxxxxxxxxx
              3. xxxxxxxxxxxxxxxxxxxxxxxxxxxxxxxx

Painting will be finished xxxxxxxxxxxxxxxxxxxxxxxxxxxxxxxxxxxxxxxxxxxxxxxxxxxxxxxx
xxxxxxxxxxxxxxxxxxxxxxxxxxxxxxxxxxxxxxxxxxxxxxxxxxx

                                              Jake   (7)

Fig. 6–4. The shape of an interoffice memorandum.

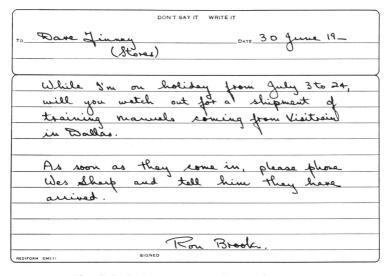

Fig. 6–5. A short memorandum written on a form. (Form illustration by permission of Moore Business Forms.)

255

Index